SECOND EDITION

Developing Web Apps with Haskell and Yesod

Michael Snoyman

Beijing · Cambridge · Farnham · Köln · Sebastopol · Tokyo

Developing Web Apps with Haskell and Yesod, Second Edition
by Michael Snoyman

Copyright © 2015 Michael Snoyman. All rights reserved.

Printed in the United States of America.

Published by O'Reilly Media, Inc., 1005 Gravenstein Highway North, Sebastopol, CA 95472.

O'Reilly books may be purchased for educational, business, or sales promotional use. Online editions are also available for most titles (*http://safaribooksonline.com*). For more information, contact our corporate/institutional sales department: 800-998-9938 or *corporate@oreilly.com*.

Editors: Simon St. Laurent and Allyson MacDonald
Production Editor: Nicole Shelby
Copyeditor: Jasmine Kwityn
Proofreader: Rachel Head

Indexer: Ellen Troutman
Interior Designer: David Futato
Cover Designer: Ellie Volckhausen
Illustrator: Rebecca Demarest

February 2015:   Second Edition

Revision History for the Second Edition
2015-02-09:   First Release

See *http://oreilly.com/catalog/errata.csp?isbn=9781491915592* for release details.

978-1-491-91559-2

[LSI]

Table of Contents

Preface... xi

Part I.   Basics

1. Introduction.. 1
   Type Safety   1
   Concise Code   2
   Performance   2
   Modularity   3
   A Solid Foundation   3

2. Haskell... 5
   Terminology   5
   Tools   7
   Language Pragmas   8
   Overloaded Strings   8
   Type Families   9
   Template Haskell   10
   QuasiQuotes   12
   API Documentation   12
   Summary   13

3. Basics... 15
   Hello, World   15
   Routing   16
   Handler Function   18
   The Foundation   18

Running   19
Resources and Type-Safe URLs   19
Non-HTML Responses   21
The Scaffolded Site   21
Development Server   22
Summary   22

4. Shakespearean Templates. 23
Synopsis   23
   Hamlet (HTML)   24
   Lucius (CSS)   24
   Cassius (CSS)   24
   Julius (JavaScript)   24
Types   25
   Type-Safe URLs   26
Syntax   27
   Hamlet Syntax   28
   Lucius Syntax   33
   Cassius Syntax   35
   Julius Syntax   35
Calling Shakespeare   35
   Alternative Hamlet Types   37
Other Shakespeare   39
General Recommendations   40

5. Widgets. 41
Synopsis   41
What's in a Widget?   43
Constructing Widgets   44
Combining Widgets   45
Generating IDs   46
whamlet   46
   Types   47
Using Widgets   48
Using Handler Functions   50
Summary   51

6. The Yesod Typeclass. 53
Rendering and Parsing URLs   53
   joinPath   55
   cleanPath   55
defaultLayout   57

getMessage   58

Custom Error Pages   59

External CSS and JavaScript   60

Smarter Static Files   61

Authentication/Authorization   62

Some Simple Settings   63

Summary   63

7. Routing and Handlers. **65**

Route Syntax   65

Pieces   66

Resource Name   68

Handler Specification   69

Dispatch   70

Return Type   70

Arguments   71

The Handler Functions   72

Application Information   73

Request Information   73

Short-Circuiting   73

Response Headers   74

I/O and Debugging   75

Query String and Hash Fragments   76

Summary   77

8. Forms. **79**

Synopsis   79

Kinds of Forms   81

Types   82

Converting   84

Creating AForms   84

Optional Fields   85

Validation   86

More Sophisticated Fields   87

Running Forms   88

i18n   89

Monadic Forms   89

Input Forms   92

Custom Fields   93

Values That Don't Come from the User   95

Summary   97

9. Sessions. **99**
  clientsession   99
  Controlling Sessions   100
  Session Operations   101
  Messages   102
  Ultimate Destination   104
  Summary   106

10. Persistent. **107**
  Synopsis   108
  Solving the Boundary Issue   109
    Types   110
    Code Generation   111
    PersistStore   114
  Migrations   115
  Uniqueness   118
  Queries   119
    Fetching by ID   119
    Fetching by Unique Constraint   120
    Select Functions   120
  Manipulation   122
    Insert   122
    Update   124
    Delete   125
  Attributes   125
  Relations   128
  A Closer Look at Types   129
    More Complicated, More Generic   130
  Custom Fields   131
  Persistent: Raw SQL   132
  Integration with Yesod   134
  More Complex SQL   136
  Something Besides SQLite   136
  Summary   137

11. Deploying Your Web App. **139**
  Keter   139
  Compiling   140
  Files to Deploy   140
  SSL and Static Files   141
  Warp   141
    Nginx Configuration   142

    Server Process   144

Nginx + FastCGI   144

Desktop   145

CGI on Apache   146

FastCGI on lighttpd   146

CGI on lighttpd   147

Part II. Advanced

12. RESTful Content.   151

Request Methods   151

Representations   152

    JSON Conveniences   154

    New Data Types   156

Other Request Headers   160

Summary   160

13. Yesod's Monads.   161

Monad Transformers   161

The Three Transformers   162

Example: Database-Driven Navbar   163

Example: Request Information   165

Performance and Error Messages   167

Adding a New Monad Transformer   168

Summary   172

14. Authentication and Authorization.   173

Overview   173

Authenticate Me   174

Email   178

Authorization   182

Summary   184

15. Scaffolding and the Site Template.   187

How to Scaffold   187

File Structure   188

    Cabal File   188

    Routes and Entities   189

    Foundation and Application Modules   189

    Import   190

    Handler Modules   191

widgetFile   191
defaultLayout   192
Static Files   192
Summary   193

16. Internationalization. **195**
Synopsis   195
Overview   197
Message Files   198
   Specifying Types   199
RenderMessage typeclass   199
Interpolation   200
Phrases, Not Words   201

17. Creating a Subsite. **203**
Hello, World   203

18. Understanding a Request. **207**
Handlers   207
   Layers   208
   Content   209
   Short-Circuit Responses   210
Dispatch   210
   toWaiApp, toWaiAppPlain, and warp   211
   Generated Code   212
   Complete Code   216
Summary   218

19. SQL Joins. **219**
Multiauthor Blog   219
Database Queries in Widgets   221
Joins   222
Esqueleto   223
Streaming   224
Summary   226

20. Yesod for Haskellers. **229**
Hello, Warp   229
What About Yesod?   234
The HandlerT Monad Transformer   236
   (To)Content, (To)TypedContent   239
   HasContentType and Representations   240

Convenience warp Function   242
Writing Handlers   242
Getting Request Parameters   242
Short-Circuiting   243
Streaming   243
Dynamic Parameters   245
Routing with Template Haskell   246
LiteApp   248
Shakespeare   249
The URL Rendering Function   251
Widgets   251
Details We Won't Cover   252

Part III. Examples

21. Initializing Data in the Foundation Data Type. **255**
Step 1: Define Your Foundation   256
Step 2: Use the Foundation   256
Step 3: Create the Foundation Value   256
Summary   257

22. Blog: i18n, Authentication, Authorization, and Database. **259**

23. Wiki: Markdown, Chat Subsite, Event Source. **269**
Subsite: Data   269
Subsite: Handlers   270
Subsite: Widget   273
Master Site: Data   275
Master Site: Instances   276
Master Site: Wiki Handlers   277
Master Site: Running   278
Summary   279

24. JSON Web Service. **281**
Server   281
Client   282

25. Case Study: Sphinx-Based Search. **285**
Sphinx Setup   285
Basic Yesod Setup   286
Searching   289

Streaming xmlpipe Output   292
Full Code   294

26. Visitor Counter... **301**

27. Single-Process Pub/Sub.... **303**
Foundation Data Type   303
Allocate a Job   304
Fork Our Background Job   304
View Progress   305
Complete Application   305

28. Environment Variables for Configuration............................... **309**

29. Route Attributes.... **311**
Alternative Approach: Hierarchical Routes   313

Part IV.   Appendices

A. monad-control.... **319**

B. Web Application Interface... **329**

C. Settings Types.... **337**

D. http-conduit.... **339**

E. xml-conduit... **345**

Index... **361**

Preface

It's fair to say that dynamic languages currently dominate the web development scene. Ruby, Python, and PHP are common choices for quickly creating a powerful web application. They provide a much faster and more comfortable development setting than standard static languages in the C family, like Java.

But some of us are looking for a bit more in our development toolbox. We want a language that gives us guarantees that our code is doing what it should. Instead of writing up a unit test to cover every bit of functionality in our application, wouldn't it be wonderful if the compiler could *automatically* ensure that our code is correct? And as an added bonus, wouldn't it be nice if our code ran quickly too?

These are the goals of Yesod. Yesod is a web framework bringing the strengths of the Haskell programming language to the web development world. Yesod not only uses a pure language to interact with an impure world, but allows safe interactions with the outside world by automatically sanitizing incoming and outgoing data. It helps us avoid basic mistakes such as mixing up integers and strings, and even allows us to statically prevent many cases of security holes like cross-site scripting (XSS) attacks.

Who This Book Is For

In general, there are two groups of people coming to Yesod. The first group is comprised of longtime Haskell users—already convinced of the advantages of Haskell—who are looking for a powerful framework for creating web applications. The second consists of web developers who either are dissatisfied with their existing tools or are looking to expand their horizons into the functional world.

This book assumes a basic familiarity with both web development and Haskell. We don't use many complicated Haskell concepts, and those we do use are introduced separately. For the most part, understanding the basics of the syntax of the language should be sufficient.

If you want to come up to speed on Haskell, I recommend another wonderful O'Reilly book: *Real World Haskell* by Bryan O'Sullivan, John Goerzen, and Donald Bruce Stewart.

Conventions Used in This Book

The following typographical conventions are used in this book:

Italic

Indicates new terms, URLs, email addresses, filenames, and file extensions.

`Constant width`

Used for program listings, as well as within paragraphs to refer to program elements such as variable or function names, databases, data types, environment variables, statements, commands, libraries, packages, tools, and keywords.

`Constant width bold`

Shows commands or other text that should be typed literally by the user.

`Constant width italic`

Shows text that should be replaced with user-supplied values or by values determined by context.

This icon signifies a tip, suggestion, or general note.

Using Code Examples

This book is here to help you get your job done. In general, you may use the code in this book in your programs and documentation. You do not need to contact us for permission unless you're reproducing a significant portion of the code. For example, writing a program that uses several chunks of code from this book does not require permission. Selling or distributing a CD-ROM of examples from O'Reilly books does require permission. Answering a question by citing this book and quoting example code does not require permission. Incorporating a significant amount of example code from this book into your product's documentation does require permission.

We appreciate, but do not require, attribution. An attribution usually includes the title, author, publisher, and ISBN. For example: "*Developing Web Apps with Haskell and Yesod*, Second Edition by Michael Snoyman (O'Reilly). Copyright 2015 Michael Snoyman, 978-1-449-31697-6."

If you feel your use of code examples falls outside fair use or the permission given above, feel free to contact us at *permissions@oreilly.com*.

Safari® Books Online

 *Safari Books Online* is an on-demand digital library that delivers expert content in both book and video form from the world's leading authors in technology and business.

Technology professionals, software developers, web designers, and business and creative professionals use Safari Books Online as their primary resource for research, problem solving, learning, and certification training.

Safari Books Online offers a range of plans and pricing for enterprise, government, education, and individuals.

Members have access to thousands of books, training videos, and prepublication manuscripts in one fully searchable database from publishers like O'Reilly Media, Prentice Hall Professional, Addison-Wesley Professional, Microsoft Press, Sams, Que, Peachpit Press, Focal Press, Cisco Press, John Wiley & Sons, Syngress, Morgan Kaufmann, IBM Redbooks, Packt, Adobe Press, FT Press, Apress, Manning, New Riders, McGraw-Hill, Jones & Bartlett, Course Technology, and hundreds more. For more information about Safari Books Online, please visit us online.

How to Contact Us

Please address comments and questions concerning this book to the publisher:

> O'Reilly Media, Inc.
> 1005 Gravenstein Highway North
> Sebastopol, CA 95472
> 800-998-9938 (in the United States or Canada)
> 707-829-0515 (international or local)
> 707-829-0104 (fax)

We have a web page for this book, where we list errata, examples, and any additional information. You can access this page at *http://bit.ly/dwa-haskell-yesod*.

To comment or ask technical questions about this book, send email to *bookquestions@oreilly.com*.

For more information about our books, courses, conferences, and news, see our website at *http://www.oreilly.com*.

Find us on Facebook: *http://facebook.com/oreilly*

Follow us on Twitter: *http://twitter.com/oreillymedia*

Watch us on YouTube: *http://www.youtube.com/oreillymedia*

Acknowledgments

Yesod was created by an entire community of developers, all of whom have put in significant effort to make sure that the final product is as polished and user-friendly as possible. Everyone from the core development team to the person making an API request on the mailing list has had an impact on bringing Yesod to where it is today.

In particular, I'd like to thank Greg Weber, who has shared the maintenance burden of the project; Kazu Yamamoto and Matt Brown, who transformed Warp from a simple testing server to one of the fastest application servers available today; and Felipe Lessa, Patrick Brisbin, and Luite Stegeman for their numerous contributions across the board.

A big thank you to my editor, Simon St. Laurent, for all of his guidance and support. Mark Lentczner, Johan Tibell, and Adam Turoff provided incredibly thorough reviews of this book, cleaning up many of my mistakes. Additionally, there have been dozens of readers who have looked over the content of this book online, and provided feedback on where either the prose or the message was not coming through clearly— not to mention numerous spelling errors.

But finally, and most importantly, I'd like to thank my wife, Miriam, for enduring all of the time spent on both this book and Yesod in general. She has been my editor and sounding board, though I'm sure the intricacies of Template Haskell sometimes worked more as a sedative than any meaningful conversation. Without her support, neither the Yesod project nor this book would have been able to happen.

Also, you'll notice that I use my kids' names (Eliezer and Gavriella) in some examples throughout the book. They deserve special mention in a Haskell text, as I think they're the youngest people to ever use the word "monad" in a sentence.

PART I

Basics

CHAPTER 1

Introduction

Since web programming began, people have been trying to make the development process a more pleasant one. As a community, we have continually pushed new techniques in an effort to solve some of the lingering difficulties of security threats, the stateless nature of HTTP, the multiple languages (HTML, CSS, JavaScript) necessary to create a powerful web application, and more.

Yesod attempts to ease the web development process by playing to the strengths of the Haskell programming language. Haskell's strong compile-time guarantees of correctness do not encompass only types; referential transparency ensures that we don't have any unintended side effects. Pattern matching on algebraic data types can help guarantee we've accounted for every possible case. By building upon Haskell, entire classes of bugs disappear.

Unfortunately, using Haskell isn't enough. The Web, by its very nature, is *not* type safe. Even the simplest case of distinguishing between an integer and a string is impossible: all data on the Web is transferred as raw bytes, evading our best efforts at type safety. Every app writer is left with the task of validating all input. I call this problem the boundary issue: however type safe your application is on the inside, every boundary with the outside world still needs to be sanitized.

Type Safety

This is where Yesod comes in. By using high-level declarative techniques, you can specify the exact input types you are expecting. And the process works the other way as well: by using type-safe URLs, you can make sure that the data you send out is also guaranteed to be well formed.

The boundary issue is not just a problem when dealing with the client: the same problem exists when persisting and loading data. Once again, Yesod saves you on the boundary by performing the marshaling of data for you. You can specify your entities in a high-level definition and remain blissfully ignorant of the details.

Concise Code

We all know that there is a lot of boilerplate coding involved in web applications. Wherever possible, Yesod tries to use Haskell's features to save your fingers the work:

- The forms library reduces the amount of code used for common cases by leveraging the Applicative typeclass.
- Routes are declared in a very terse format, without sacrificing type safety.
- Serializing your data to and from a database is handled automatically via code generation.

In Yesod, we have two kinds of code generation. To get your project started, we provide a scaffolding tool to set up your file and folder structure. However, most code generation is done at compile time via metaprogramming. This means your generated code will never get stale, as a simple library upgrade will bring all your generated code up to date.

But if you prefer to retain more control, and you want to know exactly what your code is doing, you can always run closer to the compiler and write all your code yourself.

Performance

Haskell's main compiler, the Glasgow Haskell Compiler (GHC), has amazing performance characteristics and is improving all the time. This choice of language by itself gives Yesod a large performance advantage over other offerings. But that's not enough: we need an architecture designed for performance.

Our approach to templates is one example: by allowing HTML, CSS, and JavaScript to be analyzed at compile time, Yesod both avoids costly disk I/O at runtime and can optimize the rendering of this code. But the architectural decisions go deeper: we use advanced techniques such as conduits and builders in the underlying libraries to make sure our code runs in constant memory, without exhausting precious file handles and other resources. By offering high-level abstractions, you can get highly compressed and properly cached CSS and JavaScript.

Yesod's flagship web server, Warp, is the fastest Haskell web server around. When these two pieces of technology are combined, it produces one of the fastest web application deployment solutions available.

Modularity

Yesod has spawned the creation of dozens of packages, most of which are usable in a context outside of Yesod itself. One of the goals of the project is to contribute back to the community as much as possible; as such, even if you are not planning on using Yesod in your next project, a large portion of this book may still be relevant for your needs.

Of course, these libraries have all been designed to integrate well together. Using the Yesod framework should give you a strong feeling of consistency throughout the various APIs.

A Solid Foundation

I remember once seeing a PHP framework advertising support for UTF-8. This struck me as surprising: you mean having UTF-8 support isn't automatic? In the Haskell world, issues like character encoding are already well addressed and fully supported. In fact, we usually have the opposite problem: there are a number of packages providing powerful and well-designed support for the problem. The Haskell community is constantly pushing the boundaries to find the cleanest, most efficient solutions for each challenge.

The downside of such a powerful ecosystem is the complexity of choice. By using Yesod, you will already have most of the tools chosen for you, and you can be guaranteed they work together. And of course, you always have the option of pulling in your own solution.

As a real-life example, Yesod and Hamlet (the default templating language) use `blaze-builder` for textual content generation. This choice was made because `blaze-builder` provides the fastest interface for generating UTF-8 data. Anyone who wants to use one of the other great libraries out there, such as `text`, should have no problem dropping it in.

CHAPTER 2

Haskell

Haskell is a powerful, fast, type-safe, functional programming language. This book takes as an assumption that you are already familiar with most of the basics of Haskell. There are two wonderful books for learning Haskell, both of which are available for reading online:

- *Learn You a Haskell for Great Good!* (*http://learnyouahaskell.com*) by Miran Lipovača (No Starch Press)
- *Real World Haskell* (*http://bit.ly/rw-haskell*) by Bryan O'Sullivan, John Goerzen, and Donald Bruce Stewart (O'Reilly)

Additionally, there are a number of great articles on School of Haskell (*https://www.fpcomplete.com/school*).

In order to use Yesod, you're going to have to know at least the basics of Haskell. Additionally, Yesod uses some features of Haskell that aren't covered in most introductory texts. While this book assumes the reader has a basic familiarity with Haskell, this chapter is intended to fill in the gaps.

If you are already fluent in Haskell, feel free to completely skip this chapter. Also, if you would prefer to start off by getting your feet wet with Yesod, you can always come back to this chapter later as a reference.

Terminology

Even for those familiar with Haskell as a language, there can occasionally be some confusion about terminology. Let's establish some base terms that we can use throughout this book:

Data type

This is one of the core building blocks for a strongly typed language like Haskell. Some data types (e.g., `Int`) can be treated as primitive values, while other data types will build on top of these to create more complicated values. For example, you might represent a person with:

```
data Person = Person Text Int
```

Here, the `Text` would give the person's name, and the `Int` would give the person's age. Due to its simplicity, this specific example type will recur throughout the book.

There are essentially three ways you can create a new data type:

- A `type` declaration such as `type GearCount = Int`. This merely creates a synonym for an existing type. The type system will do nothing to prevent you from using an `Int` where you asked for a `GearCount`. Using this can make your code more self-documenting.

- A `newtype` declaration such as `newtype Make = Make Text`. In this case, you cannot accidentally use a `Text` in place of a `Make`; the compiler will stop you. The `newtype` wrapper always disappears during compilation and will introduce no overhead.

- A `data` declaration such as `Person`. You can also create algebraic data types (ADTs)—for example, `data Vehicle = Bicycle GearCount | Car Make Model`.

Data constructor

In our examples, `Person`, `Make`, `Bicycle`, and `Car` are all data constructors.

Type constructor

In our examples, `Person`, `Make`, and `Vehicle` are all type constructors.

Type variables

Consider the data type `data Maybe a = Just a | Nothing`. In this case, `a` is a type variable.

 In both our `Person` and `Make` data types, our data type and data constructor share the same name. This is a common practice when dealing with a data type with a single data constructor. However, it is not a requirement; you can always name the data types and data constructors differently.

Tools

There are two main tools you'll need for Haskell development. The Glasgow Haskell Compiler (GHC) is the standard Haskell compiler, and the only one officially supported by Yesod. You'll also need Cabal, which is the standard Haskell build tool. Not only do we use Cabal for building our local code, but it can automatically download and install dependencies from Hackage, the Haskell package repository.

The Yesod website keeps an up-to-date quick start guide (*http://www.yesodweb.com/page/quickstart*) that includes information on how to install and configure the various tools. It's highly recommended that you follow these instructions. In particular, these steps make use of Stackage (*http://www.stackage.org/*) to avoid many common dependency-resolution issues.

If you decide to install your tools yourself, make sure to avoid these common pitfalls:

- Some JavaScript tools that ship with Yesod require the build tools `alex` and `happy` to be installed. These can be added with `cabal install alex happy`.
- Cabal installs an executable to a user-specific directory, which needs to be added to your `PATH`. The exact location is OS-specific; be sure to add the correct directory (*http://www.stackage.org/install*).
- On Windows, it's difficult to install the `network` package from source, as it requires a POSIX shell. Installing the Haskell Platform (*http://hackage.haskell.org/platform/*) avoids this issue.
- On Mac OS X, there are multiple C preprocessors available: one from Clang, and one from GCC. Many Haskell libraries depend on the GCC preprocessor. Again, the Haskell Platform sets things up correctly.
- Some Linux distributions—Ubuntu in particular—typically have outdated packages for GHC and the Haskell Platform. These may no longer be supported by the current version of Yesod. Check the quick start guide for minimum version requirements.
- Make sure you have all necessary system libraries installed. This is usually handled automatically by the Haskell Platform, but may require extra work on Linux distros. If you get error messages about missing libraries, you usually just need to `apt-get install` or `yum install` the relevant libraries.

Once you have your toolchain set up correctly, you'll need to install a number of Haskell libraries. For the vast majority of the book, the following command will install all the libraries you need:

```
cabal update && cabal install yesod yesod-bin persistent-sqlite yesod-static
```

Again, refer to the quick start guide (*http://www.yesodweb.com/page/quickstart*) for the most up-to-date and accurate information.

Language Pragmas

GHC will run by default in something very close to Haskell98 mode. It also ships with a large number of language extensions, allowing more powerful typeclasses, syntax changes, and more. There are multiple ways to tell GHC to turn on these extensions. For most of the code snippets in this book, you'll see language pragmas, which look like this:

```
{-# LANGUAGE MyLanguageExtension #-}
```

These should always appear at the top of your source file. Additionally, there are two other common approaches:

- On the GHC command line, pass an extra argument: -XMyLanguageExtension.
- In your cabal file, add a default-extensions block.

I personally never use the GHC command-line argument approach. It's a personal preference, but I like to have my settings clearly stated in a file. In general, it's recommended to avoid putting extensions in your cabal file; however, this rule mostly applies when writing publicly available libraries. When you're writing an application that you and your team will be working on, having all of your language extensions defined in a single location makes a lot of sense. The Yesod scaffolded site specifically uses this approach to avoid the boilerplate of specifying the same language pragmas in every source file.

We'll end up using quite a few language extensions in this book (at the time of writing, the scaffolding uses 13). We will not cover the meaning of all of them. Instead, see the GHC documentation (*http://bit.ly/ghc-docs*).

Overloaded Strings

What's the type of "hello"? Traditionally, it's String, which is defined as type String = [Char]. Unfortunately, there are a few limitations with this:

- It's a very inefficient implementation of textual data. We need to allocate extra memory for each cons cell, plus the characters themselves each take up a full machine word.
- Sometimes we have string-like data that's not actually text, such as ByteStrings and HTML.

To work around these limitations, GHC has a language extension called Overloaded Strings. When enabled, literal strings no longer have the monomorphic type String; instead, they have the type IsString a -> a, where IsString is defined as:

```
class IsString a where
    fromString :: String -> a
```

There are IsString instances available for a number of types in Haskell, such as Text (a much more efficient packed String type), ByteString, and Html. Virtually every example in this book will assume that this language extension is turned on.

Unfortunately, there is one drawback to this extension: it can sometimes confuse GHC's type checker. For example, imagine we use the following code:

```
{-# LANGUAGE OverloadedStrings, TypeSynonymInstances, FlexibleInstances #-}
import Data.Text (Text)

class DoSomething a where
    something :: a -> IO ()

instance DoSomething String where
    something _ = putStrLn "String"

instance DoSomething Text where
    something _ = putStrLn "Text"

myFunc :: IO ()
myFunc = something "hello"
```

Will the program print out String or Text? It's not clear. So instead, you'll need to give an explicit type annotation to specify whether "hello" should be treated as a String or Text.

 In some cases, you can overcome these problems by using the ExtendedDefaultRules language extension, though we'll instead try to be explicit in the book and not rely on defaulting.

Type Families

The basic idea of a type family is to state some association between two different types. Suppose we want to write a function that will safely take the first element of a list. But we don't want it to work just on lists; we'd like it to treat a ByteString like a list of Word8s. To do so, we need to introduce some associated type to specify what the contents of a certain type are:

```
{-# LANGUAGE TypeFamilies, OverloadedStrings #-}
import Data.Word (Word8)
```

```
import qualified Data.ByteString as S
import Data.ByteString.Char8 () -- get an orphan IsString instance

class SafeHead a where
    type Content a
    safeHead :: a -> Maybe (Content a)

instance SafeHead [a] where
    type Content [a] = a
    safeHead [] = Nothing
    safeHead (x:_) = Just x

instance SafeHead S.ByteString where
    type Content S.ByteString = Word8
    safeHead bs
        | S.null bs = Nothing
        | otherwise = Just $ S.head bs

main :: IO ()
main = do
    print $ safeHead ("" :: String)
    print $ safeHead ("hello" :: String)

    print $ safeHead ("" :: S.ByteString)
    print $ safeHead ("hello" :: S.ByteString)
```

The new syntax is the ability to place a `type` inside of a `class` and `instance`. We can also use `data` instead, which will create a new data type instead of referencing an existing one.

There are other ways to use associated types outside the context of a typeclass. For more information on type families, see the Haskell wiki page (*http://bit.ly/ghc-type-fam*).

Template Haskell

Template Haskell (TH) is an approach to *code generation*. We use it in Yesod in a number of places to reduce boilerplate, and to ensure that the generated code is correct. Template Haskell is essentially Haskell that generates a Haskell abstract syntax tree (AST).

There's actually more power in TH than that, as it can in fact introspect code. We don't use these facilities in Yesod, however.

Writing TH code can be tricky, and unfortunately there isn't very much type safety involved. You can easily write TH that will generate code that won't compile. This is only an issue for the developers of Yesod, not for its users. During development, we use a large collection of unit tests to ensure that the generated code is correct. As a user, all you need to do is call these already existing functions. For example, to include an externally defined Hamlet template (discussed in Chapter 4), you can write:

```
$(hamletFile "myfile.hamlet")
```

The dollar sign immediately followed by parentheses tell GHC that what follows is a Template Haskell function. The code inside is then run by the compiler and generates a Haskell AST, which is then compiled. And yes, it's even possible to go meta with this (*http://bit.ly/haskell-temp*).

A nice trick is that TH code is allowed to perform arbitrary IO actions, and therefore we can place some input in external files and have it parsed at compile time. One example usage is to have compile-time–checked HTML, CSS, and JavaScript templates.

If our Template Haskell code is being used to generate declarations and is being placed at the top level of our file, we can leave off the dollar sign and parentheses. In other words:

```
{-# LANGUAGE TemplateHaskell #-}

-- Normal function declaration, nothing special
myFunction = ...

-- Include some TH code
$(myThCode)

-- Or equivalently
myThCode
```

It can be useful to see what code is being generated by Template Haskell for you. To do so, you should use the -ddump-splices GHC option.

> There are many other features of Template Haskell not covered here. For more information, see the Haskell wiki page (*http://bit.ly/temp-haskell*).

Template Haskell introduces something called the *stage restriction*, which essentially means that code before a Template Haskell splice cannot refer to code in the Template Haskell, or what follows. This will sometimes require you to rearrange your code a bit. The same restriction applies to QuasiQuotes.

Out of the box, Yesod is really geared for using code generation to avoid boilerplate, but it's perfectly acceptable to use Yesod in a Template Haskell–free way. There's more information on that in Chapter 20.

QuasiQuotes

QuasiQuotes (QQ) are a minor extension of Template Haskell that let us embed arbitrary content within our Haskell source files. For example, we mentioned previously the hamletFile TH function, which reads the template contents from an external file. We also have a quasiquoter named hamlet that takes the content inline:

```
{-# LANGUAGE QuasiQuotes #-}

[hamlet|<p>This is quasi-quoted Hamlet.|]
```

The syntax is set off using square brackets and pipes. The name of the quasiquoter is given between the opening bracket and the first pipe, and the content is given between the pipes.

Throughout the book, we will frequently use the QQ approach over a TH-powered external file, as the former is simpler to copy and paste. However, in production, external files are recommended for all but the shortest of inputs, as it gives a nice separation of the non-Haskell syntax from your Haskell code.

API Documentation

The standard API documentation program in Haskell is called Haddock. The standard Haddock search tool is called Hoogle. I recommend using FP Complete's Hoogle search (*https://www.fpcomplete.com/hoogle*) and its accompanying Haddocks for searching and browsing documentation, because the database covers a very large number of open source Haskell packages, and the documentation provided is always fully generated and known to link to other working Haddocks.

The more commonly used sources for these are Hackage (*http://hackage.haskell.org/*) itself, and Haskell.org's Hoogle instance (*http://www.haskell.org/hoogle*). The downsides to these are that—based on build issues on the server—documentation is sometimes not generated, and the Hoogle search defaults to searching only a subset of available packages. Most importantly for us, Yesod is indexed by FP Complete's Hoogle, but not by Haskell.org's.

If you run into types or functions that you do not understand, try doing a Hoogle search with FP Complete's Hoogle to get more information.

Summary

You don't need to be an expert in Haskell to use Yesod—a basic familiarity will suffice. This chapter hopefully gave you just enough extra information to feel more comfortable as you follow along throughout the rest of the book.

CHAPTER 3

Basics

The first step with any new technology is getting it running. The goal of this chapter is to get you started with a simple Yesod application and cover some of the basic concepts and terminology.

Hello, World

Let's get this book started properly with a simple web page that says "Hello, World":

```
{-# LANGUAGE OverloadedStrings     #-}
{-# LANGUAGE QuasiQuotes           #-}
{-# LANGUAGE TemplateHaskell       #-}
{-# LANGUAGE TypeFamilies          #-}
import            Yesod

data HelloWorld = HelloWorld

mkYesod "HelloWorld" [parseRoutes|
/ HomeR GET
|]

instance Yesod HelloWorld

getHomeR :: Handler Html
getHomeR = defaultLayout [whamlet|Hello, World!|]

main :: IO ()
main = warp 3000 HelloWorld
```

If you save the preceding code in *helloworld.hs* and run it with `runhaskell hello world.hs`, you'll get a web server running on port 3000. If you point your browser to *http://localhost:3000*, you'll get the following HTML:

```
<!DOCTYPE html>
<html><head><title></title></head><body>Hello, World!</body></html>
```

We'll refer back to this example throughout the rest of the chapter.

Routing

Like most modern web frameworks, Yesod follows a front controller pattern. This means that every request to a Yesod application enters at the same point and is routed from there. As a contrast, in systems like PHP and ASP, you usually create a number of different files, and the web server automatically directs requests to the relevant file.

In addition, Yesod uses a declarative style for specifying routes. In our earlier example, this looked like:

```
mkYesod "HelloWorld" [parseRoutes|
/ HomeR GET
|]
```

mkYesod is a Template Haskell function, and parseRoutes is a quasiquoter.

In other words, the preceding code simply creates a route in the Hello, World application called HomeR. It should listen for requests to / (the root of the application) and should answer GET requests. We call HomeR a *resource*, which is where the R suffix comes from.

The R suffix on resource names is simply convention, but it's a fairly universally followed convention. It makes it just a bit easier to read and understand code.

The mkYesod TH function generates quite a bit of code here: a route data type, parser/render functions, a dispatch function, and some helper types. We'll look at this in more detail in Chapter 7, but by using the -ddump-splices GHC option we can get an immediate look at the generated code. Here's a cleaned-up version of it:

```
instance RenderRoute HelloWorld where
    data Route HelloWorld = HomeR
        deriving (Show, Eq, Read)
    renderRoute HomeR = ([], [])

instance ParseRoute HelloWorld where
    parseRoute ([], _) = Just HomeR
```

```
    parseRoute _          = Nothing

instance YesodDispatch HelloWorld where
    yesodDispatch env req =
        yesodRunner handler env mroute req
      where
        mroute = parseRoute (pathInfo req, textQueryString req)
        handler =
            case mroute of
                Nothing -> notFound
                Just HomeR ->
                    case requestMethod req of
                        "GET" -> getHomeR
                        _      -> badMethod

type Handler = HandlerT HelloWorld IO
```

 In addition to using -ddump-splices, it can often be useful to generate Haddock documentation for your application to see which functions and data types were generated for you.

We can see that the RenderRoute class defines an *associated data type* providing the routes for our application. In this simple example, we have just one route: HomeR. In real-life applications, we'll have many more, and they will be more complicated than our HomeR.

renderRoute takes a route and turns it into path segments and query string parameters. Again, our example is simple, so the code is likewise simple: both values are empty lists.

ParseRoute provides the inverse function, parseRoute. Here we see the first strong motivation for our reliance on Template Haskell: it ensures that the parsing and rendering of routes correspond correctly with each other. This kind of code can easily become difficult to keep in sync when written by hand. By relying on code generation, we're letting the compiler (and Yesod) handle those details for us.

YesodDispatch provides a means of taking an input request and passing it to the appropriate handler function. The process is essentially:

1. Parse the request.
2. Choose a handler function.
3. Run the handler function.

The code generation follows a simple format for matching routes to handler function names, which I'll describe in the next section.

Finally, we have a simple type synonym defining `Handler` to make our code a little easier to write.

There's a lot more going on here than we've described. The generated dispatch code actually uses the view patterns language extension for efficiency; also, more typeclass instances are created, and there are other cases to handle, such as subsites. We'll get into the details later in the book, especially in Chapter 18.

Handler Function

So we have a route named `HomeR`, and it responds to `GET` requests. How do you define your response? You write a handler function. Yesod follows a standard naming scheme for these functions: it's the lowercase method name (e.g., `GET` becomes `get`) followed by the route name. In this case, the function name would be `getHomeR`.

Most of the code you write in Yesod lives in handler functions. This is where you process user input, perform database queries, and create responses. In our simple example, we create a response using the `defaultLayout` function. This function wraps up the content it's given in your site's template. By default, it produces an HTML file with a doctype and <html>, <head>, and <body> tags. As we'll see in Chapter 6, this function can be overridden to do much more.

In our example, we pass [whamlet|Hello, World!|] to `defaultLayout`. `whamlet` is another quasiquoter. In this case, it converts Hamlet syntax into a widget. Hamlet is the default HTML templating engine in Yesod. Together with its siblings Cassius, Lucius, and Julius, you can create HTML, CSS, and JavaScript in a fully type-safe and compile-time-checked manner. We'll see much more about this in Chapter 4.

Widgets are another cornerstone of Yesod. They allow you to create modular components of a site consisting of HTML, CSS, and JavaScript and reuse them throughout your site. Widgets are covered in more depth in Chapter 5.

The Foundation

The string `HelloWorld` shows up a number of times in our example. Every Yesod application has a foundation data type. This data type must be an instance of the `Yesod` typeclass, which provides a central place for declaring a number of different settings controlling the execution of our application.

In our case, this data type is pretty boring: it doesn't contain any information. Nonetheless, the foundation is central to how our example runs: it ties together the routes with the instance declaration and lets it all be run. We'll see throughout this book that the foundation pops up in a whole bunch of places.

But foundations don't have to be boring. They can be used to store lots of useful information—usually stuff that needs to be initialized at program launch and used throughout. Here are some very common examples:

- A database connection pool
- Settings loaded from a config file
- An HTTP connection manager
- A random number generator

 By the way, the word Yesod (יסוד) means *foundation* in Hebrew.

Running

We mention HelloWorld again in our main function. Our foundation contains all the information we need to route and respond to requests in our application; now we just need to convert it into something that can run. A useful function for this in Yesod is warp, which runs the Warp web server with a number of default settings enabled on the specified port (here, it's 3000).

One of the features of Yesod is that you aren't tied down to a single deployment strategy. Yesod is built on top of the Web Application Interface (WAI), allowing it to run on FastCGI, SCGI, Warp, or even as a desktop application using the WebKit library. We'll discuss some of these options in Chapter 11. And at the end of this chapter, we will explain the development server.

Warp is the premier deployment option for Yesod. It is a lightweight, highly efficient web server developed specifically for hosting Yesod. It is also used outside of Yesod for other Haskell development (both framework and nonframework applications), and as a standard file server in a number of production environments.

Resources and Type-Safe URLs

In our Hello, World application we defined just a single resource (HomeR), but real-life web applications are usually much more exciting and include more than one page. Let's take a look at another example:

```
{-# LANGUAGE OverloadedStrings    #-}
{-# LANGUAGE QuasiQuotes          #-}
{-# LANGUAGE TemplateHaskell      #-}
{-# LANGUAGE TypeFamilies         #-}
```

```
import           Yesod

data Links = Links

mkYesod "Links" [parseRoutes|
/ HomeR GET
/page1 Page1R GET
/page2 Page2R GET
|]

instance Yesod Links

getHomeR  = defaultLayout [whamlet|<a href=@{Page1R}>Go to page 1!|]
getPage1R = defaultLayout [whamlet|<a href=@{Page2R}>Go to page 2!|]
getPage2R = defaultLayout [whamlet|<a href=@{HomeR}>Go home!|]

main = warp 3000 Links
```

Overall, this is very similar to Hello, World. Our foundation is now Links instead of HelloWorld, and in addition to the HomeR resource, we've added Page1R and Page2R. As such, we've also added two more handler functions: getPage1R and getPage2R.

The only truly new feature is inside the whamlet quasiquotation. We'll delve into syntax in Chapter 4, but we can see the following creates a link to the Page1R resource:

```
<a href=@{Page1R}>Go to page 1!
```

The important thing to note here is that Page1R is a data constructor. By making each resource a data constructor, we have a feature called *type-safe URLs*. Instead of splicing together strings to create URLs, we simply create a plain old Haskell value. By using at-sign interpolation (@{...}), Yesod automatically renders those values to textual URLs before sending things off to the user. We can see how this is implemented by looking again at the -ddump-splices output:

```
instance RenderRoute Links where
    data Route Links = HomeR | Page1R | Page2R
        deriving (Show, Eq, Read)

    renderRoute HomeR  = ([], [])
    renderRoute Page1R = (["page1"], [])
    renderRoute Page2R = (["page2"], [])
```

In the Route associated type for Links, we have additional constructors for Page1R and Page2R. We also now have a better glimpse of the return values for renderRoute. The first part of the tuple gives the path pieces for the given route. The second part gives the query string parameters; for almost all use cases, this will be an empty list.

It's hard to overestimate the value of type-safe URLs. They give you a huge amount of flexibility and robustness when developing your application. You can move URLs around at will without ever breaking links. In Chapter 7, we'll see that routes can take parameters, such as a blog entry URL taking the blog post ID.

Let's say you want to switch from routing on the numerical post ID to a year/month/ slug setup. In a traditional web framework, you would need to go through every single reference to your blog post route and update appropriately. If you miss one, you'll have 404s at runtime. In Yesod, all you do is update your route and compile: GHC will pinpoint every single line of code that needs to be corrected.

Non-HTML Responses

Yesod can serve up any kind of content you want, and has first-class support for many commonly used response formats. You've seen HTML so far, but JSON data is just as easy, via the `aeson` package:

```
{-# LANGUAGE ExtendedDefaultRules #-}
{-# LANGUAGE OverloadedStrings    #-}
{-# LANGUAGE QuasiQuotes          #-}
{-# LANGUAGE TemplateHaskell      #-}
{-# LANGUAGE TypeFamilies         #-}
import Yesod

data App = App

mkYesod "App" [parseRoutes|
/ HomeR GET
|]

instance Yesod App

getHomeR = return $ object ["msg" .= "Hello, World"]

main = warp 3000 App
```

We'll cover JSON responses in more detail in later chapters, including how to automatically switch between HTML and JSON representations depending on the `Accept` request header.

The Scaffolded Site

Installing Yesod will give you both the Yesod library, and a *yesod* executable. This executable accepts a few commands, but the first one you'll want to be acquainted with is `yesod init`. It will ask you some questions, and then generate a folder containing the default scaffolded site. Inside that directory, you can run `cabal install --only-dependencies` to build any extra dependencies (such as your database backends), and then `yesod devel` to run your site.

The scaffolded site gives you a lot of best practices out of the box, setting up files and dependencies in a time-tested approach used by most production Yesod sites. However, all this convenience can get in the way of actually learning Yesod. Therefore, most of this book will avoid the scaffolding tool, and instead deal directly with Yesod as a library. But if you're going to build a real site, I strongly recommend using the scaffolding.

We will cover the structure of the scaffolded site in Chapter 15.

Development Server

One of the advantages interpreted languages have over compiled languages is fast prototyping: you save changes to a file and hit refresh. If we want to make any changes to our Yesod apps, we'll need to call runhaskell from scratch, which can be a bit tedious.

Fortunately, there's a solution to this: yesod devel automatically rebuilds and reloads your code for you. This can be a great way to develop your Yesod projects, and when you're ready to move to production, you still get to compile down to incredibly efficient code. The Yesod scaffolding automatically sets things up for you. This gives you the best of both worlds: rapid prototyping *and* fast production code.

It's a little bit more involved to set up your code to be used by yesod devel, so our examples will just use warp. Fortunately, the scaffolded site is fully configured to use the development server, so when you're ready to move over to the real world, it will be waiting for you.

Summary

Every Yesod application is built around a foundation data type. We associate some resources with that data type and define some handler functions, and Yesod handles all of the routing. These resources are also data constructors, which lets us have type-safe URLs.

By being built on top of WAI, Yesod applications can run with a number of different backends. For simple apps, the warp function provides a convenient way to use the Warp web server. For rapid development, using yesod devel is a good choice. And when you're ready to move to production, you have the full power and flexibility to configure Warp (or any other WAI handler) to suit your needs.

When developing in Yesod, we get a number of choices for coding style: quasiquotation or external files, warp or yesod devel, and so on. The examples in this book deliberately use the choices that are easiest to copy and paste, but more powerful options will be available when you start building real Yesod applications.

CHAPTER 4

Shakespearean Templates

Yesod uses the Shakespearean family of template languages as its standard approach to HTML, CSS, and JavaScript creation. This language family shares some common syntax, as well as a few overarching principles:

- As little interference to the underlying language as possible, while providing conveniences where unobtrusive
- Compile-time guarantees on well-formed content
- Static type safety, greatly helping the prevention of XSS (cross-site scripting) attacks
- Automatic validation of interpolated links, whenever possible, through type-safe URLs

There is nothing inherently tying Yesod to these languages, or the other way around: each can be used independently of the other. This chapter will address these template languages on their own, while the remainder of the book will use them to enhance Yesod application development.

Synopsis

There are four main languages at play: Hamlet is an HTML templating language, Julius is for JavaScript, and Cassius and Lucius are both for CSS. Hamlet and Cassius are both whitespace-sensitive formats, using indentation to denote nesting. By contrast, Lucius is a superset of CSS, keeping CSS's braces for denoting nesting. Julius is a simple passthrough language for producing JavaScript; the only added feature is variable interpolation.

Cassius is, in fact, just an alternative syntax for Lucius. They both use the same processing engine underneath, but Cassius files have indentation converted into braces before processing. The choice between the two is purely one of syntactical preference.

Hamlet (HTML)

```
$doctype 5
<html>
    <head>
        <title>#{pageTitle} - My Site
        <link rel=stylesheet href=@{Stylesheet}>
    <body>
        <h1 .page-title>#{pageTitle}
        <p>Here is a list of your friends:
        $if null friends
            <p>Sorry, I lied, you don't have any friends.
        $else
            <ul>
                $forall Friend name age <- friends
                    <li>#{name} (#{age} years old)
        <footer>^{copyright}
```

Lucius (CSS)

```
section.blog {
    padding: 1em;
    border: 1px solid #000;
    h1 {
        color: #{headingColor};
        background-image: url(@{MyBackgroundR});
    }
}
```

Cassius (CSS)

The following is equivalent to the Lucius example:

```
section.blog
    padding: 1em
    border: 1px solid #000
    h1
        color: #{headingColor}
        background-image: url(@{MyBackgroundR})
```

Julius (JavaScript)

```
$(function(){
    $("section.#{sectionClass}").hide();
    $("#mybutton").click(function(){document.location = "@{SomeRouteR}";});
```

```
        ^{addBling}
    });
```

Types

Before we jump into syntax, let's take a look at the various types involved. We mentioned in the introduction that types help protect us from XSS attacks. For example, let's say that we have an HTML template that should display someone's name. It might look like this:

```
<p>Hello, my name is #{name}
```

 {…} is how we do variable interpolation in Shakespeare.

What should happen to `name`, and what should its data type be? A naive approach would be to use a `Text` value, and insert it verbatim. But that would give us quite a problem when `name` is equal to something like:

```
<script src='http://nefarious.com/evil.js'></script>
```

What we want is to be able to entity-encode the name, so that < becomes <.

An equally naive approach is to simply entity-encode *every* piece of text that gets embedded. What happens when you have some preexisting HTML generated from another process? For example, on the Yesod website, all Haskell code snippets are run through a colorizing function that wraps up words in appropriate `span` tags. If we entity-escaped everything, code snippets would be completely unreadable!

Instead, we have an `Html` data type. In order to generate an `Html` value, we have two options for APIs. The `ToMarkup` typeclass provides a way to convert `String` and `Text` values into `Html` via its `toHtml` function, automatically escaping entities along the way. This would be the approach we'd want for `name`. For the code snippet example, we would use the `preEscapedToMarkup` function.

When you use variable interpolation in Hamlet (the HTML Shakespeare language), it automatically applies a `toHtml` call to the value inside. So, if you interpolate a `String`, it will be entity-escaped, but if you provide an `Html` value, it will appear unmodified. In the code snippet example, we might interpolate with something like #{preEscaped ToMarkup myHaskellHtml}.

The Html data type and the functions mentioned are all provided by the blaze-html package. This allows Hamlet to interact with all other blaze-html packages, and lets Hamlet provide a general solution for producing blaze-html values. Also, we get to take advantage of blaze-html's amazing performance.

Similarly, we have Css/ToCss, as well as Javascript/ToJavascript. These provide some compile-time sanity checks to ensure we haven't accidentally stuck some HTML in our CSS.

One other advantage on the CSS side is some helper data types for colors and units. For example:

    .red { color: #{colorRed} }

Refer to the Haddock documentation (*http://www.stackage.org/pack age/shakespeare*) for more details.

Type-Safe URLs

Possibly the most unique feature in Yesod is type-safe URLs, and the ability to use them conveniently is provided directly by Shakespeare. Usage is nearly identical to variable interpolation; we just use the at sign (@) instead of the hash (#). We'll cover the syntax later, but first let's clarify the intuition.

Suppose we have an application with two routes: *http://example.com/profile/home* is the homepage, and *http://example.com/display/time* displays the current time. If we want to link from the homepage to the time, there are three different ways of constructing the URL:

- As a relative link (e.g., *../display/time*)
- As an absolute link, without a domain (e.g., */display/time*)
- As an absolute link, with a domain (e.g., *http://example.com/display/time*)

But there are problems with each approach. The first will break if either URL changes. Also, it's not suitable for all use cases; RSS and Atom feeds, for instance, require absolute URLs. The second is more resilient to change than the first, but still won't be acceptable for RSS and Atom. And while the third works fine for all use cases, you'll need to update every single URL in your application whenever your domain name changes. You think that doesn't happen often? Just wait till you move from using a development server to a staging server and finally into production.

But more importantly, there is one huge issue with all three approaches: if you change your routes at all, the compiler won't warn you about the broken links. Not to mention that typos can wreak havoc as well.

The goal of type-safe URLs is to let the compiler check things for us as much as possible. In order to facilitate this, our first step must be to move away from plain old text, which the compiler doesn't understand, to some well-defined data types. For our simple application, let's model our routes with a sum type:

```
data MyRoute = Home | Time
```

Instead of placing a link like *display/time* in our template, we can use the `Time` constructor. But at the end of the day, HTML is made up of text, not data types, so we need some way to convert these values to text. We call this a *URL rendering function* —here's a simple example:

```
renderMyRoute :: MyRoute -> Text
renderMyRoute Home = "http://example.com/profile/home"
renderMyRoute Time = "http://example.com/display/time"
```

 URL rendering functions are actually a bit more complicated than this. They need to address query string parameters, handle records within the constructor, and more intelligently handle the domain name. But in practice, you don't need to worry about this, because Yesod will automatically create your render functions. The one thing to point out is that the type signature is actually a little more complicated to handle query strings:

```
type Query = [(Text, Text)]
type Render url = url -> Query -> Text
renderMyRoute :: Render MyRoute
renderMyRoute Home _ = ...
renderMyRoute Time _ = ...
```

OK, we have our render function, and we have type-safe URLs embedded in the templates. How exactly does this fit together? Instead of generating an `Html` (or `Css` or `Javascript`) value directly, Shakespearean templates actually produce a function, which takes the render function and produces HTML. Let's take a quick peek to see how Hamlet would work under the surface. Supposing we had a template:

```
<a href=@{Time}>The time
```

this would translate roughly into the Haskell code:

```
\render -> mconcat ["<a href='", render Time, "'>The time</a>"]
```

Syntax

All Shakespearean languages share the same interpolation syntax and are able to utilize type-safe URLs. They differ in the syntax specific for their target language (HTML, CSS, or JavaScript). Let's explore each language in turn.

Hamlet Syntax

Hamlet is the most sophisticated of the languages. Not only does it provide syntax for generating HTML, but it also allows for basic control structures: conditionals, looping, and maybes.

Tags

Obviously, tags will play an important part in any HTML template language. In Hamlet, we try to stick very close to existing HTML syntax to make the language more comfortable. However, instead of using closing tags to denote nesting, we use indentation. So, something like this in HTML:

```
<body>
<p>Some paragraph.</p>
<ul>
<li>Item 1</li>
<li>Item 2</li>
</ul>
</body>
```

would be:

```
<body>
    <p>Some paragraph.
    <ul>
        <li>Item 1
        <li>Item 2
```

In general, we find this to be easier to follow than HTML once you get accustomed to it. The only tricky part arises when dealing with whitespace before and after tags. For example, let's say we want to create the following HTML:

```
<p>Paragraph <i>italic</i> end.</p>
```

We want to make sure that whitespace is preserved after the word "Paragraph" and before the word "end." To do so, we use two simple escape characters:

```
<p>
    Paragraph #
    <i>italic
    \ end.
```

The whitespace escape rules are actually quite simple:

- If the first non-space character in a line is a backslash, the backslash is ignored. (Note: this will also cause any tag on this line to be treated as plain text.)
- If the last character in a line is a hash, it is ignored.

One other thing: Hamlet does *not* escape entities within its content. This is done on purpose to allow existing HTML to be more easily copied in. So, the preceding example could also be written as:

```
<p>Paragraph <i>italic</i> end.
```

Notice that the first tag will be automatically closed by Hamlet, while the inner `<i>` tag will not. You are free to use whichever approach you want; there is no penalty for either choice. Be aware, however, that the *only* time you use closing tags in Hamlet is for such inline tags; normal tags are not closed.

Another outcome of this is that any tags after the first tag do not have special treatment for IDs and classes. For example, the following Hamlet snippet:

```
<p #firstid>Paragraph <i #secondid>italic end.
```

generates the HTML:

```
<p id="firstid">Paragraph <i #secondid>italic</i> end.</p>
```

Notice how the `<p>` tag is automatically closed, and its attributes get special treatment, whereas the `<i>` tag is treated as plain text.

Interpolation

What we have so far is nice, simplified HTML, but it doesn't let us interact with our Haskell code at all. How do we pass in variables? The answer is simple—by using interpolation:

```
<head>
    <title>#{title}
```

The hash followed by a pair of braces denotes *variable interpolation*. In this case, the `title` variable from the scope in which the template was called will be used. Let me state that again: Hamlet automatically has access to the variables in scope when it's called. There is no need to specifically pass variables in.

You can apply functions within an interpolation. You can use string and numeric literals in an interpolation. You can also use qualified modules. Both parentheses and the dollar sign can be used to group statements together. And at the end, the `toHtml` function is applied to the result, meaning *any* instance of `ToHtml` can be interpolated. Take, for instance, the following code:

```
-- Just ignore the QuasiQuote stuff for now, and that shamlet thing.
-- It will be explained later.
{-# LANGUAGE QuasiQuotes #-}
import Text.Hamlet (shamlet)
import Text.Blaze.Html.Renderer.String (renderHtml)
import Data.Char (toLower)
import Data.List (sort)
```

```
data Person = Person
    { name :: String
    , age  :: Int
    }

main :: IO ()
main = putStrLn $ renderHtml [shamlet|
<p>Hello, my name is #{name person} and I am #{show $ age person}.
<p>
    Let's do some funny stuff with my name: #
    <b>#{sort $ map toLower (name person)}
<p>Oh, and in 5 years I'll be #{show ((+) 5 (age person))} years old.
|]
  where
    person = Person "Michael" 26
```

What about our much-touted type-safe URLs? They are almost identical to variable interpolation in every way, except they start with an at sign (@) instead. In addition, there is embedding via a caret (^), which allows you to embed another template of the same type. The next code sample demonstrates both of these:

```
{-# LANGUAGE QuasiQuotes #-}
{-# LANGUAGE OverloadedStrings #-}
import Text.Hamlet (HtmlUrl, hamlet)
import Text.Blaze.Html.Renderer.String (renderHtml)
import Data.Text (Text)

data MyRoute = Home

render :: MyRoute -> [(Text, Text)] -> Text
render Home _ = "/home"

footer :: HtmlUrl MyRoute
footer = [hamlet|
<footer>
    Return to #
    <a href=@{Home}>Homepage
    .
|]

main :: IO ()
main = putStrLn $ renderHtml $ [hamlet|
<body>
    <p>This is my page.
    ^{footer}
|] render
```

Additionally, there is a variant of URL interpolation that allows you to embed query string parameters. This can be useful, for example, for creating paginated responses. Instead of using @{...}, you add a question mark (@?{...}) to indicate the presence of a query string. The value you provide must be a two-tuple with the first value being a type-safe URL and the second being a list of query string parameter pairs. The following code snippet shows an example:

```
{-# LANGUAGE QuasiQuotes #-}
{-# LANGUAGE OverloadedStrings #-}
import Text.Hamlet (HtmlUrl, hamlet)
import Text.Blaze.Html.Renderer.String (renderHtml)
import Data.Text (Text, append, pack)
import Control.Arrow (second)
import Network.HTTP.Types (renderQueryText)
import Data.Text.Encoding (decodeUtf8)
import Blaze.ByteString.Builder (toByteString)

data MyRoute = SomePage

render :: MyRoute -> [(Text, Text)] -> Text
render SomePage params = "/home" `append`
    decodeUtf8 (toByteString $ renderQueryText True (map (second Just) params))

main :: IO ()
main = do
    let currPage = 2 :: Int
    putStrLn $ renderHtml $ [hamlet|
<p>
    You are currently on page #{currPage}.
    <a href=@?{(SomePage, [("page", pack $ show $ currPage - 1)])}>Previous
    <a href=@?{(SomePage, [("page", pack $ show $ currPage + 1)])}>Next
|] render
```

This generates the expected HTML:

```
<p>You are currently on page ?
<a href="/home?page=1">Previous</a>
<a href="/home?page=3">Next</a>
</p>
```

Attributes

In the preceding example, we put an `href` attribute on the `<a>` tag. Let's elaborate on the syntax:

- You can have interpolations within the attribute value.
- The equal sign and value for an attribute are optional, just like in HTML. So, `<input type=checkbox checked>` is perfectly valid.
- There are two convenience attributes: for `id`, you can use the hash, and for classes, the period (in other words, `<p #paragraphid .class1 .class2>`).
- Although quotes around the attribute value are optional, they are required if you want to embed spaces.

- You can add an attribute optionally by using colons. To make a checkbox only checked if the variable isChecked is True, you would write <input type=check box :isChecked:checked>. To have a paragraph be optionally red, you could use <p :isRed:style="color:red">. (This also works for class names—for example, <p :isCurrent:.current> will set the class current to True.)

Conditionals

Eventually, you'll want to put some logic in your page. The goal of Hamlet is to make the logic as minimalistic as possible, pushing the heavy lifting into Haskell. As such, our logical statements are very basic... so basic, that it's if, elseif, and else:

```
$if isAdmin
    <p>Welcome to the admin section.
$elseif isLoggedIn
    <p>You are not the administrator.
$else
    <p>I don't know who you are. Please log in so I can decide if you get access.
```

All the same rules of normal interpolation apply to the content of the conditionals.

maybe

Similarly, we have a special construct for dealing with maybe values. These could technically be dealt with using if, isJust, and fromJust, but this is more convenient and avoids partial functions:

```
$maybe name <- maybeName
    <p>Your name is #{name}
$nothing
    <p>I don't know your name.
```

In addition to simple identifiers, you can use a few other, more complicated values on the lefthand side, such as constructors and tuples:

```
$maybe Person firstName lastName <- maybePerson
    <p>Your name is #{firstName} #{lastName}
```

The righthand side follows the same rules as interpolations and allows variables, function application, and so on.

forall

And what about looping over lists? We have you covered there too:

```
$if null people
    <p>No people.
$else
    <ul>
```

```
$forall person <- people
    <li>#{person}
```

case

Pattern matching is one of the great strengths of Haskell. Sum types allow you to cleanly model many real-world types, and `case` statements let you safely match, enabling the compiler to warn you if a case was missed. Hamlet gives you the same power:

```
$case foo
    $of Left bar
        <p>It was left: #{bar}
    $of Right baz
        <p>It was right: #{baz}
```

with

Rounding out our statements, we have `with`. It's basically just a convenience for declaring a synonym for a long expression:

```
$with foo <- some very (long ugly) expression that $ should only $ happen once
    <p>But I'm going to use #{foo} multiple times. #{foo}
```

doctype

One last bit of syntactic sugar: the `doctype` statement. There is support for a number of different versions of `doctype`, though we recommend `$doctype 5` for modern web applications, which generates `<!DOCTYPE html>`:

```
$doctype 5
<html>
    <head>
        <title>Hamlet is Awesome
    <body>
        <p>All done.
```

 There is an older and still supported syntax: three exclamation points (!!!). You may still see this in code out there. There are no plans to remove support for this, but in general the $doctype approach is easier to read.

Lucius Syntax

Lucius is one of two CSS templating languages in the Shakespeare family. It is intended to be a superset of CSS, leveraging the existing syntax while adding in a few more features. Here are some key points:

- Like Hamlet, it allows both variable and URL interpolation.

- CSS blocks are allowed to nest.

- You can declare variables in your templates.

- A set of CSS properties can be created as a mixin and reused in multiple declarations.

Starting with the second point, let's say you want to have special styling for some tags within your `article`. In plain ol' CSS, you'd have to write:

```
article code { background-color: grey; }
article p { text-indent: 2em; }
article a { text-decoration: none; }
```

In this case, there aren't that many clauses, but having to type out `article` each time is still a bit of a nuisance. Imagine if you had a dozen or so of these—not the worst thing in the world, but a bit of an annoyance. Lucius helps you out here:

```
article {
    code { background-color: grey; }
    p { text-indent: 2em; }
    a { text-decoration: none; }
    > h1 { color: green; }
}
```

Having Lucius variables allows you to avoid repeating yourself. A simple example would be to define a commonly used color:

```
@textcolor: #ccc; /* just because we hate our users */
body { color: #{textcolor} }
a:link, a:visited { color: #{textcolor} }
```

Mixins are a relatively new addition to Lucius. The idea is to declare a mixin providing a collection of properties, and then embed that mixin in a template using caret interpolation (^). The following example demonstrates how we could use a mixin to deal with vendor prefixes:

```
{-# LANGUAGE QuasiQuotes #-}
import Text.Lucius
import qualified Data.Text.Lazy.IO as TLIO

-- Dummy render function.
render = undefined

-- Our mixin, which provides a number of vendor prefixes for transitions.
transition val =
    [luciusMixin|
        -webkit-transition: #{val};
        -moz-transition: #{val};
        -ms-transition: #{val};
        -o-transition: #{val};
        transition: #{val};
    |]
```

```
-- Our actual Lucius template, which uses the mixin.
myCSS =
    [lucius|
        .some-class {
            ^{transition "all 4s ease"}
        }
    |]

main = TLIO.putStrLn $ renderCss $ myCSS render
```

Cassius Syntax

Cassius is a whitespace-sensitive alternative to Lucius. As mentioned in the synopsis, it uses the same processing engine as Lucius but preprocesses all input to insert braces to enclose subblocks and semicolons to terminate lines. This means you can leverage all features of Lucius when writing Cassius. Here's a simple example:

```
#banner
    border: 1px solid #{bannerColor}
    background-image: url(@{BannerImageR})
```

Julius Syntax

Julius is the simplest of the languages discussed here. In fact, some might even say it's really just JavaScript. Julius allows the three forms of interpolation we've mentioned so far, and otherwise applies no transformations to your content.

 If you use Julius with the scaffolded Yesod site, you may notice that your JavaScript is automatically minified. This is not a feature of Julius; instead, Yesod uses the `hjsmin` package to minify Julius output.

Calling Shakespeare

The question, of course, arises at some point: how do I actually use this stuff? There are three different ways to call out to Shakespeare from your Haskell code:

QuasiQuotes
> QuasiQuotes allow you to embed arbitrary content within your Haskell that is converted into Haskell code at compile time.

External file
> In this case, the template code is in a separate file that is referenced via Template Haskell.

Reload mode

Both of the preceding modes require a full recompile to see any changes. In reload mode, your template is kept in a separate file and referenced via Template Haskell. But at runtime, the external file is reparsed from scratch each time.

 Reload mode is not available for Hamlet but is for Cassius, Lucius, and Julius. There are too many sophisticated features in Hamlet that rely directly on the Haskell compiler and could not feasibly be reimplemented at runtime.

One of the first two approaches should be used in production. They both embed the entirety of the template in the final executable, simplifying deployment and increasing performance. The advantage of the QuasiQuotes approach is the simplicity: everything stays in a single file. For short templates, this can be a very good fit. However, in general, the external file approach is recommended because:

- It follows nicely in the tradition of separating logic from presentation.
- You can easily switch between external file and debug mode with some simple C preprocessor macros, meaning you can keep development rapid and still achieve high performance in production.

Because special quasiquoters and Template Haskell functions are involved, you need to be sure to enable the appropriate language extensions and use correct syntax. You can see a simple example of each approach in the following code snippets:

```
{-# LANGUAGE OverloadedStrings #-} -- we're using Text below
{-# LANGUAGE QuasiQuotes #-}
import Text.Hamlet (HtmlUrl, hamlet)
import Data.Text (Text)
import Text.Blaze.Html.Renderer.String (renderHtml)

data MyRoute = Home | Time | Stylesheet

render :: MyRoute -> [(Text, Text)] -> Text
render Home _ = "/home"
render Time _ = "/time"
render Stylesheet _ = "/style.css"

template :: Text -> HtmlUrl MyRoute
template title = [hamlet|
$doctype 5
<html>
    <head>
        <title>#{title}
        <link rel=stylesheet href=@{Stylesheet}>
    <body>
        <h1>#{title}
```

```
|]

main :: IO ()
main = putStrLn $ renderHtml $ template "My Title" render

{-# LANGUAGE OverloadedStrings #-} -- we're using Text below
{-# LANGUAGE TemplateHaskell #-}
{-# LANGUAGE CPP #-} -- to control production versus debug
import Text.Lucius (CssUrl, luciusFile, luciusFileDebug, renderCss)
import Data.Text (Text)
import qualified Data.Text.Lazy.IO as TLIO

data MyRoute = Home | Time | Stylesheet

render :: MyRoute -> [(Text, Text)] -> Text
render Home _ = "/home"
render Time _ = "/time"
render Stylesheet _ = "/style.css"

template :: CssUrl MyRoute
#if PRODUCTION
template = $(luciusFile "template.lucius")
#else
template = $(luciusFileDebug "template.lucius")
#endif

main :: IO ()
main = TLIO.putStrLn $ renderCss $ template render

-- @template.lucius
foo { bar: baz }
```

The naming scheme for the functions is very consistent:

Language	Quasiquoter	External file	Reload
Hamlet	hamlet	hamletFile	N/A
Cassius	cassius	cassiusFile	cassiusFileReload
Lucius	lucius	luciusFile	luciusFileReload
Julius	julius	juliusFile	juliusFileReload

Alternative Hamlet Types

So far, we've seen how to generate an HtmlUrl value from Hamlet, which is a piece of HTML with embedded type-safe URLs. There are currently three other values we can generate using Hamlet: plain HTML, HTML with URLs, and internationalized messages/widgets. That last one will be covered in more detail in Chapter 5.

To generate plain HTML without any embedded URLs, we use "simplified Hamlet." There are a few changes:

- We use a different set of functions, prefixed with an "s". So, the quasiquoter is shamlet and the external file function is shamletFile. How we pronounce those is still up for debate.

- No URL interpolation is allowed. Doing so will result in a compile-time error.

- Embedding (the caret interpolator) no longer allows arbitrary HtmlUrl values. The rule is that the embedded value must have the same type as the template itself, so in this case it must be Html. That means that for shamlet, embedding can be completely replaced with normal variable interpolation (with a hash).

Dealing with internationalization (i18n) in Hamlet is a bit complicated. Hamlet supports i18n via a message data type, very similar in concept and implementation to a type-safe URL. As an example, let's say we want to create an application that says "hello" and indicates how many apples you've eaten. Those messages can be represented with a data type:

```
data Msg = Hello | Apples Int
```

Next, we need to convert that into something human readable, so we define some render functions:

```
renderEnglish :: Msg -> Text
renderEnglish Hello = "Hello"
renderEnglish (Apples 0) = "You did not buy any apples."
renderEnglish (Apples 1) = "You bought 1 apple."
renderEnglish (Apples i) = T.concat ["You bought ", T.pack $ show i, " apples."]
```

Now we want to interpolate those Msg values directly in the template. For that, we use underscore interpolation:

```
$doctype 5
<html>
    <head>
        <title>i18n
    <body>
        <h1>_{Hello}
        <p>_{Apples count}
```

This kind of a template now needs some way to turn those values into HTML. So, just like with type-safe URLs, we pass in a render function. To represent this, we define a new type synonym:

```
type Render url = url -> [(Text, Text)] -> Text
type Translate msg = msg -> Html
type HtmlUrlI18n msg url = Translate msg -> Render url -> Html
```

At this point, you can pass `renderEnglish`, `renderSpanish`, or `renderKlingon` to this template, and it will generate nicely translated output (depending, of course, on the quality of your translators). Here's the complete program:

```
{-# LANGUAGE QuasiQuotes #-}
{-# LANGUAGE OverloadedStrings #-}
import Data.Text (Text)
import qualified Data.Text as T
import Text.Hamlet (HtmlUrlI18n, ihamlet)
import Text.Blaze.Html (toHtml)
import Text.Blaze.Html.Renderer.String (renderHtml)

data MyRoute = Home | Time | Stylesheet

renderUrl :: MyRoute -> [(Text, Text)] -> Text
renderUrl Home _ = "/home"
renderUrl Time _ = "/time"
renderUrl Stylesheet _ = "/style.css"

data Msg = Hello | Apples Int

renderEnglish :: Msg -> Text
renderEnglish Hello = "Hello"
renderEnglish (Apples 0) = "You did not buy any apples."
renderEnglish (Apples 1) = "You bought 1 apple."
renderEnglish (Apples i) = T.concat ["You bought ", T.pack $ show i, " apples."]

template :: Int -> HtmlUrlI18n Msg MyRoute
template count = [ihamlet|
$doctype 5
<html>
    <head>
        <title>i18n
    <body>
        <h1>_{Hello}
        <p>_{Apples count}
|]

main :: IO ()
main = putStrLn $ renderHtml
    $ (template 5) (toHtml . renderEnglish) renderUrl
```

Other Shakespeare

In addition to HTML, CSS, and JavaScript helpers, there is also some more general-purpose Shakespeare available. shakespeare-text provides a simple way to create interpolated strings, much like people are accustomed to in scripting languages like Ruby and Python. This package's utility is definitely not limited to Yesod:

```
{-# LANGUAGE QuasiQuotes, OverloadedStrings #-}
import Text.Shakespeare.Text
```

```
import qualified Data.Text.Lazy.IO as TLIO
import Data.Text (Text)
import Control.Monad (forM_)

data Item = Item
    { itemName :: Text
    , itemQty :: Int
    }

items :: [Item]
items =
    [ Item "apples" 5
    , Item "bananas" 10
    ]

main :: IO ()
main = forM_ items $ \item -> TLIO.putStrLn
    [lt|You have #{show $ itemQty item} #{itemName item}.|]
```

Some quick points about this simple example:

- Notice that we have three different textual data types involved (String, strict Text, and lazy Text). They all play together well.

- We use a quasiquoter named lt, which generates lazy text. There is also st.

- Also, there are longer names for these quasiquoters (ltext and stext).

General Recommendations

Here are some general hints from the Yesod community on how to get the most out of Shakespeare:

- For actual sites, use external files. For libraries, it's OK to use quasiquoters, assuming they aren't too long.

- Patrick Brisbin has put together an immensely helpful Vim code highlighter (*http://bit.ly/vim-highlite*).

- You should almost always start Hamlet tags on their own line instead of embedding start/end tags after an existing tag. The only exception to this is the occasional <i> or <b> tag inside a large block of text.

CHAPTER 5

Widgets

One of the challenges in web development is that we have to coordinate three different client-side technologies: HTML, CSS, and JavaScript. Worse still, we have to place these components in different locations on the page: CSS in a `<style>` tag in the head, JavaScript in a `<script>` tag in the head, and HTML in the body. And never mind if you want to put your CSS and JavaScript in separate files!

In practice, this works out fairly nicely when building a single page, because we can separate our structure (HTML), style (CSS), and logic (JavaScript). But when we want to build modular pieces of code that can be easily composed, it can be a headache to coordinate all three pieces separately. Widgets are Yesod's solution to the problem. They also help with the issue of including libraries, such as jQuery, one time only.

Our four template languages—Hamlet, Cassius, Lucius, and Julius—provide the raw tools for constructing our output. Widgets provide the glue that allows them to work together seamlessly.

Synopsis

```
{-# LANGUAGE OverloadedStrings #-}
{-# LANGUAGE QuasiQuotes       #-}
{-# LANGUAGE TemplateHaskell   #-}
{-# LANGUAGE TypeFamilies      #-}
import          Yesod

data App = App
mkYesod "App" [parseRoutes|
/ HomeR GET
|]
instance Yesod App

getHomeR = defaultLayout $ do
```

```
setTitle "My Page Title"
toWidget [lucius| h1 { color: green; } |]
addScriptRemote
  "https://ajax.googleapis.com/ajax/libs/jquery/1.6.2/jquery.min.js"
toWidget
    [julius|
        $(function() {
            $("h1").click(function(){
                alert("You clicked on the heading!");
            });
        });
    |]
toWidgetHead
    [hamlet|
        <meta name=keywords content="some sample keywords">
    |]
toWidget
    [hamlet|
        <h1>Here's one way of including content
    |]
[whamlet|<h2>Here's another |]
toWidgetBody
    [julius|
        alert("This is included in the body itself");
    |]

main = warp 3000 App
```

This produces the following HTML (indentation added):

```
<!DOCTYPE html>
<html>
  <head>
    <title>My Page Title</title>
    <meta name="keywords" content="some sample keywords">
    <style>h1{color:green}</style>
  </head>
  <body>
    <h1>Here's one way of including content</h1>
    <h2>Here's another</h2>
    <script>
      alert("This is included in the body itself");
    </script>
    <script src="
     https://ajax.googleapis.com/ajax/libs/jquery/1.6.2/jquery.min.js">
    </script><script>
      $(function() {
        $('h1').click(function() {
          alert("You clicked on the heading!");
        });
      });
    </script>
```

```
    </body>
</html>
```

What's in a Widget?

At a very superficial level, an HTML document is just a bunch of nested tags. This is the approach most HTML-generation tools take: you define hierarchies of tags and are done with it. But let's imagine that we want to write a component of a page for displaying the navbar. We want this to be "plug and play": the function is called at the right time, and the navbar is inserted at the correct point in the hierarchy.

This is where our superficial HTML generation breaks down. Our navbar likely consists of some CSS and JavaScript in addition to HTML. By the time we call the navbar function, we have already rendered the `<head>` tag, so it is too late to add a new `<style>` tag for our CSS declarations. Under normal strategies, we would need to break up our navbar function into three parts—HTML, CSS, and JavaScript—and make sure that we always call all three pieces.

Widgets take a different approach. Instead of viewing an HTML document as a monolithic tree of tags, widgets see a number of distinct components in the page. In particular, widgets are interested in the following:

- The title
- External stylesheets
- External JavaScript
- CSS declarations
- JavaScript code
- Arbitrary `<head>` content
- Arbitrary `<body>` content

Different components have different semantics. For example, there can only be one title, but there can be multiple external scripts and stylesheets. However, those external scripts and stylesheets should only be included once. Arbitrary head and body content, on the other hand, has no limitation (someone may want to have five lorem ipsum blocks, after all).

The job of a widget is to hold onto these disparate components and apply proper logic for combining different widgets. This consists of things like taking the last title set and ignoring others, filtering duplicates from the list of external scripts and stylesheets, and concatenating head and body content.

Constructing Widgets

In order to use widgets, you'll obviously need to be able to get your hands on them. The most common way will be via the `ToWidget` typeclass and its `toWidget` method. This allows you to convert your Shakespearean templates directly to a `Widget`: Hamlet code will appear in the body, Julius scripts inside a `<script>`, and Cassius and Lucius in a `<style>` tag.

 You can actually override the default behavior and have the script and style code appear in a separate file. The scaffolded site provides this for you automatically.

But what if you want to add some `<meta>` tags, which need to appear in the head? Or if you want some JavaScript to appear in the body instead of the head? For these purposes, Yesod provides two additional typeclasses: `ToWidgetHead` and `ToWidgetBody`. These work exactly as they seem they should. One example use case for this is to have fine-grained control over where your `<script>` tags end up getting inserted:

```
{-# LANGUAGE OverloadedStrings #-}
{-# LANGUAGE QuasiQuotes       #-}
{-# LANGUAGE TemplateHaskell   #-}
{-# LANGUAGE TypeFamilies      #-}
import           Yesod

data App = App

mkYesod "App" [parseRoutes|
/       HomeR   GET
|]

instance Yesod App where

getHomeR :: Handler Html
getHomeR = defaultLayout $ do
    setTitle "toWidgetHead and toWidgetBody"
    toWidgetBody
        [hamlet|<script src=/included-in-body.js>|]
    toWidgetHead
        [hamlet|<script src=/included-in-head.js>|]

main :: IO ()
main = warp 3001 App
```

Note that even though `toWidgetHead` was called after `toWidgetBody`, the latter `<script>` tag appears first in the generated HTML.

In addition, there are a number of other functions for creating specific kinds of widgets:

setTitle
: Turns an HTML value into the page title.

toWidgetMedia
: Works the same as toWidget, but takes an additional parameter to indicate what kind of media this applies to. Useful for creating print stylesheets, for instance.

addStylesheet
: Adds a reference, via a <link> tag, to an external stylesheet. Takes a type-safe URL.

addStylesheetRemote
: Same as addStylesheet, but takes a normal URL. Useful for referring to files hosted on a content distribution network (CDN), like Google's jQuery UI CSS files.

addScript
: Adds a reference, via a <script> tag, to an external script. Takes a type-safe URL.

addScriptRemote
: Same as addScript, but takes a normal URL. Useful for referring to files hosted on a CDN, like Google's jQuery.

Combining Widgets

The whole idea of widgets is to increase composability. You can take individual pieces of HTML, CSS, and JavaScript, combine them into something more complicated, and then combine these larger entities into complete pages. This all works naturally through the Monad instance of Widget, meaning you can use do notation to compose pieces:

```
myWidget1 = do
    toWidget [hamlet|<h1>My Title|]
    toWidget [lucius|h1 { color: green } |]

myWidget2 = do
    setTitle "My Page Title"
    addScriptRemote "http://www.example.com/script.js"

myWidget = do
    myWidget1
    myWidget2

-- or, if you want
myWidget' = myWidget1 >> myWidget2
```

If you're so inclined, there's also a `Monoid` instance of `Widget`, meaning you can use `mconcat` or a `Writer` monad to build things up. In my experience, it's easiest and most natural to just use `do` notation.

Generating IDs

If we're really going for true code reuse here, we're eventually going to run into name conflicts. Let's say that there are two helper libraries that both use the class name "foo" to affect styling. We want to avoid such a possibility. Therefore, we have the `newIdent` function. This function automatically generates a word that is unique for this handler:

```
getRootR = defaultLayout $ do
    headerClass <- newIdent
    toWidget [hamlet|<h1 .#{headerClass}>My Header|]
    toWidget [lucius| .#{headerClass} { color: green; } |]
```

whamlet

Let's say we've got a fairly standard Hamlet template that embeds another Hamlet template to represent the footer:

```
page =
    [hamlet|
        <p>This is my page. I hope you enjoyed it.
        ^{footer}
    |]

footer =
    [hamlet|
        <footer>
            <p>That's all folks!
    |]
```

That works fine if the footer is plain old HTML, but what if we want to add some style? Well, we can easily spice up the footer by turning it into a widget:

```
footer = do
    toWidget
        [lucius|
            footer {
                font-weight: bold;
                text-align: center
            }
        |]
    toWidget
        [hamlet|
            <footer>
```

```
      <p>That's all folks!
    |]
```

But now we've got a problem: a Hamlet template can only embed another Hamlet template; it knows nothing about a widget. This is where whamlet comes in. It takes exactly the same syntax as normal Hamlet, and variable (#{…}) and URL (@{…}) interpolation are unchanged. But embedding (^{…}) takes a Widget, and the final result is a Widget. To use it, we can just do:

```
page =
    [whamlet|
        <p>This is my page. I hope you enjoyed it.
        ^{footer}
    |]
```

There is also whamletFile, if you prefer to keep your template in a separate file.

> The scaffolded site has an even more convenient function, widget File, which will also include your Lucius, Cassius, and Julius files automatically. We'll cover that in Chapter 15.

Types

You may have noticed that I've been avoiding type signatures so far. Why? The simple answer is that each widget is a value of type Widget. But if you look through the Yesod libraries, you'll find no definition of the Widget type. What gives?

Yesod defines a very similar type: data WidgetT site m a. This data type is a *monad transformer*. The last two arguments are the underlying monad and the monadic value, respectively. The site parameter is the specific foundation type for your individual application. Because this type varies for each and every site, it's impossible for the libraries to define a single Widget data type that would work for every application.

Instead, the mkYesod Template Haskell function generates this type synonym for you. Assuming your foundation data type is called MyApp, your Widget synonym is defined as follows:

```
type Widget = WidgetT MyApp IO ()
```

We set the monadic value to be (), as a widget's value will ultimately be thrown away. IO is the standard base monad, and will be used in almost all cases. The only exception is when writing a *subsite*. Subsites are a more advanced topic and will be covered later, in Chapter 17.

Once we know about our Widget type synonym, it's easy to add signatures to our previous code samples:

```
footer :: Widget
footer = do
    toWidget
        [lucius|
            footer {
                font-weight: bold;
                text-align: center
            }
        |]
    toWidget
        [hamlet|
            <footer>
                <p>That's all folks!
        |]

page :: Widget
page =
    [whamlet|
        <p>This is my page. I hope you enjoyed it.
        ^{footer}
    |]
```

When we start digging into handler functions some more, we'll encounter a similar situation with the `HandlerT` and `Handler` types.

Using Widgets

It's all well and good that we have these beautiful `Widget` data types, but how exactly do we turn them into something the user can interact with? The most commonly used function is `defaultLayout`, which essentially has the type signature `Widget ->` `Handler Html`.

`defaultLayout` is actually a typeclass method, which can be overridden for each application. This is how Yesod apps are themed. So we're still left with the question: when we're inside `defaultLayout`, how do we unwrap a `Widget`? The answer is `widgetToPageContent`. Let's look at some (simplified) types:

```
data PageContent url = PageContent
    { pageTitle :: Html
    , pageHead :: HtmlUrl url
    , pageBody :: HtmlUrl url
    }
widgetToPageContent :: Widget -> Handler (PageContent url)
```

This is getting closer to what we need. We now have direct access to the HTML making up the head and body, as well as the title. At this point, we can use Hamlet to combine them all into a single document, along with our site layout, and we use `with` `UrlRenderer` to convert that Hamlet result into actual HTML that's ready to be shown to the user. The next example demonstrates this process:

```
{-# LANGUAGE OverloadedStrings #-}
{-# LANGUAGE QuasiQuotes       #-}
{-# LANGUAGE TemplateHaskell   #-}
{-# LANGUAGE TypeFamilies      #-}
import             Yesod

data App = App
mkYesod "App" [parseRoutes|
/ HomeR GET
|]

myLayout :: Widget -> Handler Html
myLayout widget = do
    pc <- widgetToPageContent widget
    withUrlRenderer
        [hamlet|
            $doctype 5
            <html>
                <head>
                    <title>#{pageTitle pc}
                    <meta charset=ulf-8>
                    <style>body { font-family: verdana }
                    ^{pageHead pc}
                <body>
                    <article>
                        ^{pageBody pc}
        |]

instance Yesod App where
    defaultLayout = myLayout

getHomeR :: Handler Html
getHomeR = defaultLayout
    [whamlet|
        <p>Hello, World!
    |]

main :: IO ()
main = warp 3000 App
```

But there's still one thing that bothers me: that `<style>` tag. There are a few problems with it:

- Unlike with Lucius or Cassius, it doesn't get compile-time checked for correctness.
- Granted, the current example is very simple, but in something more complicated we could get into character escaping issues.
- We'll now have two `<style>` tags instead of one: the one produced by `myLayout`, and the one generated in the `pageHead` based on the styles set in the widget.

We have one more trick in our bag to address this: we apply some last-minute adjustments to the widget itself before calling `widgetToPageContent`. It's actually very easy to do—we just use do notation again:

```
{-# LANGUAGE OverloadedStrings #-}
{-# LANGUAGE QuasiQuotes       #-}
{-# LANGUAGE TemplateHaskell   #-}
{-# LANGUAGE TypeFamilies      #-}
import            Yesod

data App = App
mkYesod "App" [parseRoutes|
/ HomeR GET
|]

myLayout :: Widget -> Handler Html
myLayout widget = do
    pc <- widgetToPageContent $ do
        widget
        toWidget [lucius| body { font-family: verdana } |]
    withUrlRenderer
        [hamlet|
            $doctype 5
            <html>
                <head>
                    <title>#{pageTitle pc}
                    <meta charset=utf-8>
                    ^{pageHead pc}
                <body>
                    <article>
                        ^{pageBody pc}
        |]

instance Yesod App where
    defaultLayout = myLayout

getHomeR :: Handler Html
getHomeR = defaultLayout
    [whamlet|
        <p>Hello, World!
    |]

main :: IO ()
main = warp 3000 App
```

Using Handler Functions

We haven't covered too much of the handler functionality yet, but once we do, the question arises: how do we use those functions in a widget? For example, what if your widget needs to look up a query string parameter using `lookupGetParam`?

The first answer is the function `handlerToWidget`, which can convert a `Handler` action into a `Widget` answer. However, in many cases, this won't be necessary. Consider the type signature of `lookupGetParam`:

```
lookupGetParam :: MonadHandler m => Text -> m (Maybe Text)
```

This function will live in *any* instance of `MonadHandler`. And conveniently, `Widget` is also a `MonadHandler` instance. This means that most code can be run in either `Handler` or `Widget`. And if you need to explicitly convert from `Handler` to `Widget`, you can always use `handlerToWidget`.

 This is a significant departure from how Yesod worked in versions 1.1 and earlier. Previously, there was no `MonadHandler` typeclass, and all functions needed to be explicitly converted using `lift`, not `handlerToWidget`. The new system is not only easier to use, but also avoids any strange monad transformer tricks that were previously employed.

Summary

The basic building block of each page is the widget. Individual snippets of HTML, CSS, and JavaScript can be turned into widgets via the polymorphic `toWidget` function. Using do notation, you can combine these individual widgets into larger widgets, eventually containing all the content of your page.

Unwrapping these widgets is usually performed within the `defaultLayout` function, which can be used to apply a unified look and feel to all your pages.

The Yesod Typeclass

Every one of our Yesod applications requires an instance of the Yesod typeclass. So far, we've just relied on default implementations of the methods of the Yesod typeclass. In this chapter, we'll explore the meaning of many of these methods Yesod typeclass.

The Yesod typeclass gives us a central place for defining settings for our application. Everything has a default definition, which is often the right thing. But in order to build a powerful, customized application, you'll usually end up wanting to override at least a few of these methods.

 A common question I hear is, "Why use a typeclass instead of a record type?" There are two main advantages:

- The methods of the Yesod typeclass may wish to call other methods. With typeclasses, this kind of usage is trivial. It becomes slightly more complicated with a record type.

- Simplicity of syntax. We want to provide default implementations and allow users to override just the necessary functionality. Typeclasses make this both easy and syntactically nice. Records have a slightly larger overhead.

Rendering and Parsing URLs

We've already mentioned how Yesod is able to automatically render type-safe URLs into textual URLs that can be inserted into an HTML page. Let's say we have a route definition that looks like the following:

```
mkYesod "MyApp" [parseRoutes|
/some/path SomePathR GET
]
```

If we place `SomePathR` into a Hamlet template, how does Yesod render it? Yesod always tries to construct *absolute* URLs. This is especially useful once we start creating XML sitemaps and Atom feeds, or sending emails. But in order to construct an absolute URL, we need to know the domain name of the application.

You might think we could get that information from the user's request, but we still need to deal with ports. And even if we get the port number from the request, are we using HTTP or HTTPS? And even if we know *that*, such an approach would mean that, depending on how the user submitted a request, different URLs would be generated. For example, a different URL would be generated if the user connected to *example.com* versus *www.example.com*. For search engine optimization, we want to be able to consolidate on a single canonical URL.

And finally, Yesod doesn't make any assumption about *where* you host your application. For example, you may have a mostly static site (*http://static.example.com/*), but want to stick a Yesod-powered wiki at */wiki/*. There is no reliable way for an application to determine what subpath it is being hosted from. So instead of doing all of this guesswork, Yesod needs you to tell it the application root.

Using the wiki example, you would write your `Yesod` instance as follows:

```
instance Yesod MyWiki where
    approot = ApprootStatic "http://static.example.com/wiki"
```

Notice that there is no trailing slash there. Next, when Yesod wants to construct a URL for `SomePathR`, it determines that the relative path for `SomePathR` is */some/path*, appends that to your approot, and creates *http://static.example.com/wiki/some/path*.

The default value of `approot` is `ApprootRelative`, which essentially means "don't add any prefix." In that case, the generated URL would be */some/path*. This works fine for the common case of a link within your application, and your application being hosted at the root of your domain. But if you have any use cases that demand absolute URLs (e.g., sending an email), it's best to use `ApprootStatic`.

In addition to the `ApprootStatic` constructor just demonstrated, you can also use the `ApprootMaster` and `ApprootRequest` constructors. The former allows you to determine the approot from the foundation value, which would let you load up the approot from a config file, for instance. The latter allows you to additionally use the request value to determine the approot; using this, you could, for example, provide a different domain name depending on how the user requested the site in the first place.

The scaffolded site uses `ApprootMaster` by default, and pulls your approot from either the `APPROOT` environment variable or a config file on launch. Additionally, it loads different settings for testing and production builds, so you can easily test on one domain (e.g., *localhost*) and serve from a different domain. You can modify these values from the config file.

joinPath

In order to convert a type-safe URL into a text value, Yesod uses two helper functions. The first is the `renderRoute` method of the `RenderRoute` typeclass. Every type-safe URL is an instance of this typeclass. `renderRoute` converts a value into a list of path pieces. For example, the `SomePathR` we used earlier would be converted into `["some", "path"]`.

 Actually, `renderRoute` produces both the path pieces and a list of query string parameters. The default instances of `renderRoute` always provide an empty list of query string parameters. However, it is possible to override this. One notable case is the static subsite, which puts a hash of the file contents in the query string for caching purposes.

The other function is the `joinPath` method of the `Yesod` typeclass. This function takes four arguments:

- The foundation value
- The application root
- A list of path segments
- A list of query string parameters

It returns a textual URL. The default implementation does the "right thing": it separates the path pieces by forward slashes, prepends the application root, and appends the query string.

If you are happy with the default URL rendering, you should not need to modify it. However, if you want to modify URL rendering to do things like append a trailing slash, this would be the place to do it.

cleanPath

The flip side of `joinPath` is `cleanPath`. Let's look at how it gets used in the dispatch process:

1. The path info requested by the user is split into a series of path pieces.

2. We pass the path pieces to the `cleanPath` function.

3. If `cleanPath` indicates a redirect (a `Left` response), then a 301 response is sent to the client. This is used to force canonical URLs (e.g., remove extra slashes).

4. Otherwise, we try to dispatch using the response from `cleanPath` (a `Right`). If this works, we return a response. Otherwise, we return a 404.

This combination allows subsites to retain full control over how their URLs appear, yet allows master sites to have modified URLs. As a simple example, let's see how we could modify Yesod to always produce trailing slashes on URLs:

```
{-# LANGUAGE MultiParamTypeClasses #-}
{-# LANGUAGE OverloadedStrings     #-}
{-# LANGUAGE QuasiQuotes           #-}
{-# LANGUAGE TemplateHaskell       #-}
{-# LANGUAGE TypeFamilies          #-}
import           Blaze.ByteString.Builder.Char.Utf8 (fromText)
import           Control.Arrow                      ((***))
import           Data.Monoid                        (mappend)
import qualified Data.Text                          as T
import qualified Data.Text.Encoding                 as TE
import           Network.HTTP.Types                 (encodePath)
import           Yesod

data Slash = Slash

mkYesod "Slash" [parseRoutes|
/ RootR GET
/foo FooR GET
|]

instance Yesod Slash where
    joinPath _ ar pieces' qs' =
        fromText ar `mappend` encodePath pieces qs
      where
        qs = map (TE.encodeUtf8 *** go) qs'
        go "" = Nothing
        go x = Just $ TE.encodeUtf8 x
        pieces = pieces' ++ [""]

    -- We want to keep canonical URLs. Therefore, if the URL is missing a
    -- trailing slash, redirect. But the empty set of pieces always stays the
    -- same.
    cleanPath _ [] = Right []
    cleanPath _ s
        | dropWhile (not . T.null) s == [""] =
            -- the only empty string is the last one
            Right $ init s
        -- Because joinPath will append the missing trailing slash, we
        -- simply remove empty pieces.
        | otherwise = Left $ filter (not . T.null) s

getRootR :: Handler Html
```

```
getRootR = defaultLayout
    [whamlet|
        <p>
            <a href=@{RootR}>RootR
        <p>
            <a href=@{FooR}>FooR
    |]

getFooR :: Handler Html
getFooR = getRootR

main :: IO ()
main = warp 3000 Slash
```

First, let's look at our `joinPath` implementation. This is copied almost verbatim from the default Yesod implementation, with one difference: we append an extra empty string to the end. When dealing with path pieces, an empty string will append another slash, so adding an extra empty string will force a trailing slash.

`cleanPath` is a little bit trickier. First, we check for the empty path like before, and if found, we pass it through as is. We use `Right` to indicate that a redirect is not necessary. The next clause is actually checking for two different possible URL issues:

- There is a double slash, which would show up as an empty string in the middle of our paths.
- There is a missing trailing slash, which would show up as the last piece not being an empty string.

Assuming neither of those conditions hold, then only the last piece is empty, and we should dispatch based on all but the last piece. However, if this is not the case, we want to redirect to a canonical URL. In this case, we strip out all empty pieces and do not bother appending a trailing slash, as `joinPath` will do that for us.

defaultLayout

Most websites like to apply some general template to all of their pages. `defaultLay out` is the recommended approach for this. While you could just as easily define your own function and call that instead, when you override `defaultLayout` all of the Yesod-generated pages (error pages, authentication pages) automatically get this style.

Overriding is very straightforward: we use `widgetToPageContent` to convert a `Widget` to a title, `<head>` tags, and `<body>` tags, and then use `withUrlRenderer` to convert a Hamlet template into an `Html` value. We can even add extra widget components, like a Lucius template, from within `defaultLayout`. For more information, see Chapter 5.

If you are using the scaffolded site, you can modify the files *templates/default-layout.hamlet* and *templates/default-layout-wrapper.hamlet*. The former contains most of the contents of the <body> tag, while the latter has the rest of the HTML, such as the doctype and the <head> tag. See those files for more details.

getMessage

Even though we haven't covered sessions yet, I'd like to mention `getMessage` here. A common pattern in web development is setting a message in one handler and displaying it in another. For example, if a user POSTs a form, you may want to redirect her to another page along with a "Form submission complete" message. This is commonly known as Post/Redirect/Get.

To facilitate this, Yesod comes with a pair of functions built in: `setMessage` sets a message in the user session, and `getMessage` retrieves the message (and clears it, so it doesn't appear a second time). It's recommended that you put the result of `getMessage` into your `defaultLayout`. For example:

```
{-# LANGUAGE OverloadedStrings    #-}
{-# LANGUAGE QuasiQuotes          #-}
{-# LANGUAGE TemplateHaskell      #-}
{-# LANGUAGE TypeFamilies         #-}
import           Yesod
import Data.Time (getCurrentTime)

data App = App

mkYesod "App" [parseRoutes|
/ HomeR GET
|]

instance Yesod App where
    defaultLayout contents = do
        PageContent title headTags bodyTags <- widgetToPageContent contents
        mmsg <- getMessage
        withUrlRenderer [hamlet|
            $doctype 5

            <html>
                <head>
                    <title>#{title}
                    ^{headTags}
                <body>
                    $maybe msg <- mmsg
                        <div #message>#{msg}
                    ^{bodyTags}
        |]

getHomeR :: Handler Html
```

```
getHomeR = do
    now <- liftIO getCurrentTime
    setMessage $ toHtml $ "You previously visited at: " ++ show now
    defaultLayout [whamlet|<p>Try refreshing|]

main :: IO ()
main = warp 3000 App
```

We'll cover `getMessage/setMessage` in more detail when we discuss sessions in Chapter 9.

Custom Error Pages

One of the marks of a professional website is a properly designed error page. Yesod gets you a long way there by automatically using your `defaultLayout` for displaying error pages. But sometimes you'll want to go even further. For this, you'll want to override the `errorHandler` method:

```
{-# LANGUAGE OverloadedStrings    #-}
{-# LANGUAGE QuasiQuotes          #-}
{-# LANGUAGE TemplateHaskell      #-}
{-# LANGUAGE TypeFamilies         #-}
import            Yesod

data App = App

mkYesod "App" [parseRoutes|
/ HomeR GET
/error ErrorR GET
/not-found NotFoundR GET
|]

instance Yesod App where
    errorHandler NotFound = fmap toTypedContent $ defaultLayout $ do
        setTitle "Request page not located"
        toWidget [hamlet|
<h1>Not Found
<p>
We apologize for the inconvenience, but the requested page could not be located.
|]
    errorHandler other = defaultErrorHandler other

getHomeR :: Handler Html
getHomeR = defaultLayout
    [whamlet|
        <p>
            <a href=@{ErrorR}>Internal server error
            <a href=@{NotFoundR}>Not found
    |]

getErrorR :: Handler ()
```

```
getErrorR = error "This is an error"

getNotFoundR :: Handler ()
getNotFoundR = notFound

main :: IO ()
main = warp 3000 App
```

Here we specify a custom 404 error page. We can also use the `defaultErrorHandler` when we don't want to write a custom handler for each error type. Due to type constraints, we need to start off our methods with `fmap toTypedContent`, but otherwise we can write a typical handler function. (We'll learn more about `TypedContent` in the next chapter.)

In fact, you could even use special responses like redirects:

```
errorHandler NotFound = redirect HomeR
errorHandler other = defaultErrorHandler other
```

Although you *can* do this, I don't actually recommend such practices. A 404 should be a 404.

External CSS and JavaScript

One of the most powerful, and most intimidating, methods in the `Yesod` typeclass is `addStaticContent`. Remember that a widget consists of multiple components, including CSS and JavaScript. How exactly does that CSS/JS arrive in the user's browser? By default, these resources are served in the `<head>` of the page, inside `<style>` and `<script>` tags, respectively.

The functionality described here is automatically included in the scaffolded site, so you don't need to worry about implementing this yourself.

That might be simple, but it's far from efficient. Every page load will now require loading up the CSS/JS from scratch, even if nothing has changed! What we really want is to store this content in an external file and then refer to it from the HTML.

This is where `addStaticContent` comes in. It takes three arguments: the filename extension of the content (*.css* or *.js*), the MIME type of the content (`text/css` or `text/javascript`), and the content itself. It will then return one of three possible results:

Nothing

No static file saving occurred; embed this content directly in the HTML. This is the default behavior.

`Just (Left Text)`

This content was saved in an external file. The given textual link should be used to refer to it.

`Just (Right (Route a, Query))`

Same as `Just (Left Text)`, but now a type-safe URL should be used along with some query string parameters.

The `Left` result is useful if you want to store your static files on an external server, such as a CDN or memory-backed server. The `Right` result is more commonly used, and ties in very well with the static subsite. This is the recommended approach for most applications, and is provided by the scaffolded site by default.

 You might be wondering: if this is the recommended approach, why isn't it the default? The problem is that it makes a number of assumptions that don't universally hold, such as the presence of a static subsite and the location of your static files.

The scaffolded `addStaticContent` does a number of intelligent things to help you out:

- It automatically minifies your JavaScript using the `hjsmin` package.
- It names the output files based on a hash of the file contents. This means you can set your cache headers to far in the future without fears of stale content.
- Because filenames are based on hashes, you can be guaranteed that a file doesn't need to be written if a file with the same name already exists. The scaffold code automatically checks for the existence of that file, and avoids the costly disk I/O of a write if it's not necessary.

Smarter Static Files

Google recommends an important optimization: serve static files from a separate domain (*http://bit.ly/gdev-comp*). The advantage to this approach is that cookies set on your main domain are not sent when retrieving static files, thus saving on a bit of bandwidth.

To facilitate this, we have the urlRenderOverride method. This method intercepts the normal URL rendering and sets a special value for some routes. For example, the scaffolding defines this method as:

```
urlRenderOverride y (StaticR s) =
    Just $ uncurry (joinPath y (Settings.staticRoot $ settings y))
        $ renderRoute s

urlRenderOverride _ _ = Nothing
```

This means that static routes are served from a special static root, which you can configure to be a different domain. This is a great example of the power and flexibility of type-safe URLs: with a single line of code, you're able to change the rendering of static routes throughout all of your handlers.

Authentication/Authorization

For simple applications, checking permissions inside each handler function can be a simple, convenient approach. However, it doesn't scale well. Eventually, you're going to want to have a more declarative approach. Many systems out there define access control lists, special config files, and a lot of other hocus-pocus. In Yesod, it's just plain old Haskell. There are three methods involved:

isWriteRequest

Determines if the current request is a "read" or "write" operation. By default, Yesod follows RESTful principles and assumes GET, HEAD, OPTIONS, and TRACE requests are read-only, while all others are writable.

isAuthorized

Takes a route (i.e., type-safe URL) and a Boolean indicating whether or not the request is a write request. It returns an AuthResult, which can have one of the following three values. By default, it returns Authorized for all requests.

- Authorized
- AuthenticationRequired
- Unauthorized

authRoute

If isAuthorized returns AuthenticationRequired, then redirects to the given route. If no route is provided (the default), returns a 401 "authentication required" message.

These methods tie in nicely with the yesod-auth package, which is used by the scaffolded site to provide a number of authentication options, such as OpenID,

Mozilla Persona, email, username, and Twitter. We'll cover more concrete examples in Chapter 14.

Some Simple Settings

Not everything in the Yesod typeclass is complicated. Some methods are simple functions. Let's just go through the list:

maximumContentLength

> To prevent denial-of-service (DoS) attacks, Yesod will limit the size of request bodies. Some of the time, you'll want to bump that limit for some routes (e.g., a file upload page). This is where you'd do that.

fileUpload

> Determines how uploaded files are treated, based on the size of the request. The two most common approaches are saving the files in memory, or streaming to temporary files. By default, small requests are kept in memory and large ones are stored to disk.

shouldLog

> Determines if a given log message (with associated source and level) should be sent to the log. This allows you to put lots of debugging information into your app, but only turn it on as necessary.

For the most up-to-date information, see the Haddock API documentation for the Yesod typeclass (*http://www.stackage.org/package/yesod-core*).

Summary

The Yesod typeclass has a number of overrideable methods that allow you to configure your application. They are all optional, and provide sensible defaults. By using built-in Yesod constructs like defaultLayout and getMessage, you'll get a consistent look and feel throughout your site, including pages automatically generated by Yesod such as error pages and authentication.

We haven't covered all the methods in the Yesod typeclass in this chapter. For a full listing of methods available, you should consult the Haddock documentation (*http://www.stackage.org/package/yesod-core*).

CHAPTER 7

Routing and Handlers

If we look at Yesod as a model-view-controller framework, routing and handlers make up the controller. For contrast, let's describe two other routing approaches used in other web development environments:

- Dispatch based on filename. This is how PHP and ASP work, for example.
- Have a centralized routing function that parses routes based on regular expressions. Django and Rails follow this approach.

Yesod is closer in principle to the latter technique. Even so, there are significant differences. Instead of using regular expressions, Yesod matches on pieces of a route. Instead of having a one-way route-to-handler mapping, Yesod has an intermediate data type (called the route or type-safe URL data type) and creates two-way conversion functions.

Coding this more advanced system manually is tedious and error prone. Therefore, Yesod defines a domain-specific language (DSL) for specifying routes, and provides Template Haskell functions to convert this DSL to Haskell code. This chapter will explain the syntax of the routing declarations, give you a glimpse of what code is generated for you, and explain the interaction between routing and handler functions.

Route Syntax

Instead of trying to shoehorn route declarations into an existing syntax, Yesod's approach is to use a simplified syntax designed just for routes. This has the advantage of making the code not only easy to write, but simple enough that someone with no Yesod experience can read and understand the sitemap of your application.

A basic example of this syntax is:

```
/              HomeR     GET
/blog          BlogR     GET POST
/blog/#BlogId BlogPostR GET POST

/static        StaticR   Static getStatic
```

The next few sections explain the full details of what goes on in the route declaration.

Pieces

One of the first things Yesod does when it gets a request is split up the requested path into pieces. The pieces are tokenized at all forward slashes. For example:

```
toPieces "/" = []
toPieces "/foo/bar/baz/" = ["foo", "bar", "baz", ""]
```

You may notice that there are some funny things going on with trailing slashes, or double slashes (/foo//bar//), or a few other things. Yesod believes in having canonical URLs; if users request a URL with a trailing slash, or with a double slash, they are automatically redirected to the canonical version. This ensures you have one URL for one resource, and can help with your search rankings.

What this means for you is that you needn't concern yourself with the exact structure of your URLs: you can safely think about pieces of a path, and Yesod automatically handles intercalating the slashes and escaping problematic characters.

If, by the way, you want more fine-tuned control of how paths are split into pieces and joined together again, you'll want to look at the `cleanPath` and `joinPath` methods in Chapter 6.

Types of pieces

When you are declaring your routes, you have three types of pieces at your disposal:

Static
> This is a plain string that must be matched against precisely in the URL.

Dynamic single
> This is a single piece (i.e., between two forward slashes), but represents a user-submitted value. This is the primary method of receiving extra user input on a page request. These pieces begin with a hash (#) and are followed by a data type. The data type must be an instance of `PathPiece`.

Dynamic multi
> The same as the previous type, but can receive multiple pieces of the URL. This must always be the last piece in a resource pattern. It is specified by an asterisk (*) followed by a data type, which must be an instance of `PathMultiPiece`. Multi-

pieces are not as common as the other two, though they are very important for implementing features like static trees representing file structure or wikis with arbitrary hierarchies.

Since Yesod 1.4, you can additionally use a + to indicate a dynamic multi. This is important, because the C preprocessor can be confused by the /* character combination.

Let us take a look at some standard kinds of resource patterns you may want to write. Starting simply, the root of an application will just be /. Similarly, you may want to place your FAQ at */page/faq*.

Now let's say we are going to write a Fibonacci website. We might construct our URLs like */fib/#Int*. But there's a slight problem with this: we do not want to allow negative numbers or zero to be passed into our application. Fortunately, the type system can protect us:

```
newtype Natural = Natural Int
instance PathPiece Natural where
    toPathPiece (Natural i) = T.pack $ show i
    fromPathPiece s =
        case reads $ T.unpack s of
            (i, ""):_
                | i < 1 -> Nothing
                | otherwise -> Just $ Natural i
            []  ▸ Nothing
```

On line 1 we define a simple `newtype` wrapper around `Int` to protect ourselves from invalid input. We can see that `PathPiece` is a typeclass with two methods. `toPath Piece` does nothing more than convert to a `Text`. `fromPathPiece` *attempts* to convert a `Text` to our data type, returning `Nothing` when this conversion is impossible. By using this data type, we can ensure that our handler function is only ever given natural numbers, allowing us to once again use the type system to battle the boundary issue.

In a real-life application, we would also want to ensure we never accidentally constructed an invalid `Natural` value internally to our app. To do so, we could use an approach like smart constructors (*http://www.haskell.org/haskellwiki/Smart_constructors*). For the purposes of this example, we've kept the code simple.

Defining a `PathMultiPiece` is just as simple. Let's say we want to have a wiki with at least two levels of hierarchy. We might define a data type such as:

```
data Page = Page Text Text [Text] -- 2 or more
instance PathMultiPiece Page where
    toPathMultiPiece (Page x y z) = x : y : z
    fromPathMultiPiece (x:y:z) = Just $ Page x y z
    fromPathMultiPiece _ = Nothing
```

Overlap checking

By default, Yesod will ensure that no two routes have the potential to overlap with each other. So, for example, consider the following routes:

```
/foo/bar    Foo1R GET
/foo/#Text Foo2R GET
```

This route declaration will be rejected as overlapping, because /foo/bar will match both routes. However, there are two cases where you may wish to allow overlapping:

- If you know by the definition of your data type that the overlap can never happen. For example, if you replace Text with Int in the preceding example, it's easy to convince yourself that there's no route that exists that will overlap. Yesod is currently not capable of performing such an analysis.

- If you have some extra knowledge about how your application operates, and know that such a situation should never be allowed—for example, if the Foo2R route should never be allowed to receive the parameter bar.

You can turn off overlap checking by using an exclamation mark at the beginning of your route. For example, the following will be accepted by Yesod:

```
/foo/bar     Foo1R GET
!/foo/#Int  Foo2R GET
!/foo/#Text Foo3R GET
```

> You can also place the exclamation point at the beginning of any of the path pieces, or following the #, *, or + characters. However, this newer syntax should be preferred as it's clearer what the goal is.

One issue that overlapping routes introduces is ambiguity. In the preceding example, should /foo/bar route to Foo1R or Foo3R? And should /foo/42 route to Foo2R or Foo3R? Yesod's rule for this is simple: the first route wins.

Resource Name

Each resource pattern also has a name associated with it. That name will become the constructor for the type-safe URL data type associated with your application. Therefore, it has to start with a capital letter. By convention, these resource names all end with a capital R. There is nothing forcing you to do this; it is just common practice.

The exact definition of our constructor depends on the resource pattern it is attached to. Whatever data types are used as single pieces or multipieces of the pattern become arguments to the data type. This gives us a one-to-one correspondence between our type-safe URL values and valid URLs in our application.

 This doesn't necessarily mean that *every* value is a working page, just that it is a potentially valid URL. As an example, the value PersonR "Michael" may not resolve to a valid page if there is no Michael in the database.

Let's get some real examples going here. If you had the resource patterns /person/ #Text named PersonR, /year/#Int named YearR, and /page/faq named FaqR, you would end up with a route data type roughly looking like:

```
data MyRoute = PersonR Text
             | YearR Int
             | FaqR
```

If a user requests /year/2009, Yesod will convert it into the value YearR 2009. /person/Michael becomes PersonR "Michael", and /page/faq becomes FaqR. On the other hand, /year/two-thousand-nine, /person/michael/snoyman, and / page/FAQ would all result in 404 errors without ever seeing your code.

Handler Specification

The last piece of the puzzle when declaring your resources is how they will be handled. There are three options in Yesod:

- A single handler function for all request methods on a given route.
- A separate handler function for each request method on a given route. Any other request method will generate a 405 Method Not Allowed response.
- You want to pass off to a subsite.

The first two can be easily specified. A single handler function will be a line with just a resource pattern and the resource name, such as /page/faq FaqR. In this case, the handler function must be named handleFaqR.

A separate handler for each request method will be the same, plus a list of request methods. The request methods must be in all capital letters; for example, /person/ #String PersonR GET POST DELETE. In this case, you would need to define three handler functions: getPersonR, postPersonR, and deletePersonR.

Subsites are a very useful—but more complicated—topic in Yesod. We will cover writing subsites later, but using them is not too difficult. The most commonly used subsite is the static subsite, which serves static files for your application. In order to serve static files from /static, you would need a resource line like:

```
/static StaticR Static getStatic
```

In this line, /static just says where in your URL structure to serve the static files from. There is nothing magical about the word "static"; you could easily replace it with /my/non-dynamic/files.

The next word, StaticR, gives the resource name. The next two words specify that we are using a subsite. Static is the name of the subsite foundation data type, and get Static is a function that gets a Static value from a value of your master foundation data type.

Let's not get too caught up in the details of subsites now. We will look more closely at the static subsite in Chapter 15.

Dispatch

Once you have specified your routes, Yesod will take care of all the pesky details of URL dispatch for you. You just need to make sure to provide the appropriate handler functions. For subsite routes, you do not need to write any handler functions, but you do for the other two. We mentioned the naming rules earlier (MyHandlerR GET becomes getMyHandlerR, MyOtherHandlerR becomes handleMyOtherHandlerR).

Now that we know which functions we need to write, let's figure out what their type signatures should be.

Return Type

Let's look at a simple handler function:

```
mkYesod "Simple" [parseRoutes|
/ HomeR GET
|]

getHomeR :: Handler Html
getHomeR = defaultLayout [whamlet|<h1>This is simple|]
```

There are two components to this return type: Handler and Html. Let's analyze each in more depth.

Handler monad

Like the Widget type, the Handler data type is not defined anywhere in the Yesod libraries. Instead, the libraries provide the data type:

```
data HandlerT site m a
```

And like `WidgetT`, this has three arguments: a base monad `m`, a monadic value `a`, and the foundation data type `site`. Each application defines a `Handler` synonym that constrains `site` to that application's foundation data type, and sets `m` to `IO`. If your foundation is `MyApp`, in other words, you'd have the synonym:

```
type Handler = HandlerT MyApp IO
```

We need to be able to modify the underlying monad when writing subsites, but otherwise we'll use `IO`.

The `HandlerT` monad provides access to information about the user request (e.g., query string parameters), allows modifying the response (e.g., response headers), and more. This is the monad that most of your Yesod code will live in.

In addition, there's a typeclass called `MonadHandler`. Both `HandlerT` and `WidgetT` are instances of this typeclass, allowing many common functions to be used in both monads. If you see `MonadHandler` in any API documentation, you should remember that the function can be used in your `Handler` functions.

Html

There's nothing too surprising about this type. This function returns some HTML content, represented by the `Html` data type. But clearly Yesod would not be useful if it only allowed HTML responses to be generated. We want to respond with CSS, JavaScript, JSON, images, and more. So the question is: what data types can be returned?

In order to generate a response, we need to know two pieces of information: the content type (e.g., `text/html`, `image/png`) and how to serialize it to a stream of bytes. This is represented by the `TypedContent` data type:

```
data TypedContent = TypedContent !ContentType !Content
```

We also have a typeclass for all data types, which can be converted to a `TypedContent`:

```
class ToTypedContent a where
    toTypedContent :: a -> TypedContent
```

Many common data types are instances of this typeclass, including `Html`, `Value` (from the aeson package, representing JSON), `Text`, and even `()` (for representing an empty response).

Arguments

Let's return to our simple example:

```
mkYesod "Simple" [parseRoutes|
/ HomeR GET
|]
```

```
getHomeR :: Handler Html
getHomeR = defaultLayout [whamlet|<h1>This is simple|]
```

Not every route is as simple as this HomeR. Take, for instance, our PersonR route from earlier. The name of the person needs to be passed to the handler function. This translation is very straightforward, and hopefully intuitive. For example:

```
{-# LANGUAGE OverloadedStrings #-}
{-# LANGUAGE QuasiQuotes       #-}
{-# LANGUAGE TemplateHaskell   #-}
{-# LANGUAGE TypeFamilies      #-}
{-# LANGUAGE ViewPatterns      #-}
import           Data.Text (Text)
import qualified Data.Text as T
import           Yesod

data App = App
instance Yesod App

mkYesod "App" [parseRoutes|
/person/#Text PersonR GET
/year/#Integer/month/#Text/day/#Int DateR
/wiki/*Texts WikiR GET
|]

getPersonR :: Text -> Handler Html
getPersonR name = defaultLayout [whamlet|<h1>Hello #{name}!|]

handleDateR :: Integer -> Text -> Int -> Handler Text -- text/plain
handleDateR year month day =
    return $
        T.concat [month, " ", T.pack $ show day, ", ", T.pack $ show year]

getWikiR :: [Text] -> Handler Text
getWikiR = return . T.unwords

main :: IO ()
main = warp 3000 App
```

The arguments have the types of the dynamic pieces for each route, in the order specified. Also notice how we are able to use both Html and Text return values.

The Handler Functions

Because the majority of your code will live in the Handler monad, it's important to invest some time in understanding it better. The remainder of this chapter will give a brief introduction to some of the most common functions living in the Handler monad. I am specifically *not* covering any of the session functions; those will be addressed in Chapter 9.

Application Information

There are a number of functions that return information about your application as a whole, and give no information about individual requests. Some of these are:

getYesod
> Returns your application foundation value. If you store configuration values in your foundation, you will probably end up using this function a lot. (If you're so inclined, you can also use ask from Control.Monad.Reader; getYesod is simply a type-constrained synonym for it.)

getUrlRender
> Returns the URL rendering function, which converts a type-safe URL into a Text. Most of the time—like with Hamlet—Yesod calls this function for you, but you may occasionally need to call it directly.

getUrlRenderParams
> A variant of getUrlRender that converts both a type-safe URL and a list of query string parameters. This function handles all percent-encoding necessary.

Request Information

The most common information you will want to get about the current request is the requested path, the query string parameters, and POSTed form data. The first of those is dealt with in the routing, as described earlier. The other two are best dealt with using the forms module.

That said, you will sometimes need to get the data in a more raw format. For this purpose, Yesod exposes the YesodRequest data type along with the getRequest function to retrieve it. This gives you access to the full list of GET parameters, cookies, and preferred languages. There are some convenient functions to make these lookups easier, such as lookupGetParam, lookupCookie, and languages. For raw access to the POST parameters, you should use runRequestBody.

If you need even more raw data, like request headers, you can use waiRequest to access the Web Application Interface (WAI) request value. See Appendix B for more details.

Short-Circuiting

The following functions immediately end execution of a handler function and return a result to the user:

redirect
> Sends a redirect response to the user (a 303 response). If you want to use a different response code (e.g., a permanent 301 redirect), you can use redirectWith.

Yesod uses a 303 response for HTTP/1.1 clients, and a 302 response for HTTP/1.0 clients. You can read up on this sordid saga in the HTTP spec (*http://bit.ly/stat-codes*).

notFound
> Returns a 404 response. This can be useful if a user requests a database value that doesn't exist.

permissionDenied
> Returns a 403 response with a specific error message.

invalidArgs
> Returns a 400 response with a list of invalid arguments.

sendFile
> Sends a file from the filesystem with a specified content type. This is the preferred way to send static files, because the underlying WAI handler may be able to optimize this to a sendfile system call. Using readFile for sending static files should not be necessary.

sendResponse
> Sends a normal response with a 200 status code. This is really just a convenience for when you need to break out of some deeply nested code with an immediate response. Any instance of ToTypedContent may be used.

sendWaiResponse
> Used when you need to get low-level and send out a raw WAI response. This can be especially useful for creating streaming responses or for a technique like server-sent events.

Response Headers

The following functions allow you to generate various response headers:

setCookie
> Sets a cookie on the client. Instead of taking an expiration date, this function takes a cookie duration in minutes. Remember, you won't see this cookie using lookupCookie until the *following* request.

deleteCookie
> Tells the client to remove a cookie. Once again, lookupCookie will not reflect this change until the next request.

setHeader
> Sets an arbitrary response header.

setLanguage

Sets the preferred user language, which will show up in the result of the languages function.

cacheSeconds

Sets a Cache-Control header to indicate how many seconds this response can be cached. This can be particularly useful if you are using Varnish on your server (*http://www.varnish-cache.org*).

neverExpires

Sets the Expires header to the year 2037. You can use this for content that should never expire, such as when the request path has a hash value associated with it.

alreadyExpired

Sets the Expires header to the past.

expiresAt

Sets the Expires header to the specified date/time.

I/O and Debugging

The HandlerT and WidgetT monad transformers are both instances of a number of typeclasses. For this section, the important typeclasses are MonadIO and MonadLogger. The former allows you to perform arbitrary IO actions inside your handler, such as reading from a file. In order to achieve this, you just need to prepend liftIO to the call.

MonadLogger provides a built-in logging system. There are many ways you can customize this system, including what messages get logged and where logs are sent. By default, logs are sent to standard output. In development, all messages are logged, and in production, warnings and errors are logged.

When logging, we often want to know where in the source code the logging occurred. For this, MonadLogger provides a number of convenience Template Haskell functions that will automatically insert the source code location into the log messages. These functions are $logDebug, $logInfo, $logWarn, and $logError. Let's look at a short example of some of these functions:

```
{-# LANGUAGE OverloadedStrings #-}
{-# LANGUAGE QuasiQuotes       #-}
{-# LANGUAGE TemplateHaskell   #-}
{-# LANGUAGE TypeFamilies      #-}
import           Control.Exception (IOException, try)
import           Control.Monad     (when)
import           Yesod

data App = App
```

```
instance Yesod App where
    -- This function controls which messages are logged
    shouldLog App src level =
        True -- good for development
        -- level == LevelWarn || level == LevelError -- good for production

mkYesod "App" [parseRoutes|
/ HomeR GET
|]

getHomeR :: Handler Html
getHomeR = do
    $logDebug "Trying to read data file"
    edata <- liftIO $ try $ readFile "datafile.txt"
    case edata :: Either IOException String of
        Left e -> do
            $logError $ "Could not read datafile.txt"
            defaultLayout [whamlet|An error occurred|]
        Right str -> do
            $logInfo "Reading of data file succeeded"
            let ls = lines str
            when (length ls < 5) $ $logWarn "Less than 5 lines of data"
            defaultLayout
                [whamlet|
                    <ol>
                        $forall l <- ls
                            <li>#{l}
                |]

main :: IO ()
main = warp 3000 App
```

Query String and Hash Fragments

We've seen a number of functions that work on URL-like things, such as `redirect`. These functions all work with type-safe URLs, but what else do they work with? There's a typeclass called `RedirectUrl` that contains the logic for converting some type into a textual URL. This includes type-safe URLs, textual URLs, and two special instances:

- A tuple of a URL and a list of key/value pairs of query string parameters
- The `Fragment` data type, used for adding a hash fragment to the end of a URL

Both of these instances allow you to "add on" extra information to a type-safe URL. Let's see some examples of how these can be used:

```
{-# LANGUAGE OverloadedStrings #-}
{-# LANGUAGE QuasiQuotes       #-}
{-# LANGUAGE TemplateHaskell   #-}
```

```
{-# LANGUAGE TypeFamilies      #-}
import          Data.Set         (member)
import          Data.Text        (Text)
import          Yesod
import          Yesod.Auth
import          Yesod.Auth.Dummy

data App = App

mkYesod "App" [parseRoutes|
/       HomeR   GET
/link1 Link1R GET
/link2 Link2R GET
/link3 Link3R GET
/link4 Link4R GET
|]

instance Yesod App where

getHomeR :: Handler Html
getHomeR = defaultLayout $ do
    setTitle "Redirects"
    [whamlet|
        <p>
            <a href=@{Link1R}>Click to start the redirect loop!
    |]

getLink1R, getLink2R, getLink3R :: Handler ()
getLink1R = redirect Link2R -- /link1
getLink2R = redirect (Link3R, [("foo", "bar")]) -- /link3?foo=bar
getLink3R = redirect $ Link4R :#: ("baz" :: Text) -- /link4#baz

getLink4R :: Handler Html
getLink4R = defaultLayout
    [whamlet|
        <p>You made it!
    |]

main :: IO ()
main = warp 3000 App
```

Of course, inside a Hamlet template this is usually not necessary, as you can simply include the hash after the URL directly. For example:

```
<a href=@{Link1R}#somehash>Link to hash
```

Summary

Routing and dispatch is arguably the core of Yesod: it is from here that our type-safe URLs are defined, and the majority of our code is written within the Handler monad.

This chapter covered some of the most important and central concepts of Yesod, so it is important that you properly digest it.

This chapter also hinted at a number of more complex Yesod topics that we will be covering later, but you should be able to write some very sophisticated web applications with just the knowledge you have learned up until this point.

CHAPTER 8

Forms

I've mentioned the boundary issue already: whenever data enters or leaves an application, we need to validate it. Probably the most difficult place this occurs is in forms. Coding forms is complex; in an ideal world, we'd like a solution that can do all of the following:

- Ensure data is valid.
- Marshal string data in the form submission to Haskell data types.
- Generate HTML code for displaying the form.
- Generate JavaScript to do client-side validation and provide more user-friendly widgets, such as date pickers.
- Build up more complex forms by combining together simpler forms.
- Automatically assign names to our fields that are guaranteed to be unique.

The yesod-form package provides all these features in a simple, declarative API. It builds on top of Yesod's widgets to simplify styling of forms and applying JavaScript appropriately. And like the rest of Yesod, it uses Haskell's type system to make sure everything is working correctly.

Synopsis

```
{-# LANGUAGE MultiParamTypeClasses #-}
{-# LANGUAGE OverloadedStrings     #-}
{-# LANGUAGE QuasiQuotes           #-}
{-# LANGUAGE TemplateHaskell       #-}
{-# LANGUAGE TypeFamilies          #-}
import           Control.Applicative ((<$>), (<*>))
import           Data.Text           (Text)
import           Data.Time           (Day)
```

```
import          Yesod
import          Yesod.Form.Jquery

data App = App

mkYesod "App" [parseRoutes|
/ HomeR GET
/person PersonR POST
|]

instance Yesod App

-- Tells our application to use the standard English messages.
-- If you want i18n, then you can supply a translating function instead.
instance RenderMessage App FormMessage where
    renderMessage _ _ = defaultFormMessage

-- And tell us where to find the jQuery libraries. We'll just use the defaults,
-- which point to the Google CDN.
instance YesodJquery App

-- The data type we wish to receive from the form
data Person = Person
    { personName          :: Text
    , personBirthday      :: Day
    , personFavoriteColor :: Maybe Text
    , personEmail         :: Text
    , personWebsite       :: Maybe Text
    }
  deriving Show

-- Declare the form. The type signature is a bit intimidating, but here's the
-- overview:
--
-- * The Html parameter is used for encoding some extra information. See the
-- discussion regarding runFormGet and runFormPost below for further
-- explanation.
--
-- * We have our Handler as the inner monad, which indicates which site this is
-- running in.
--
-- * FormResult can be in three states: FormMissing (no data available),
-- FormFailure (invalid data), and FormSuccess.
--
-- * The Widget is the viewable form to place into the web page.
--
-- Note that the scaffolded site provides a convenient Form type synonym,
-- so that our signature could be written as:
--
-- > personForm :: Form Person
--
-- For our purposes, it's good to see the long version.
```

```
personForm :: Html -> MForm Handler (FormResult Person, Widget)
personForm = renderDivs $ Person
    <$> areq textField "Name" Nothing
    <*> areq (jqueryDayField def
        { jdsChangeYear = True -- give a year drop-down
        , jdsYearRange = "1900:-5" -- 1900 to five years ago
        }) "Birthday" Nothing
    <*> aopt textField "Favorite color" Nothing
    <*> areq emailField "Email address" Nothing
    <*> aopt urlField "Website" Nothing

-- The GET handler displays the form
getHomeR :: Handler Html
getHomeR = do
    -- Generate the form to be displayed
    (widget, enctype) <- generateFormPost personForm
    defaultLayout
        [whamlet|
            <p>
                The widget generated contains only the contents
                of the form, not the form tag itself. So...
            <form method=post action=@{PersonR} enctype=#{enctype}>
                ^{widget}
                <p>It also doesn't include the submit button.
                <button>Submit
        |]

-- The POST handler processes the form. If it is successful, it displays the
-- parsed person. Otherwise, it displays the form again with error messages.
postPersonR :: Handler Html
postPersonR = do
    ((result, widget), enctype) <- runFormPost personForm
    case result of
        FormSuccess person -> defaultLayout [whamlet|<p>#{show person}|]
        _ -> defaultLayout
            [whamlet|
                <p>Invalid input, let's try again.
                <form method=post action=@{PersonR} enctype=#{enctype}>
                    ^{widget}
                    <button>Submit
            |]

main :: IO ()
main = warp 3000 App
```

Kinds of Forms

Before jumping into the types themselves, we should begin with an overview of the
different kinds of forms. There are three categories:

Applicative

These are the most commonly used (it's what appeared in the preceding code). This approach has some nice properties: it lets error messages coalesce and remains a very high-level, declarative approach. (For more information on applicative code, see the Haskell wiki (*http://bit.ly/app-functor*).)

Monadic

A more powerful alternative to the applicative style. Although this approach allows for more flexibility, it does so at the cost of being more verbose. However, it's useful if you want to create forms that don't fit into the standard two-column look.

Input

Used only for receiving input. No HTML is generated for receiving the user input. Useful for interacting with existing forms.

In addition, there are a number of different variables that come into play for each form and field you will want to set up:

- Is the field required or optional?
- Should it be submitted with GET or POST?
- Does it have a default value, or not?

An overriding goal is to minimize the number of field definitions and let them work in as many contexts as possible. One result of this is that we end up with a few extra words for each field. In the synopsis, you may have noticed things like areq and that extra Nothing parameter. We'll cover why all of those exist in the course of this chapter, but for now realize that by making these parameters explicit, we are able to reuse the individual fields (like intField) in many different ways.

A quick note on naming conventions: each form type has a one-letter prefix (A, M, or I) that is used in a few places, such as MForm. We also use req and opt to mean required and optional. Combining these, we create a required applicative field with areq, or an optional input field with iopt.

Types

The Yesod.Form.Types module declares a few types. We won't cover all the types available, but will instead focus on the most crucial. Let's start with some of the simple ones:

enctype

The encoding type, either UrlEncoded or Multipart. This data type declares an instance of ToHtml, so you can use the enctype directly in Hamlet.

FormResult

> This data type has one of three possible states: FormMissing if no data was submitted, FormFailure if there was an error parsing the form (e.g., missing a required field or including invalid content), or FormSuccess if everything went smoothly.

FormMessage

> Represents all of the different messages that can be generated as a data type. For example, MsgInvalidInteger is used by the library to indicate that the textual value provided is not an integer. By keeping this data highly structured, you are able to provide any kind of rendering function you want, which allows for internationalization (i18n) of your application.

Next, we have some data types used for defining individual fields. We define a field as a single piece of information, such as a number, a string, or an email address. Fields are combined to build forms. The two key data types here are:

Field

> Defines two pieces of functionality: how to parse the text input from a user into a Haskell value, and how to create the widget to be displayed to the user. yesod-form defines a number of individual Field+s in +Yesod.Form.Fields.

FieldSettings

> Contains basic information on how a field should be displayed, such as the display name, an optional tooltip, and possibly hardcoded id and name attributes. (If none are provided, they are automatically generated.) Note that FieldSettings provides an IsString instance, so when you need to provide a FieldSettings value, you can actually type in a literal string. That's how we interacted with it in the synopsis.

And finally, we get to the important stuff: the forms themselves. There are three types: MForm is for monadic forms, AForm for applicative, and FormInput for input. MForm is actually a type synonym for a monad stack that provides the following features:

- A Reader monad giving us the parameters submitted by the user, the foundation data type, and the list of languages the user supports. The last two are used for rendering of the FormMessages to support i18n (more on this later).

- A Writer monad keeping track of the Enctype. A form will be UrlEncoded by default unless there is a file input field, which will force us to use Multipart instead.

- A State monad keeping track of generated names and identifiers for fields.

An AForm is pretty similar. However, there are a few major differences:

- It produces a list of FieldViews, which are used for tracking what we will display to the user. This allows us to keep an abstract idea of the form display, and then at the end of the day choose an appropriate function for laying it out on the page. In the synopsis, we used renderDivs, which creates a bunch of <div> tags. Two other options are renderBootstrap and renderTable.

- It does not provide a Monad instance. The goal of Applicative is to allow the entire form to run, grab as much information on each field as possible, and then create the final result. This cannot work in the context of Monad.

A FormInput is even simpler: it returns either a list of error messages or a result.

Converting

"But wait a minute," you say. "You said the synopsis code uses an applicative form, but I'm sure the type signature said MForm. Shouldn't it be monadic?" That's true; the final form we produced was monadic. But what really happened is that we converted an applicative form to a monadic one.

Again, our goal is to reuse code as much as possible, and minimize the number of functions in the API. And monadic forms are more powerful than applicative forms, if a bit clumsy, so anything that can be expressed in an applicative form could also be expressed in a monadic form. There are two core functions that help out with this: aformToForm converts any applicative form to a monadic one, and formToAForm converts certain kinds of monadic forms to applicative forms.

"But wait *another* minute," you insist. "I didn't see any aformToForm!" Also true. The renderDivs function takes care of that for us.

Creating AForms

Now that I've (hopefully) convinced you that we were really dealing with applicative forms, let's have a look and try to understand how these things get created. Let's take a simple example:

```
data Car = Car
    { carModel :: Text
    , carYear  :: Int
    }
  deriving Show

carAForm :: AForm Handler Car
carAForm = Car
    <$> areq textField "Model" Nothing
    <*> areq intField "Year" Nothing
```

```
carForm :: Html -> MForm Handler (FormResult Car, Widget)
carForm = renderTable carAForm
```

Here, we've explicitly split up applicative and monadic forms. In carAForm, we use the <$> and <*> operators. This should not be surprising; these are almost always used in applicative-style code. And we have one line for each record in our Car data type. Perhaps also unsurprisingly, we have a textField for the Text record, and an intField for the Int record.

Let's look a bit more closely at the areq function. Its (simplified) type signature is Field a -> FieldSettings -> Maybe a -> AForm a. That first argument specifies the data type of this field, how to parse it, and how to render it. The next argument, FieldSettings, tells us the label, tooltip, name, and ID of the field. In this case, we're using the previously mentioned IsString instance of FieldSettings.

And what's up with that Maybe a? It provides the optional default value. For example, if we wanted our form to fill in "2007" as the default car year, we would use areq int Field "Year" (Just 2007). We can even take this to the next level, and have a form that takes an optional parameter giving the default values:

```
carAForm :: Maybe Car -> AForm Handler Car
carAForm mcar = Car
    <$> areq textField "Model" (carModel <$> mcar)
    <*> areq intField  "Year"  (carYear  <$> mcar)
```

Optional Fields

Suppose we wanted to have an optional field (like the car color). All we do for this is use the aopt function:

```
carAForm :: AForm Handler Car
carAForm = Car
    <$> areq textField "Model" Nothing
    <*> areq intField "Year" Nothing
    <*> aopt textField "Color" Nothing
```

Like with required fields, the last argument is the optional default value. However, this has two layers of Maybe wrapping. This is actually a bit redundant, but it makes it much easier to write code that takes an optional default form parameter, such as in the next example:

```
carAForm :: Maybe Car -> AForm Handler Car
carAForm mcar = Car
    <$> areq textField "Model" (carModel <$> mcar)
    <*> areq intField  "Year"  (carYear  <$> mcar)
    <*> aopt textField "Color" (carColor <$> mcar)

carForm :: Html -> MForm Handler (FormResult Car, Widget)
carForm = renderTable $ carAForm $ Just $ Car "Forte" 2010 $ Just "gray"
```

Validation

How would we make our form only accept cars created after 1990? If you remember, the Field itself contained the information on what is a valid entry. So all we need to do is write a new Field, right? Well, that would be a bit tedious. Instead, let's just modify an existing one:

```
carAForm :: Maybe Car -> AForm Handler Car
carAForm mcar = Car
    <$> areq textField    "Model" (carModel <$> mcar)
    <*> areq carYearField "Year"  (carYear <$> mcar)
    <*> aopt textField    "Color" (carColor <$> mcar)
  where
    errorMessage :: Text
    errorMessage = "Your car is too old, get a new one!"

    carYearField = check validateYear intField

    validateYear y
        | y < 1990 = Left errorMessage
        | otherwise = Right y
```

The trick here is the check function. It takes a function (validateYear) that returns either an error message or a modified field value. In this example, we haven't modified the value at all. That is usually going to be the case. This kind of checking is very common, so we have a shortcut:

```
carYearField = checkBool (>= 1990) errorMessage intField
```

checkBool takes two parameters: a condition that must be fulfilled, and an error message to be displayed if it was not.

You may have noticed the explicit Text type signature on errorMessage. In the presence of OverloadedStrings, this is necessary. In order to support i18n, messages can have many different data types, and GHC has no way of determining which instance of IsString you intended to use.

It's great to make sure the car isn't too old. But what if we want to make sure that the year specified is not in the future? In order to look up the current year, we'll need to run some IO. For such circumstances, we'll need checkM, which allows our validation code to perform arbitrary actions:

```
carYearField = checkM inPast $ checkBool (>= 1990) errorMessage intField

inPast y = do
    thisYear <- liftIO getCurrentYear
    return $ if y <= thisYear
        then Right y
```

```
        else Left ("You have a time machine!" :: Text)

getCurrentYear :: IO Int
getCurrentYear = do
    now <- getCurrentTime
    let today = utctDay now
    let (year, _, _) = toGregorian today
    return $ fromInteger year
```

inPast is a function that will return an Either result in the Handler monad. We use
liftIO getCurrentYear to get the current year and then compare it against the user-
supplied year. Also, notice how we can chain together multiple validators.

 Because the checkM validator runs in the Handler monad, it has
access to a lot of the stuff you can normally do in Yesod. This is
especially useful for running database actions, which we'll cover in
Chapter 10.

More Sophisticated Fields

Our color entry field is nice, but it's not exactly user-friendly. What we really want is a
drop-down list:

```
data Car = Car
    { carModel :: Text
    , carYear :: Int
    , carColor :: Maybe Color
    }
  deriving Show

data Color = Red | Blue | Gray | Black
    deriving (Show, Eq, Enum, Bounded)

carAForm :: Maybe Car -> AForm Handler Car
carAForm mcar = Car
    <$> areq textField "Model" (carModel <$> mcar)
    <*> areq carYearField "Year" (carYear <$> mcar)
    <*> aopt (selectFieldList colors) "Color" (carColor <$> mcar)
  where
    colors :: [(Text, Color)]
    colors = [("Red", Red), ("Blue", Blue), ("Gray", Gray), ("Black", Black)]
```

selectFieldList takes a list of pairs. The first item in the pair is the text displayed to
the user in the drop-down list, and the second item is the actual Haskell value. Of
course, this code looks really repetitive; we can get the same result using the Enum and
Bounded instance GHC automatically derives for us:

```
colors = map (pack . show &&& id) [minBound..maxBound]
```

[minBound..maxBound] gives us a list of all the different Color values. We then apply a map and &&& (a.k.a., the to turn that into a list of pairs. And even this can be simplified by using the optionsEnum function provided by yesod-form, which would turn our original code into:

```
carAForm :: Maybe Car -> AForm Handler Car
carAForm mcar = Car
    <$> areq textField "Model" (carModel <$> mcar)
    <*> areq carYearField "Year" (carYear <$> mcar)
    <*> aopt (selectFieldList optionsEnum) "Color" (carColor <$> mcar)
```

Some people prefer radio buttons to drop-down lists. Fortunately, this is just a one-word change:

```
carAForm = Car
    <$> areq textField               "Model" Nothing
    <*> areq intField                "Year"  Nothing
    <*> aopt (radioFieldList optionsEnum) "Color" Nothing
```

Running Forms

At some point, we're going to need to take our beautiful forms and produce some results. There are a number of different functions available for this, each with its own purpose. I'll go through them, starting with the most common:

runFormPost

> This will run your form against any submitted POST parameters. If this is not a POST submission, it will return FormMissing. This automatically inserts a security token as a hidden form field to avoid cross-site request forgery (CSRF) attacks.

runFormGet

> The equivalent of runFormPost for GET parameters. In order to distinguish a normal GET page load from a GET submission, it includes an extra _hasdata hidden field in the form. Unlike runFormPost, it does not include CSRF protection.

runFormPostNoToken

> Same as runFormPost, but does not include (or require) the CSRF security token.

generateFormPost

> Instead of binding to existing POST parameters, acts as if there are none. This can be useful when you want to generate a new form after a previous form was submitted, such as in a wizard.

generateFormGet

> Same as generateFormPost, but for GET.

The return type from the first three is ((FormResult a, Widget), Enctype). The Widget will already have any validation errors and previously submitted values.

Why the nested tuple instead of a specialized data type? It's because `runFormPostNoToken` and `runFormGet` can both be used with forms that don't return a `FormResult` or `Widget`, which can be useful when dealing with more complicated monadic forms (discussed later).

i18n

There have been a few references to i18n in this chapter. The topic will get more thorough coverage in Chapter 22, but because it has such a profound effect on yesod-form, I wanted to give a brief overview here. The idea behind i18n in Yesod is to have data types represent messages. Each site can have an instance of `RenderMessage` for a given data type, which will translate that message based on a list of languages the user accepts. As a result of all this, there are a few things you should be aware of:

- There is an automatic instance of `RenderMessage` for `Text` in every site, so you can just use plain strings if you don't care about i18n support. However, you may need to use explicit type signatures occasionally.
- yesod-form expresses all of its messages in terms of the `FormMessage` data type. Therefore, to use yesod-form, you'll need to have an appropriate `RenderMessage` instance. A simple one that uses the default English translations would be:

```
instance RenderMessage App FormMessage where
    renderMessage _ _ = defaultFormMessage
```

This is provided automatically by the scaffolded site.

Monadic Forms

Oftentimes, a simple form layout is adequate, and applicative forms excel at this approach. Sometimes, however, you'll want your form to have a more customized look, such as that shown in Figure 8-1.

Hello, my name is [Michael Snoyman] and I am [26] years old. [Introduce myself]

Figure 8-1. A nonstandard form layout

For these use cases, monadic forms fit the bill. They are a bit more verbose than their applicative cousins, but this verbosity allows you to have complete control over what the form will look like. In order to generate the form in Figure 8-1, we could use code like the following:

```
{-# LANGUAGE MultiParamTypeClasses #-}
{-# LANGUAGE OverloadedStrings      #-}
```

```
{-# LANGUAGE QuasiQuotes        #-}
{-# LANGUAGE TemplateHaskell    #-}
{-# LANGUAGE TypeFamilies       #-}
import           Control.Applicative
import           Data.Text          (Text)
import           Yesod

data App = App

mkYesod "App" [parseRoutes|
/ HomeR GET
|]

instance Yesod App

instance RenderMessage App FormMessage where
    renderMessage _ _ = defaultFormMessage

data Person = Person
    { personName :: Text
    , personAge  :: Int
    }
    deriving Show

personForm :: Html -> MForm Handler (FormResult Person, Widget)
personForm extra = do
    (nameRes, nameView) <- mreq textField "this is not used" Nothing
    (ageRes, ageView) <- mreq intField "neither is this" Nothing
    let personRes = Person <$> nameRes <*> ageRes
    let widget = do
            toWidget
                [lucius|
                    ##{fvId ageView} {
                        width: 3em;
                    }
                |]
            [whamlet|
                #{extra}
                <p>
                    Hello, my name is #
                    ^{fvInput nameView}
                    \ and I am #
                    ^{fvInput ageView}
                    \ years old. #
                    <input type=submit value="Introduce myself">
            |]
    return (personRes, widget)

getHomeR :: Handler Html
getHomeR = do
    ((res, widget), enctype) <- runFormGet personForm
    defaultLayout
```

```
        [whamlet|
            <p>Result: #{show res}
            <form enctype=#{enctype}>
                ^{widget}
        |]

main :: IO ()
main = warp 3000 App
```

Similar to the applicative `areq`, we use `mreq` for monadic forms. (And yes, there's also `mopt` for optional fields.) But there's a big difference: `mreq` gives us back a pair of values. Instead of hiding away the `FieldView` value and automatically inserting it into a widget, we have the ability to insert it as we see fit.

`FieldView` has a number of pieces of information. The most important is `fvInput`, which is the actual form field. In this example, we also use `fvId`, which gives us back the HTML `id` attribute of the `<input>` tag. In our example, we use that to specify the width of the field.

You might be wondering what the story is with the "this is not used" and "neither is this" values. `mreq` takes `FieldSettings` as its second argument. `FieldSettings` provides an `IsString` instance, so the strings are essentially expanded by the compiler as follows:

```
fromString "this is not used" == FieldSettings
    { fsLabel = "this is not used"
    , fsTooltip = Nothing
    , fsId = Nothing
    , fsName = Nothing
    , fsAttrs = []
    }
```

In the case of applicative forms, the `fsLabel` and `fsTooltip` values are used when constructing your HTML. In the case of monadic forms, Yesod does not generate any of the "wrapper" HTML for you, and therefore these values are ignored. However, we still keep the `FieldSettings` parameter to allow you to override the `id` and `name` attributes of your fields if desired.

The other interesting bit is the `extra` value. GET forms include an extra field to indicate that they have been submitted, and POST forms include a security token to prevent CSRF attacks. If you don't include this extra hidden field in your form, the form submission will fail.

Other than that, things are pretty straightforward. We create our `personRes` value by combining the `nameRes` and `ageRes` values, and then return a tuple of the person and the widget. And in the `getHomeR` function, everything looks just like an applicative form. In fact, you could swap our monadic form with an applicative one and the code would still work.

Input Forms

Applicative and monadic forms handle both the generation of your HTML code and the parsing of user input. Sometimes you only want to do the latter, such as when there's an already existing form in HTML somewhere, or if you want to generate a form dynamically using JavaScript. In such a case, you'll want input forms.

These work mostly the same as applicative and monadic forms, with some differences:

- You use `runInputPost` and `runInputGet`.
- You use `ireq` and `iopt`. These functions now only take two arguments: the field type and the name (i.e., HTML `name` attribute) of the field in question.
- After running a form, it returns the value. It doesn't return a widget or an encoding type.
- If there are any validation errors, the page returns an "invalid arguments" error page.

You can use input forms to re-create the previous example. Note, however, that the input version is less user-friendly. If you make a mistake in an applicative or monadic form, you will be brought back to the same page, with your previously entered values in the form, and an error message explaining what you need to correct. With input forms, the user simply gets an error message:

```
{-# LANGUAGE MultiParamTypeClasses #-}
{-# LANGUAGE OverloadedStrings    #-}
{-# LANGUAGE QuasiQuotes          #-}
{-# LANGUAGE TemplateHaskell      #-}
{-# LANGUAGE TypeFamilies         #-}
import         Control.Applicative
import         Data.Text          (Text)
import         Yesod

data App = App

mkYesod "App" [parseRoutes|
/ HomeR GET
/input InputR GET
|]

instance Yesod App

instance RenderMessage App FormMessage where
    renderMessage _ _ = defaultFormMessage

data Person = Person
    { personName :: Text
```

```
    , personAge  :: Int
    }
    deriving Show

getHomeR :: Handler Html
getHomeR = defaultLayout
    [whamlet|
        <form action=@{InputR}>
            <p>
                My name is
                <input type=text name=name>
                and I am
                <input type=text name=age>
                years old.
                <input type=submit value="Introduce myself">
    |]

getInputR :: Handler Html
getInputR = do
    person <- runInputGet $ Person
                <$> ireq textField "name"
                <*> ireq intField "age"
    defaultLayout [whamlet|<p>#{show person}|]

main :: IO ()
main = warp 3000 App
```

Custom Fields

The fields that come built in with Yesod will likely cover the vast majority of your form needs. But occasionally, you'll need something more specialized. Fortunately, you can create new fields in Yesod yourself. The Field constructor has three values. The first, fieldParse, takes a list of values submitted by the user and returns one of three results:

- An error message saying validation failed
- The parsed value
- Nothing, indicating that no data was supplied

That last case might sound surprising. It would seem that Yesod can automatically know that no information is supplied when the input list is empty. But in reality, for some field types, the lack of any input is actually valid input. Checkboxes, for instance, indicate an unchecked state by sending in an empty list.

Also, what's up with the list? Shouldn't it be a Maybe? That's also not the case. With grouped checkboxes and multiselect lists, you'll have multiple widgets with the same name. We also use this trick in our example.

The second value in the constructor is fieldView, and it renders a widget to display to the user. This function has the following arguments:

- The id attribute.

- The name attribute.

- Any other arbitrary attributes.

- The result, given as an Either value. This will provide either the unparsed input (when parsing failed) or the successfully parsed value. intField is a great example of how this works. If you type in **42**, the value of the result will be Right 42. But if you type in **turtle**, the result will be Left "turtle". This lets you put in a value attribute on your <input> tag that will give the user a consistent experience.

- A Bool indicating if the field is required.

The final value in the constructor is fieldEnctype. If you're dealing with file uploads, this should be Multipart; otherwise, it should be UrlEncoded.

As a small example, let's create a new field type that is a password confirm field. This field has two text inputs—both with the same name attribute—and returns an error message if the values don't match. Note that, unlike most fields, it does *not* provide a value attribute on the <input> tags, as you don't ever want to send back a user-entered password in your HTML:

```
passwordConfirmField :: Field Handler Text
passwordConfirmField = Field
    { fieldParse = \rawVals _fileVals ->
        case rawVals of
            [a, b]
                | a == b -> return $ Right $ Just a
                | otherwise -> return $ Left "Passwords don't match"
            [] -> return $ Right Nothing
            _ -> return $ Left "You must enter two values"
    , fieldView = \idAttr nameAttr otherAttrs eResult isReq ->
        [whamlet|
            <input id=#{idAttr} name=#{nameAttr} *{otherAttrs} type=password>
            <div>Confirm:
            <input id=#{idAttr}-confirm name=#{nameAttr} *{otherAttrs}
                type=password>
        |]
    , fieldEnctype = UrlEncoded
    }

getHomeR :: Handler Html
getHomeR = do
    ((res, widget), enctype) <- runFormGet $ renderDivs
        $ areq passwordConfirmField "Password" Nothing
```

```
defaultLayout
    [whamlet|
        <p>Result: #{show res}
        <form enctype=#{enctype}>
            ^{widget}
            <input type=submit value="Change password">
    |]
```

Values That Don't Come from the User

Imagine you're writing a blog hosting web app, and you want to have a form for users to enter a blog post. A blog post will consist of four pieces of information:

- Title
- HTML contents
- User ID of the author
- Publication date

We want the user to enter the first two values, but not the second two. User ID should be determined automatically by authenticating the user (a topic we haven't covered yet), and the publication date should just be the current time. The question is, how do we keep our simple applicative form syntax, and yet pull in values that don't come from the user?

The answer is two separate helper functions:

- pure allows us to wrap up a plain value as an applicative form value.
- lift allows us to run arbitrary Handler actions inside an applicative form.

Let's see an example of using these two functions:

```
{-# LANGUAGE MultiParamTypeClasses #-}
{-# LANGUAGE OverloadedStrings     #-}
{-# LANGUAGE QuasiQuotes           #-}
{-# LANGUAGE TemplateHaskell       #-}
{-# LANGUAGE TypeFamilies          #-}
import           Control.Applicative
import           Data.Text           (Text)
import           Data.Time
import           Yesod

-- We'll address this properly in Chapter 14
newtype UserId = UserId Int
    deriving Show

data App = App
```

```
mkYesod "App" [parseRoutes|
/ HomeR GET POST
|]

instance Yesod App

instance RenderMessage App FormMessage where
    renderMessage _ _ = defaultFormMessage

type Form a = Html -> MForm Handler (FormResult a, Widget)

data Blog = Blog
    { blogTitle    :: Text
    , blogContents :: Textarea
    , blogUser     :: UserId
    , blogPosted   :: UTCTime
    }
    deriving Show

form :: UserId -> Form Blog
form userId = renderDivs $ Blog
    <$> areq textField "Title" Nothing
    <*> areq textareaField "Contents" Nothing
    <*> pure userId
    <*> lift (liftIO getCurrentTime)

getHomeR :: Handler Html
getHomeR = do
    let userId = UserId 5 -- again, see Chapter 14
    ((res, widget), enctype) <- runFormPost $ form userId
    defaultLayout
        [whamlet|
            <p>Previous result: #{show res}
            <form method=post action=@{HomeR} enctype=#{enctype}>
                ^{widget}
                <input type=submit>
        |]

postHomeR :: Handler Html
postHomeR = getHomeR

main :: IO ()
main = warp 3000 App
```

One trick we've introduced here is using the same handler code for both the GET and POST request methods. This is enabled by the implementation of runFormPost, which will behave exactly like generateFormPost in the case of a GET request. Using the same handler for both request methods cuts down on some boilerplate.

Summary

Forms in Yesod are broken up into three groups. Applicative is the most common, as it provides a nice user interface with an easy-to-use API. Monadic forms give you more power, but are harder to use. Input forms are intended for when you just want to read data from the user, not generate the input widgets.

Out of the box, Yesod provides a number of different Fields. In order to use these in your forms, you need to indicate the kind of form and whether the field is required or optional. The result is six helper functions: areq, aopt, mreq, mopt, ireq, and iopt.

Forms have significant power available. They can automatically insert JavaScript to help you leverage nicer UI controls, such as a jQuery UI date picker. Forms are also fully i18n-ready, so you can support a global community of users. And when you have more specific needs, you can slap some validation functions onto an existing field, or write a new one from scratch.

CHAPTER 9

Sessions

HTTP is a stateless protocol. Although some view this as a disadvantage, advocates of RESTful web development laud this as a plus. When state is removed from the picture, we get some automatic benefits, such as easier scalability and caching. You can draw many parallels with the nonmutable nature of Haskell in general.

As much as possible, RESTful applications should avoid storing state about an interaction with a client. However, it is sometimes unavoidable. Features like shopping carts are the classic example, but other, more mundane interactions like proper login handling can be greatly enhanced by correct usage of sessions.

This chapter will describe how Yesod stores session data, how you can access this data, and some special functions to help you make the most of sessions.

clientsession

One of the earliest packages spun off from Yesod was clientsession. This package uses encryption and signatures to store data in a client-side cookie. The encryption prevents the user from inspecting the data, and the signature ensures that the session cannot be tampered with.

It might sound like a bad idea from an efficiency standpoint to store data in a cookie. After all, this means that the data must be sent on every request. However, in practice, clientsession can be a great boon for performance:

- No server-side database lookup is required to service a request.
- We can easily scale horizontally: each request contains all the information we need to send a response.

- To avoid undue bandwidth overhead, production sites can serve their static content from a separate domain name, thereby skipping transmission of the session cookie for each request.

Storing megabytes of information in the session will be a bad idea. But for that matter, most session implementations recommend against such practices. If you really need massive storage for a user, it is best to store a lookup key in the session and put the actual data in a database.

All of the interaction with clientsession is handled by Yesod internally, but there are a few spots where you can tweak the behavior just a bit.

Controlling Sessions

By default, your Yesod application will use clientsession for its session storage, getting the encryption key from the client *client-session-key.aes* and giving a session a two-hour timeout. (Note: timeout is measured from the last time the client sent a request to the site, *not* from when the session was first created.) However, all of those points can be modified by overriding the makeSessionBackend method in the Yesod typeclass.

One simple way to override this method is to simply turn off session handling. To do so, return Nothing:

```
instance Yesod App where
    makeSessionBackend _ = return Nothing
```

If your app has absolutely no session needs, disabling them can give a bit of a performance increase. But be careful about disabling sessions: this will also disable such features as cross-site request forgery protection.

Another common approach is to modify the filepath or timeout value, but continue using clientsession. In order to do so, use the defaultClientSessionBackend helper function:

```
instance Yesod App where
    makeSessionBackend _ = do
        let minutes = 24 * 60 -- 1 day
            filepath = "mykey.aes"
        backend <- defaultClientSessionBackend minutes filepath
```

There are a few other functions to grant you more fine-grained control over client session, but they will rarely be necessary. Refer to Yesod.Core's documentation (*https://hackage.haskell.org/package/yesod-core-1.2.4/docs/Yesod-Core.html?*) if you are interested. It's also possible to implement some other form of session, such as a server-side session. To my knowledge, at the time of writing, no other such implementations exist.

If the given key file does not exist, it will be created and populated with a randomly generated key. When you deploy your app to production, you should include a pregenerated key with it; otherwise, all existing sessions will be invalidated when your new key file is generated. The scaffolding addresses this for you.

Session Operations

As in most frameworks, a session in Yesod is a key/value store. The base session API boils down to four functions: lookupSession gets a value for a key (if available), get Session returns all of the key/value pairs, setSession sets a value for a key, and deleteSession clears a value for a key. Let's look at an example:

```
{-# LANGUAGE OverloadedStrings      #-}
{-# LANGUAGE QuasiQuotes            #-}
{-# LANGUAGE TemplateHaskell        #-}
{-# LANGUAGE TypeFamilies           #-}
{-# LANGUAGE MultiParamTypeClasses #-}
import                Control.Applicative ((<$>), (<*>))
import qualified Web.ClientSession   as CS
import                Yesod

data App = App

mkYesod "App" [parseRoutes|
/ HomeR GET POST
|]

getHomeR :: Handler Html
getHomeR = do
    sess <- getSession
    defaultLayout
        [whamlet|
            <form method=post>
                <input type=text name=key>
                <input type=text name=val>
                <input type=submit>
            <h1>#{show sess}
        |]

postHomeR :: Handler ()
postHomeR = do
    (key, mval) <- runInputPost $ (,)
        <$> ireq textField "key"
        <*> iopt textField "val"
    case mval of
        Nothing -> deleteSession key
        Just val -> setSession key val
    liftIO $ print (key, mval)
    redirect HomeR
```

```
instance Yesod App where
    -- Make the session timeout 1 minute so that it's easier to play with
    makeSessionBackend _ = do
        backend <- defaultClientSessionBackend 1 "keyfile.aes"
        return $ Just backend

instance RenderMessage App FormMessage where
    renderMessage _ _ = defaultFormMessage

main :: IO ()
main = warp 3000 App
```

Messages

One usage of sessions previously alluded to is for messages. They solve a common problem in web development: the user performs a POST request, the web app makes a change, and then the web app wants to *simultaneously* redirect the user to a new page and send the user a success message. (This is known as Post/Redirect/Get.)

Yesod provides a pair of functions to enable this workflow: setMessage stores a value in the session, and getMessage both reads the value most recently put into the session and clears the old value so it is not displayed twice.

It is recommended to have a call to getMessage in defaultLayout so that any available message is shown to the user immediately, without having to add getMessage calls to every handler:

```
{-# LANGUAGE MultiParamTypeClasses #-}
{-# LANGUAGE OverloadedStrings     #-}
{-# LANGUAGE QuasiQuotes           #-}
{-# LANGUAGE TemplateHaskell       #-}
{-# LANGUAGE TypeFamilies          #-}
import           Yesod

data App = App

mkYesod "App" [parseRoutes|
/            HomeR       GET
/set-message SetMessageR POST
|]

instance Yesod App where
    defaultLayout widget = do
        pc <- widgetToPageContent widget
        mmsg <- getMessage
        withUrlRenderer
            [hamlet|
                $doctype 5
                <html>
```

```
                      <head>
                          <title>#{pageTitle pc}
                          ^{pageHead pc}
                      <body>
                          $maybe msg <- mmsg
                              <p>Your message was: #{msg}
                          ^{pageBody pc}
              |]

instance RenderMessage App FormMessage where
    renderMessage _ _ = defaultFormMessage

getHomeR :: Handler Html
getHomeR = defaultLayout
    [whamlet|
        <form method=post action=@{SetMessageR}>
            My message is: #
            <input type=text name=message>
            <button>Go
    |]

postSetMessageR :: Handler ()
postSetMessageR = do
    msg <- runInputPost $ ireq textField "message"
    setMessage $ toHtml msg
    redirect HomeR

main :: IO ()
main = warp 3000 App
```

The screenshots in Figures 9-1 through 9-4 demonstrate how you would interact with this program.

My message is: [   ] Submit

Figure 9-1. Initial page load, no message

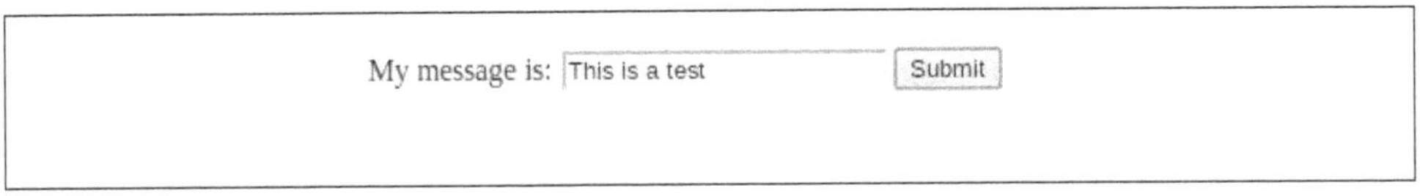

My message is: [This is a test] Submit

Figure 9-2. New message entered in text box

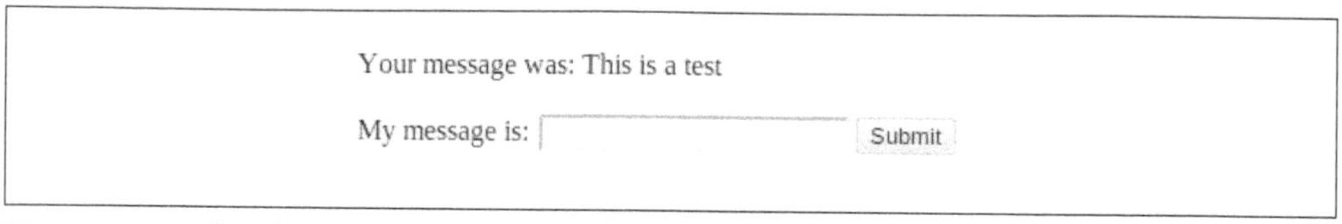

> Your message was: This is a test
>
> My message is: [   ] [Submit]

Figure 9-3. After form submit, message appears at top of page

> My message is: [   ] [Submit]

Figure 9-4. After refresh, message is cleared

Ultimate Destination

Not to be confused with a horror film, "ultimate destination" is a technique that was originally developed for Yesod's authentication framework, but which has more general usefulness. Suppose a user requests a page that requires authentication. If the user is not yet logged in, you need to send him to the login page. A well-designed web app will then *send the user back to the first page he requested*. That's what we call the ultimate destination.

`redirectUltDest` sends the user to the ultimate destination set in that user's session, clearing that value from the session. It takes a default destination as well, in case there is no destination set. For setting the session, there are three options:

- `setUltDest` sets the destination to the given URL, which can be provided either as a textual URL or a type-safe URL.
- `setUltDestCurrent` sets the destination to the currently requested URL.
- `setUltDestReferer` sets the destination based on the `Referer` header (the page that led the user to the current page).

Additionally, there is the `clearUltDest` function, to drop the ultimate destination value from the session if present.

Let's look at a small sample app. It will allow the user to set her name in the session, and then tell the user her name from another route. If the name hasn't been set yet, the user will be redirected to the set name page, with an ultimate destination set to come back to the current page:

```
{-# LANGUAGE MultiParamTypeClasses #-}
{-# LANGUAGE OverloadedStrings     #-}
{-# LANGUAGE QuasiQuotes           #-}
{-# LANGUAGE TemplateHaskell       #-}
{-# LANGUAGE TypeFamilies          #-}
import          Yesod
```

```
data App = App

mkYesod "App" [parseRoutes|
/         HomeR      GET
/setname  SetNameR   GET POST
/sayhello SayHelloR  GET
|]

instance Yesod App

instance RenderMessage App FormMessage where
    renderMessage _ _ = defaultFormMessage

getHomeR :: Handler Html
getHomeR = defaultLayout
    [whamlet|
        <p>
            <a href=@{SetNameR}>Set your name
        <p>
            <a href=@{SayHelloR}>Say hello
    |]

-- Display the set name form
getSetNameR :: Handler Html
getSetNameR = defaultLayout
    [whamlet|
        <form method=post>
            My name is #
            <input type=text name=name>
            . #
            <input type=submit value="Set name">
    |]

-- Retrieve the submitted name from the user
postSetNameR :: Handler ()
postSetNameR = do
    -- Get the submitted name and set it in the session
    name <- runInputPost $ ireq textField "name"
    setSession "name" name

    -- After we get a name, redirect to the ultimate destination.
    -- If no destination is set, default to the homepage.
    redirectUltDest HomeR

getSayHelloR :: Handler Html
getSayHelloR = do
    -- Look up the name value set in the session
    mname <- lookupSession "name"
    case mname of
        Nothing -> do
            -- No name in the session, so set the current page as
```

```
               -- the ultimate destination and redirect to the
               -- SetName page
               setUltDestCurrent
               setMessage "Please tell me your name"
               redirect SetNameR
          Just name -> defaultLayout [whamlet|<p>Welcome #{name}|]

    main :: IO ()
    main = warp 3000 App
```

Summary

Sessions are the primary means by which we bypass the statelessness imposed by HTTP. We shouldn't consider this an escape hatch to perform whatever actions we want: statelessness in web applications is a virtue, and we should respect it whenever possible. However, there are specific cases where it is vital to retain some state.

The session API in Yesod is very simple. It provides a key/value store and a few convenience functions built on top for common use cases. If used properly, with small payloads, sessions should be an unobtrusive part of your web development.

CHAPTER 10

Persistent

Forms deal with the boundary between the user and the application. Another boundary we need to deal with is between the application and the storage layer. Whether it be a SQL database, a YAML file, or a binary blob, odds are your storage layer does not natively understand your application's data types, and you'll need to perform some marshaling. Persistent is Yesod's answer to data storage—a type-safe, universal data store interface for Haskell.

Haskell has many different database bindings available. However, most of these have little knowledge of a schema and therefore do not provide useful static guarantees. They also force database-dependent APIs and data types on the programmer.

Some Haskellers have attempted a more revolutionary route: creating Haskell-specific data stores that allow one to easily store any strongly typed Haskell data. These options are great for certain use cases, but they constrain one to the storage techniques provided by the library and do not interface well with other languages.

In contrast, Persistent allows us to choose among existing databases that are highly tuned for different data storage use cases, to interoperate with other programming languages, and to use a safe and productive query interface, while still keeping the type safety of Haskell data types.

Persistent follows the guiding principles of type safety and concise, declarative syntax. Some other nice features include the following:

Database agnosticity
> There is first-class support for PostgreSQL, SQLite, MySQL, and MongoDB, and experimental Redis support.

Convenient data modeling
> Persistent lets you model relationships and use them in type-safe ways. The default type-safe persistent API does not support joins, allowing support for a wider number of storage layers. Joins and other SQL-specific functionality can be achieved through using a raw SQL layer (with very little type safety). An additional library, Esqueleto (*http://hackage.haskell.org/package/esqueleto*), builds on top of the Persistent data model, adding type-safe joins and SQL functionality.

Easy database migrations
> Persistent automatically performs database migrations.

Persistent works well with Yesod, but it is quite usable on its own as a standalone library. Most of this chapter will address Persistent on its own.

Synopsis

```
{-# LANGUAGE EmptyDataDecls             #-}
{-# LANGUAGE FlexibleContexts           #-}
{-# LANGUAGE GADTs                      #-}
{-# LANGUAGE GeneralizedNewtypeDeriving #-}
{-# LANGUAGE MultiParamTypeClasses      #-}
{-# LANGUAGE OverloadedStrings          #-}
{-# LANGUAGE QuasiQuotes                #-}
{-# LANGUAGE TemplateHaskell            #-}
{-# LANGUAGE TypeFamilies               #-}
import           Control.Monad.IO.Class  (liftIO)
import           Database.Persist
import           Database.Persist.Sqlite
import           Database.Persist.TH

share [mkPersist sqlSettings, mkMigrate "migrateAll"] [persistLowerCase|
Person
    name String
    age Int Maybe
    deriving Show
BlogPost
    title String
    authorId PersonId
    deriving Show
|]

main :: IO ()
main = runSqlite ":memory:" $ do
    runMigration migrateAll

    johnId <- insert $ Person "John Doe" $ Just 35
    janeId <- insert $ Person "Jane Doe" Nothing

    insert $ BlogPost "My fr1st p0st" johnId
    insert $ BlogPost "One more for good measure" johnId
```

```
oneJohnPost <- selectList [BlogPostAuthorId ==. johnId] [LimitTo 1]
liftIO $ print (oneJohnPost :: [Entity BlogPost])

john <- get johnId
liftIO $ print (john :: Maybe Person)

delete janeId
deleteWhere [BlogPostAuthorId ==. johnId]
```

The type annotations in the preceding snippet are *not* required to get your code to compile, but are present to clarify the types of each value.

Solving the Boundary Issue

Suppose you are storing information on people in a SQL database. Your table might look something like:

```
CREATE TABLE person(id SERIAL PRIMARY KEY, name VARCHAR NOT NULL, age INTEGER)
```

And if you are using a database like PostgreSQL, you can be guaranteed that the database will never store some arbitrary text in your age field. (The same cannot be said of SQLite, but let's forget about that for now.) To mirror this database table, you would likely create a Haskell data type that looks something like:

```
data Person = Person
    { personName :: Text
    , personAge  :: Int
    }
```

It looks like everything is type safe: the database schema matches our Haskell data types, the database ensures that invalid data can never make it into our data store, and everything is generally awesome. Well, until you encounter scenarios such as the following:

- You want to pull data from the database, and the database layer gives you the data in an untyped format.

- You want to find everyone older than 32, and you accidentally write "thirtytwo" in your SQL statement. Guess what: that will compile just fine, and you won't find out you have a problem until runtime.

- You decide you want to find the first 10 people alphabetically. No problem... until you make a typo in your SQL. Once again, you don't find out until runtime.

In dynamic languages, the answer to these issues is unit testing. For everything that *can* go wrong, make sure you write a test case. But as I am sure you are aware by now, that doesn't jive well with the Yesod approach to things. We like to take advantage of Haskell's strong typing to save us wherever possible, and data storage is no exception.

So the question remains: how can we use Haskell's type system to save the day?

Types

Like routing, there is nothing intrinsically difficult about type-safe data access. It just requires a lot of monotonous, error-prone boilerplate code. As usual, this means we can use the type system to keep us honest. And to avoid some of the drudgery, we'll use a sprinkling of Template Haskell.

`PersistValue` is the basic building block of Persistent. It is a sum type that can represent data that gets sent to and from a database. Its definition is:

```
data PersistValue
    = PersistText Text
    | PersistByteString ByteString
    | PersistInt64 Int64
    | PersistDouble Double
    | PersistRational Rational
    | PersistBool Bool
    | PersistDay Day
    | PersistTimeOfDay TimeOfDay
    | PersistUTCTime UTCTime
    | PersistNull
    | PersistList [PersistValue]
    | PersistMap [(Text, PersistValue)]
    | PersistObjectId ByteString
    -- ^ Intended especially for MongoDB backend
    | PersistDbSpecific ByteString
    -- ^ Using 'PersistDbSpecific' allows you to use types
    -- specific to a particular backend
```

Each Persistent backend needs to know how to translate the relevant values into something the database can understand. However, it would be awkward to have to express all of our data simply in terms of these basic types. The next layer is the `PersistField` typeclass, which defines how an arbitrary Haskell data type can be marshaled to and from a `PersistValue`. A `PersistField` correlates to a column in a SQL database. In our person example, name and age would be our `PersistFields`.

To tie up the user side of the code, our last typeclass is `PersistEntity`. An instance of `PersistEntity` correlates with a table in a SQL database. This typeclass defines a number of functions and some associated types. To review, we have the following correspondence between Persistent and SQL:

SQL	Persistent
Data type (VARCHAR, INTEGER, etc.)	PersistValue
Column	PersistField
Table	PersistEntity

Code Generation

In order to ensure that the PersistEntity instances match up properly with your Haskell data types, Persistent takes responsibility for both. This is also good from a DRY (Don't Repeat Yourself) perspective: you only need to define your entities once. Let's see a quick example:

```
{-# LANGUAGE GADTs                      #-}
{-# LANGUAGE GeneralizedNewtypeDeriving #-}
{-# LANGUAGE OverloadedStrings          #-}
{-# LANGUAGE QuasiQuotes                #-}
{-# LANGUAGE TemplateHaskell            #-}
{-# LANGUAGE TypeFamilies               #-}
import Database.Persist
import Database.Persist.TH
import Database.Persist.Sqlite
import Control.Monad.IO.Class (liftIO)

mkPersist sqlSettings [persistLowerCase|
Person
    name String
    age Int
    deriving Show
|]
```

We use a combination of Template Haskell and quasiquotation (like when defining routes): persistLowerCase is a quasiquoter that converts a whitespace-sensitive syntax into a list of entity definitions. LowerCase refers to the format of the generated table names. In this scheme, an entity like SomeTable would become the SQL table some_table. You can also declare your entities in a separate file using persistFile With. mkPersist takes that list of entities and declares:

- One Haskell data type for each entity
- A PersistEntity instance for each data type defined

The preceding example generates code that looks like the following:

```
{-# LANGUAGE TypeFamilies, GeneralizedNewtypeDeriving,
OverloadedStrings, GADTs #-}
import Database.Persist
```

```
import Database.Persist.Sqlite
import Control.Monad.IO.Class (liftIO)
import Control.Applicative

data Person = Person
    { personName :: !String
    , personAge :: !Int
    }
  deriving Show

type PersonId = Key Person

instance PersistEntity Person where
    newtype Key Person = PersonKey (BackendKey SqlBackend)
        deriving (PersistField, Show, Eq, Read, Ord)
    -- A generalized algebraic data type (GADT).
    -- This gives us a type-safe approach to matching fields with
    -- their data types.
    data EntityField Person typ where
        PersonId   :: EntityField Person PersonId
        PersonName :: EntityField Person String
        PersonAge  :: EntityField Person Int

    data Unique Person
    type PersistEntityBackend Person = SqlBackend

    toPersistFields (Person name age) =
        [ SomePersistField name
        , SomePersistField age
        ]

    fromPersistValues [nameValue, ageValue] = Person
        <$> fromPersistValue nameValue
        <*> fromPersistValue ageValue
    fromPersistValues _ = Left "Invalid fromPersistValues input"

    -- Information on each field, used internally to generate SQL statements
    persistFieldDef PersonId = FieldDef
        (HaskellName "Id")
        (DBName "id")
        (FTTypeCon Nothing "PersonId")
        SqlInt64
        []
        True
        NoReference
    persistFieldDef PersonName = FieldDef
        (HaskellName "name")
        (DBName "name")
        (FTTypeCon Nothing "String")
        SqlString
        []
        True
```

```
            NoReference
    persistFieldDef PersonAge = FieldDef
        (HaskellName "age")
        (DBName "age")
        (FTTypeCon Nothing "Int")
        SqlInt64
        []
        True
        NoReference
```

As you might expect, our `Person` data type closely matches the definition we gave in the original Template Haskell version. We also have a generalized algebraic data type (GADT) that gives a separate constructor for each field. This GADT encodes both the type of the entity and the type of the field. We use its constructors throughout Persistent, such as to ensure that when we apply a filter, the types of the filtering value match the field. There's another associated newtype for the database primary key of this entity.

We can use the generated `Person` type like any other Haskell type, and then pass it off to other Persistent functions:

```
{-# LANGUAGE EmptyDataDecls             #-}
{-# LANGUAGE FlexibleContexts           #-}
{-# LANGUAGE GADTs                      #-}
{-# LANGUAGE GeneralizedNewtypeDeriving #-}
{-# LANGUAGE MultiParamTypeClasses      #-}
{-# LANGUAGE OverloadedStrings          #-}
{-# LANGUAGE QuasiQuotes                #-}
{-# LANGUAGE TemplateHaskell            #-}
{-# LANGUAGE TypeFamilies               #-}
import          Control.Monad.IO.Class  (liftIO)
import          Database.Persist
import          Database.Persist.Sqlite
import          Database.Persist.TH

share [mkPersist sqlSettings, mkMigrate "migrateAll"] [persistLowerCase|
Person
    name String
    age Int Maybe
    deriving Show
|]

main :: IO ()
main = runSqlite ":memory:" $ do
    michaelId <- insert $ Person "Michael" $ Just 26
    michael <- get michaelId
    liftIO $ print michael
```

This code compiles, but will generate a runtime exception about a missing table. We'll explain and address that problem next.

We start off with some standard database connection code. In this case, we used the single-connection functions. Persistent also comes built in with connection pool functions, which we will generally want to use in production.

In this example, we have seen two functions. `insert` creates a new record in the database and returns its ID. Like everything else in Persistent, IDs are type safe. (We'll get into more details of how these IDs work later.) So, when you call `insert $ Person "Michael" 26`, it gives you a value back of type `PersonId`.

The next function we see is `get`, which attempts to load a value from the database using an `Id`. In Persistent, you never need to worry that you are using the key from the wrong table: trying to load up a different entity (like `House`) using a `PersonId` will never compile.

PersistStore

One last detail is left unexplained from the previous example: what exactly does `run Sqlite` do, and what is that monad that our database actions are running in?

All database actions require a parameter that is an instance of `PersistStore`. As its name implies, every data store (PostgreSQL, SQLite, MongoDB) has an instance of `PersistStore`. This is where all the translations from `PersistValue` to database-specific values occur, where SQL query generation happens, and so on.

As you can imagine, even though `PersistStore` provides a safe, well-typed interface to the outside world, there are a lot of database interactions that could go wrong. However, by testing this code automatically and thoroughly in a single location, we can centralize our error-prone code and make sure it is as bug-free as possible.

`runSqlite` creates a single connection to a database using its supplied connection string. For our test cases, we will use `:memory:`, which uses an in-memory database. All of the SQL backends share the same instance of `PersistStore`: `SqlBackend`. `run Sqlite` then provides the `SqlBackend` value as an environment parameter to the action via `runReaderT`.

There are actually a couple of other typeclasses: `PersistUpdate` and `PersistQuery`. Different typeclasses provide different functionality, which allows us to write backends that use simpler data stores (e.g., Redis) even though they can't provide us with all the high-level functionality available in Persistent.

One important thing to note is that everything that occurs inside a single call to `run Sqlite` runs in a single transaction. This has two important implications:

- For many databases, committing a transaction can be a costly activity. By putting multiple steps into a single transaction, you can speed up code dramatically.

- If an exception is thrown anywhere inside a single call to `runSqlite`, all actions will be rolled back (assuming your backend has rollback support).

This actually has farther-reaching impact than it may initially seem. A number of the short-circuit functions in Yesod, such as redirects, are implemented using exceptions. If you use such a call from inside a Persistent block, it will roll back the entire transaction.

Migrations

I'm sorry to tell you, but so far I have lied to you a bit: the example from the previous section does not actually work. If you try to run it, you will get an error message about a missing table.

For SQL databases, one of the major pains can be managing schema changes. Instead of leaving this to the user, Persistent steps in to help, but you have to *ask* it to help. Let's see what this looks like:

```
{-# LANGUAGE EmptyDataDecls            #-}
{-# LANGUAGE FlexibleContexts          #-}
{-# LANGUAGE GADTs                     #-}
{-# LANGUAGE GeneralizedNewtypeDeriving #-}
{-# LANGUAGE MultiParamTypeClasses     #-}
{-# LANGUAGE OverloadedStrings         #-}
{-# LANGUAGE QuasiQuotes               #-}
{-# LANGUAGE TemplateHaskell           #-}
{-# LANGUAGE TypeFamilies              #-}
import Database.Persist
import Database.Persist.TH
import Database.Persist.Sqlite
import Control.Monad.IO.Class (liftIO)
```

```
share [mkPersist sqlSettings, mkSave "entityDefs"] [persistLowerCase|
Person
    name String
    age Int
    deriving Show
|]

main :: IO ()
main = runSqlite ":memory:" $ do
    -- this line added: that's it!
    runMigration $ migrate entityDefs $ entityDef (Nothing :: Maybe Person)
    michaelId <- insert $ Person "Michael" 26
    michael <- get michaelId
    liftIO $ print michael
```

With this one little code change, Persistent will automatically create your Person table for you. This split between runMigration and migrate allows you to migrate multiple tables simultaneously.

This works when dealing with just a few entities, but can quickly get tiresome once you are dealing with a dozen entities. Instead of repeating yourself, Persistent provides a helper function, mkMigrate:

```
{-# LANGUAGE EmptyDataDecls              #-}
{-# LANGUAGE FlexibleContexts            #-}
{-# LANGUAGE GADTs                       #-}
{-# LANGUAGE GeneralizedNewtypeDeriving  #-}
{-# LANGUAGE MultiParamTypeClasses       #-}
{-# LANGUAGE OverloadedStrings           #-}
{-# LANGUAGE QuasiQuotes                 #-}
{-# LANGUAGE TemplateHaskell             #-}
{-# LANGUAGE TypeFamilies                #-}
import Database.Persist
import Database.Persist.Sqlite
import Database.Persist.TH

share [mkPersist sqlSettings, mkMigrate "migrateAll"] [persistLowerCase|
Person
    name String
    age Int
    deriving Show
Car
    color String
    make String
    model String
    deriving Show
|]

main :: IO ()
main = runSqlite ":memory:" $ do runMigration migrateAll
```

mkMigrate is a Template Haskell function that creates a new function that will automatically call migrate on all entities defined in the persist block. The share function is just a little helper that passes the information from the persist block to each Template Haskell function and concatenates the results.

Persistent has very conservative rules about what it will do during a migration. It starts by loading up table information from the database, complete with all defined SQL data types. It then compares that against the entity definition given in the code. For the following cases, it will automatically alter the schema:

- The data type of a field changed. However, the database may object to this modification if the data cannot be translated.

- A field was added. However, if the field is not null, no default value is supplied (we'll discuss defaults later), and there is already data in the database, the database will not allow this to happen.

- A field was converted from not null to null. In the opposite case, Persistent will attempt the conversion, contingent upon the database's approval.

- A brand new entity was added.

However, there are some cases that Persistent will not handle:

Field or entity renames

Persistent has no way of knowing that name has now been renamed to fullName: all it sees is an old field called name and a new field called fullName.

Field removals

Because this can result in data loss, Persistent by default will refuse to perform the action (you can force the issue by using runMigrationUnsafe instead of run Migration, though it is *not* recommended).

runMigration will print out the migrations it is running on stderr (you can bypass this by using runMigrationSilent). Whenever possible, it uses ALTER TABLE calls. However, in SQLite, ALTER TABLE has very limited abilities, and therefore Persistent must resort to copying the data from one table to another.

Finally, if instead of *performing* a migration you want Persistent to give you hints about what migrations are necessary, use the printMigration function. This function will print out the migrations that runMigration would perform for you. This may be useful for performing migrations that Persistent is not capable of, for adding arbitrary SQL to a migration, or just to log what migrations occurred.

Uniqueness

In addition to declaring fields within an entity, you can also declare uniqueness constraints. A typical example would be requiring that a username be unique:

```
User
    username Text
    UniqueUsername username
```

Each field name must begin with a lowercase letter, but the uniqueness constraint must begin with an uppercase letter because it will be represented in Haskell as a data constructor:

```
{-# LANGUAGE EmptyDataDecls            #-}
{-# LANGUAGE FlexibleContexts          #-}
{-# LANGUAGE GADTs                     #-}
{-# LANGUAGE GeneralizedNewtypeDeriving #-}
{-# LANGUAGE MultiParamTypeClasses     #-}
{-# LANGUAGE OverloadedStrings         #-}
{-# LANGUAGE QuasiQuotes               #-}
{-# LANGUAGE TemplateHaskell           #-}
{-# LANGUAGE TypeFamilies              #-}
import Database.Persist
import Database.Persist.Sqlite
import Database.Persist.TH
import Data.Time
import Control.Monad.IO.Class (liftIO)

share [mkPersist sqlSettings, mkMigrate "migrateAll"] [persistLowerCase|
Person
    firstName String
    lastName String
    age Int
    PersonName firstName lastName
    deriving Show
|]

main :: IO ()
main = runSqlite ":memory:" $ do
    runMigration migrateAll
    insert $ Person "Michael" "Snoyman" 26
    michael <- getBy $ PersonName "Michael" "Snoyman"
    liftIO $ print michael
```

To declare a unique combination of fields, we add an extra line to our declaration. Persistent knows that it is defining a unique constructor, because the line begins with a capital letter. Each following word must be a field in this entity.

The main restriction on uniqueness is that it can only be applied to non-null fields. The reason for this is that the SQL standard is ambiguous on how uniqueness should be applied to NULL (e.g., is NULL=NULL true or false?). Besides that ambiguity, most

SQL engines in fact implement rules that would be *contrary* to what the Haskell data types anticipate (e.g., PostgreSQL says that NULL=NULL is false, whereas Haskell says Nothing == Nothing is true).

In addition to providing nice guarantees at the database level about the consistency of your data, uniqueness constraints can also be used to perform some specific queries within your Haskell code, like the getBy demonstrated earlier. This happens via the Unique associated type. In the preceding example, we end up with a new constructor:

```
PersonName :: String -> String -> Unique Person
```

 With the MongoDB backend, a uniqueness constraint cannot be created: you must place a unique index on the field.

Queries

Depending on what your goal is, there are different approaches to querying the database. Some commands query based on a numeric ID, while others will filter. Queries also differ in the number of results they return: some lookups should return no more than one result (if the lookup key is unique), while others can return many results.

Persistent therefore provides a few different query functions. As usual, we try to encode as many invariants in the types as possible. For example, a query that can return only zero or one result will use a Maybe wrapper, whereas a query returning many results will return a list.

Fetching by ID

The simplest query you can perform in Persistent is getting based on an ID. Because this value may or may not exist, its return type is wrapped in a Maybe:

```
personId <- insert $ Person "Michael" "Snoyman" 26
maybePerson <- get personId
case maybePerson of
    Nothing -> liftIO $ putStrLn "Just kidding, not really there"
    Just person -> liftIO $ print person
```

This can be very useful for sites that provide URLs like */person/5*. However, in such a case, we don't usually care about the Maybe wrapper and just want the value, returning a 404 message if it is not found. Fortunately, the get404 function (provided by the yesod-persistent package) helps us out here. We'll go into more details when we look at integration with Yesod.

Fetching by Unique Constraint

getBy is almost identical to get, except:

- It takes a uniqueness constraint (i.e., instead of an ID it takes a Unique value).
- It returns an Entity instead of a value. An Entity is a combination of database ID and value:

```
personId <- insert $ Person "Michael" "Snoyman" 26
maybePerson <- getBy $ PersonName "Michael" "Snoyman"
case maybePerson of
    Nothing -> liftIO $ putStrLn "Just kidding, not really there"
    Just (Entity personId person) -> liftIO $ print person
```

Like get404, there is also a getBy404 function.

Select Functions

Most likely, you're going to want more powerful queries. You'll want to find everyone over a certain age; all cars available in blue; all users without a registered email address. For this, you need one of the select functions.

All the select functions use a similar interface, with slightly different outputs. They are:

selectSource
Returns a Source containing all the IDs and values from the database. This allows you to write streaming code.

selectList
Returns a list containing all the IDs and values from the database. All records will be loaded into memory.

selectFirst
Takes just the first ID and value from the database, if available.

selectKeys
Returns only the keys, without the values, as a Source.

A Source is a stream of data, and is part of the conduit package. I recommend reading the School of Haskell conduit tutorial (*http://bit.ly/h-conduit*) to get started.

selectList is the most commonly used, so we will cover it specifically. Understanding the others should be trivial after that.

selectList takes two arguments: a list of Filters, and a list of SelectOpts. The former is what limits your results based on characteristics; it allows for equals, less than, is member of, and such. The SelectOpts list provides for three different features:

sorting, limiting output to a certain number of rows, and offsetting results by a certain number of rows.

 The combination of limits and offsets is very important; it allows for efficient pagination in your web apps.

Let's jump straight into an example of filtering, and then analyze it:

```
people <- selectList [PersonAge >. 25, PersonAge <=. 30] []
liftIO $ print people
```

As simple as that example is, we really need to cover three points:

- PersonAge is a constructor for an associated phantom type. That might sound scary, but what's important is that it uniquely identifies the "age" column of the "person" table, and that it knows that the age field is an Int. (That's the phantom part.)
- We have a bunch of Persistent filtering operators. They're all pretty straightforward: just tack a period onto the end of what you'd expect. There are three gotchas here, which I'll explain momentarily.
- The list of filters is ANDed together, so that our constraint means "age is greater than 25 AND age is less than or equal to 30." We'll describe ORing later.

The one operator that's surprisingly named is "not equals." We use !=., because /=. is used for updates (described later). Don't worry: if you use the wrong one, the compiler will catch you. The other two surprising operators are "is member" and "is not member." They are, respectively, <-. and /<-. (both end with a period).

And regarding ORs, we use the ||. operator. For example:

```
people <- selectList
    (     [PersonAge >. 25, PersonAge <=. 30]
      ||. [PersonFirstName /<-. ["Adam", "Bonny"]]
      ||. ([PersonAge ==. 50] ||. [PersonAge ==. 60])
    )
    []
liftIO $ print people
```

This (completely nonsensical) example means: find people who are 26–30 years old, inclusive, OR whose names are neither Adam nor Bonny, OR whose age is either 50 or 60.

SelectOpt

All of our `selectList` calls have included an empty list as the second parameter. That specifies no options, meaning: sort however the database wants, return all results, and don't skip any results. A `SelectOpt` has four constructors that can be used to change all that:

Asc
> Sorts by the given column in ascending order. This uses the same phantom type as filtering, such as `PersonAge`.

Desc
> Same as `Asc`, but in descending order.

LimitTo
> Takes an `Int` argument. Only returns up to the specified number of results.

OffsetBy
> Takes an `Int` argument. Skips the specified number of results.

The following code defines a function that will break down results into pages. It returns all people aged 18 and over, and then sorts them by age (oldest person first). People with the same age are sorted alphabetically by last name, then first name:

```
resultsForPage pageNumber = do
    let resultsPerPage = 10
    selectList
        [ PersonAge >=. 18
        ]
        [ Desc PersonAge
        , Asc PersonLastName
        , Asc PersonFirstName
        , LimitTo resultsPerPage
        , OffsetBy $ (pageNumber - 1) * resultsPerPage
        ]
```

Manipulation

Querying is only half the battle. We also need to be able to add data to and modify existing data in the database.

Insert

It's all well and good to be able to play with data in the database, but how does it get there in the first place? The answer is the `insert` function. You just give it a value, and it gives back an ID.

At this point, it makes sense to explain a bit of the philosophy behind Persistent. In many other object-relational mapping (ORM) solutions, the data types used to hold data are opaque: you need to go through their defined interfaces to get at and modify the data. That's not the case with Persistent: we're using plain old algebraic data types for the whole thing. This means you still get all the great benefits of pattern matching, currying, and everything else you're used to.

There are a few things you *can't* do. For one, there's no way to automatically update values in the database every time the record is updated in Haskell. Of course, with Haskell's normal stance of purity and immutability, this wouldn't make much sense anyway, so I don't shed any tears over it.

However, there is one issue that newcomers are often bothered by: why are IDs and values completely separate? It seems like it would be very logical to embed the ID inside the value. In other words, instead of having:

```
data Person = Person { name :: String }
```

have:

```
data Person = Person { personId :: PersonId, name :: String }
```

Well, there's one problem with this right off the bat: how do we do an insert? If a Person needs to have an Id, and we get the Id by inserting, and an insert needs a Person, we have an impossible loop. We could solve this with undefined, but that's just asking for trouble.

OK, you say, let's try something a bit safer:

```
data Person = Person { personId :: Maybe PersonId, name :: String }
```

Most definitely prefer insert $ Person Nothing "Michael" to insert $ Person undefined "Michael". And now our types will be much simpler, right? For example, selectList could return a simple [Person] instead of that ugly [Entity SqlPersist Person].

The problem is that the "ugliness" is incredibly useful. Having Entity Person makes it obvious, at the type level, that we're dealing with a value that exists in the database. Let's say we want to create a link to another page that requires the PersonId (not an uncommon occurrence, as we'll discuss later). The Entity Person form gives us unambiguous access to that information; embedding PersonId within Person with a Maybe wrapper means an extra runtime check for Just, instead of a more error-proof compile-time check.

Finally, there's a semantic mismatch with embedding the ID within the value. The Person is the value. Two people are identical (in the context of Haskell) if all their fields are the same. By embedding the ID in the value, we're no longer talking about a person, but about a row in the database. Equality is no longer really equality, it's identity; we want to know if this is the *same person*, as opposed to an equivalent person.

In other words, there are some annoyances with having the ID separated out, but overall, it's the *right* approach, which in the grand scheme of things leads to better, less buggy code.

Update

Now, in the context of that discussion, let's think about updating. The simplest way to update is:

```
let michael = Person "Michael" 26
    michaelAfterBirthday = michael { personAge = 27 }
```

But that's not actually updating anything; it's just creating a new `Person` value based on the old one. When we say "update," we're *not* talking about modifications to the values in Haskell (we'd better not be, of course, because data in Haskell is immutable).

Instead, we're looking at ways of modifying rows in a table. And the simplest way to do that is with the `update` function:

```
personId <- insert $ Person "Michael" "Snoyman" 26
update personId [PersonAge =. 27]
```

`update` takes two arguments: an ID, and a list of updates. The simplest update is assignment, but it's not always the best. What if you want to increase someone's age by 1, but you don't have that person's current age? Persistent has you covered:

```
haveBirthday personId = update personId [PersonAge +=. 1]
```

And as you might expect, we have all the basic mathematical operators: `+=.`, `-=.`, `*=.`, and `/=.` (full stop). These can be convenient for updating a single record, but they are also essential for proper ACID guarantees. Imagine the alternative: pull out a `Person`, increment the age, and update the new value. If you have two threads/processes working on this database at the same time, you're in for a world of hurt (hint: race conditions).

Sometimes you'll want to update many rows at once (give all your employees a 5% pay increase, for example). `updateWhere` takes two parameters—a list of filters, and a list of updates to apply:

```
updateWhere [PersonFirstName ==. "Michael"] [PersonAge *=. 2]
-- it's been a long day
```

Occasionally, you'll just want to completely replace the value in a database with a different value. For that, you use (surprise) the `replace` function:

```
personId <- insert $ Person "Michael" "Snoyman" 26
replace personId $ Person "John" "Doe" 20
```

Delete

As much as it pains us, sometimes we must part with our data. To do so, we have three functions:

delete
> Deletes based on an ID

deleteBy
> Deletes based on a unique constraint

deleteWhere
> Deletes based on a set of filters:

```
personId <- insert $ Person "Michael" "Snoyman" 26
delete personId
deleteBy $ PersonName "Michael" "Snoyman"
deleteWhere [PersonFirstName ==. "Michael"]
```

We can even use deleteWhere to wipe out all the records in a table; we just need to give some hints to GHC as to what table we're interested in:

```
deleteWhere ([] :: [Filter Person])
```

Attributes

So far, we have seen a basic syntax for our persistLowerCase blocks: a line for the name of our entities; and then an indented line for each field with two words, the name of the field and the data type of the field. Persistent handles more than this, though you can assign an arbitrary list of attributes after the first two words on a line.

Suppose we want to have a Person entity with an (optional) age and the timestamp of when the entity was added to the system. For entities already in the database, we want to just use the current date-time for that timestamp:

```
{-# LANGUAGE EmptyDataDecls              #-}
{-# LANGUAGE FlexibleContexts            #-}
{-# LANGUAGE GADTs                       #-}
{-# LANGUAGE GeneralizedNewtypeDeriving #-}
{-# LANGUAGE MultiParamTypeClasses       #-}
{-# LANGUAGE OverloadedStrings           #-}
{-# LANGUAGE QuasiQuotes                 #-}
{-# LANGUAGE TemplateHaskell             #-}
{-# LANGUAGE TypeFamilies                #-}
import Database.Persist
import Database.Persist.Sqlite
import Database.Persist.TH
import Data.Time
import Control.Monad.IO.Class
```

```
share [mkPersist sqlSettings, mkMigrate "migrateAll"] [persistLowerCase|
Person
    name String
    age Int Maybe
    created UTCTime default=CURRENT_TIME
    deriving Show
|]

main :: IO ()
main = runSqlite ":memory:" $ do
    time <- liftIO getCurrentTime
    runMigration migrateAll
    insert $ Person "Michael" (Just 26) time
    insert $ Person "Greg" Nothing time
    return ()
```

Maybe is a built-in, single-word attribute. It makes the field optional. In Haskell, this means it is wrapped in a Maybe. In SQL, it makes the column nullable.

The default attribute is backend-specific and uses whatever syntax is understood by the database. In this case, it uses the database's built-in CURRENT_TIME function. Suppose that we now want to add a field for a person's favorite programming language:

```
{-# LANGUAGE EmptyDataDecls              #-}
{-# LANGUAGE FlexibleContexts            #-}
{-# LANGUAGE GADTs                       #-}
{-# LANGUAGE GeneralizedNewtypeDeriving  #-}
{-# LANGUAGE MultiParamTypeClasses       #-}
{-# LANGUAGE OverloadedStrings           #-}
{-# LANGUAGE QuasiQuotes                 #-}
{-# LANGUAGE TemplateHaskell             #-}
{-# LANGUAGE TypeFamilies                #-}
import Database.Persist
import Database.Persist.Sqlite
import Database.Persist.TH
import Data.Time

share [mkPersist sqlSettings, mkMigrate "migrateAll"] [persistLowerCase|
Person
    name String
    age Int Maybe
    created UTCTime default=CURRENT_TIME
    language String default='Haskell'
    deriving Show
|]

main :: IO ()
main = runSqlite ":memory:" $ do
    runMigration migrateAll
```

The `default` attribute has absolutely no impact on the Haskell code itself; you still need to fill in all values. This will only affect the database schema and automatic migrations.

We need to surround the string with single quotes so that the database can properly interpret it. Finally, Persistent can use double quotes for containing whitespace, so if we want to set someone's default home country to be El Salvador, we would use the following:

```
{-# LANGUAGE EmptyDataDecls         #-}
{-# LANGUAGE FlexibleContexts       #-}
{-# LANGUAGE GADTs                  #-}
{-# LANGUAGE GeneralizedNewtypeDeriving #-}
{-# LANGUAGE MultiParamTypeClasses  #-}
{-# LANGUAGE OverloadedStrings      #-}
{-# LANGUAGE QuasiQuotes            #-}
{-# LANGUAGE TemplateHaskell        #-}
{-# LANGUAGE TypeFamilies           #-}
import Database.Persist
import Database.Persist.Sqlite
import Database.Persist.TH
import Data.Time

share [mkPersist sqlSettings, mkMigrate "migrateAll"] [persistLowerCase|
Person
    name String
    age Int Maybe
    created UTCTime default=CURRENT_TIME
    language String default='Haskell'
    country String "default='El Salvador'"
    deriving Show
|]

main :: IO ()
main = runSqlite ":memory:" $ do
    runMigration migrateAll
```

One last trick you can do with attributes is to specify the names to be used for the SQL tables and columns. This can be convenient when interacting with existing databases:

```
share [mkPersist sqlSettings, mkMigrate "migrateAll"] [persistLowerCase|
Person sql=the-person-table id=numeric_id
    firstName String sql=first_name
    lastName String sql=fldLastName
    age Int "sql=The Age of the Person"
    PersonName firstName lastName
    deriving Show
|]
```

There are a number of other features to the entity definition syntax. An up-to-date list is maintained on the Persistent wiki (*http://bit.ly/yesod-pers*).

Relations

Persistent allows references between your data types in a manner that is consistent with supporting non-SQL databases. You do this by embedding an ID in the related entity. So if a person has many cars:

```
{-# LANGUAGE EmptyDataDecls            #-}
{-# LANGUAGE FlexibleContexts          #-}
{-# LANGUAGE GADTs                     #-}
{-# LANGUAGE GeneralizedNewtypeDeriving #-}
{-# LANGUAGE MultiParamTypeClasses     #-}
{-# LANGUAGE OverloadedStrings         #-}
{-# LANGUAGE QuasiQuotes               #-}
{-# LANGUAGE TemplateHaskell           #-}
{-# LANGUAGE TypeFamilies              #-}
import Database.Persist
import Database.Persist.Sqlite
import Database.Persist.TH
import Control.Monad.IO.Class (liftIO)
import Data.Time

share [mkPersist sqlSettings, mkMigrate "migrateAll"] [persistLowerCase|
Person
    name String
    deriving Show
Car
    ownerId PersonId
    name String
    deriving Show
|]

main :: IO ()
main = runSqlite ":memory:" $ do
    runMigration migrateAll
    bruce <- insert $ Person "Bruce Wayne"
    insert $ Car bruce "Bat Mobile"
    insert $ Car bruce "Porsche"
    -- this could go on a while
    cars <- selectList [CarOwnerId ==. bruce] []
    liftIO $ print cars
```

Using this technique, you can define one-to-many relationships. To define many-to-many relationships, you need a join entity, which has a one-to-many relationship with each of the original tables. It is also a good idea to use uniqueness constraints on these. For example, to model a situation where we want to track which people have shopped in which stores:

```
{-# LANGUAGE EmptyDataDecls              #-}
{-# LANGUAGE FlexibleContexts            #-}
{-# LANGUAGE GADTs                       #-}
{-# LANGUAGE GeneralizedNewtypeDeriving  #-}
{-# LANGUAGE MultiParamTypeClasses       #-}
{-# LANGUAGE OverloadedStrings           #-}
{-# LANGUAGE QuasiQuotes                 #-}
{-# LANGUAGE TemplateHaskell             #-}
{-# LANGUAGE TypeFamilies                #-}
import Database.Persist
import Database.Persist.Sqlite
import Database.Persist.TH
import Data.Time

share [mkPersist sqlSettings, mkMigrate "migrateAll"] [persistLowerCase|
Person
    name String
Store
    name String
PersonStore
    personId PersonId
    storeId StoreId
    UniquePersonStore personId storeId
|]

main :: IO ()
main = runSqlite ":memory:" $ do
    runMigration migrateAll

    bruce <- insert $ Person "Bruce Wayne"
    michael <- insert $ Person "Michael"

    target <- insert $ Store "Target"
    gucci <- insert $ Store "Gucci"
    sevenEleven <- insert $ Store "7-11"

    insert $ PersonStore bruce gucci
    insert $ PersonStore bruce sevenEleven

    insert $ PersonStore michael target
    insert $ PersonStore michael sevenEleven

    return ()
```

A Closer Look at Types

So far, we've spoken about Person and PersonId without really explaining what they
are. In the simplest sense, for a SQL-only system, the PersonId could just be type
PersonId = Int64. However, that means there is nothing binding a PersonId at the
type level to the Person entity. As a result, you could accidentally use a PersonId and

get a `Car`. In order to model this relationship, we could use phantom types. So, our next naive step would be:

```
newtype Key entity = Key Int64
type PersonId = Key Person
```

And that works out really well, until you get to a backend that doesn't use `Int64` for its IDs. And that's not just a theoretical possibility; MongoDB uses `ByteStrings` instead. So what we need is a key value that can contain an `Int` and a `ByteString`. Seems like a great time for a sum type:

```
data Key entity = KeyInt Int64 | KeyByteString ByteString
```

But that's just asking for trouble. Next we'll have a backend that uses timestamps, so we'll need to add another constructor to `Key`. This could go on for a while. Fortunately, we already have a sum type intended for representing arbitrary data, called `PersistValue`:

```
newtype Key entity = Key PersistValue
```

And this is (more or less) what Persistent did until version 2.0. However, this has a different problem: it throws away data. For example, when dealing with a SQL database, we know that the key type will be an `Int64` (assuming defaults are being used). However, we can't assert that at the type level with this construction. So instead, starting with Persistent 2.0, we now use an associated data type inside the `PersistEntity` class:

```
class PersistEntity record where
    data Key record
    ...
```

When you're working with a SQL backend and aren't using a custom key type, this becomes a `newtype` wrapper around an `Int64`, and the `toSqlKey`/`fromSqlKey` functions can perform that type-safe conversion for you. With MongoDB, on the other hand, it's a wrapper around a `ByteString`.

More Complicated, More Generic

By default, Persistent will hardcode your data types to work with a specific database backend. When using `sqlSettings`, this is the `SqlBackend` type. But if you want to write Persistent code that can be used on multiple backends, you can enable more generic types by replacing `sqlSettings` with `sqlSettings { mpsGeneric = True }`.

To understand why this is necessary, consider relations. Let's say we want to represent blogs and blog posts. We would use the entity definition:

```
Blog
    title Text
Post
```

```
        title Text
        blogId BlogId
```

We know that `BlogId` is just a type synonym for `Key Blog`, but how will `Key Blog` be defined? We can't use an `Int64`, as that won't work for MongoDB. And we can't use `ByteString`, because that won't work for SQL databases.

To allow for this, once `mpsGeneric` is set to `True`, our resulting data types have a type parameter to indicate the database backend they use, so that keys can be properly encoded. This looks like the following:

```
data BlogGeneric backend = Blog { blogTitle :: Text }
data PostGeneric backend = Post
    { postTitle  :: Text
    , postBlogId :: Key (BlogGeneric backend)
    }
```

Notice that we still keep the short names for the constructors and the records. Finally, to give a simple interface for normal code, we define some type synonyms:

```
type Blog   = BlogGeneric SqlBackend
type BlogId = Key Blog
type Post   = PostGeneric SqlBackend
type PostId = Key Post
```

And no, `SqlBackend` isn't hardcoded into Persistent anywhere. That `sqlSettings` parameter you've been passing to `mkPersist` is what tells it to use `SqlBackend`. Mongo code will use `mongoSettings` instead.

This might be quite complicated under the surface, but user code hardly ever touches this. Look back through this whole chapter: not once did we need to deal with the `Key` or `Generic` stuff directly. The most common place for it to pop up is in compiler error messages. So, it's important to be aware that this exists, but it shouldn't affect you on a day-to-day basis.

Custom Fields

Occasionally, you will want to define a custom field to be used in your data store. The most common case is an enumeration, such as employment status. For this, Persistent provides a helper Template Haskell function:

```
-- @Employment.hs
{-# LANGUAGE TemplateHaskell #-}
module Employment where

import Database.Persist.TH

data Employment = Employed | Unemployed | Retired
    deriving (Show, Read, Eq)
derivePersistField "Employment"
```

```
{-# LANGUAGE EmptyDataDecls             #-}
{-# LANGUAGE FlexibleContexts           #-}
{-# LANGUAGE GADTs                      #-}
{-# LANGUAGE GeneralizedNewtypeDeriving #-}
{-# LANGUAGE MultiParamTypeClasses      #-}
{-# LANGUAGE OverloadedStrings          #-}
{-# LANGUAGE QuasiQuotes                #-}
{-# LANGUAGE TemplateHaskell            #-}
{-# LANGUAGE TypeFamilies               #-}
import Database.Persist.Sqlite
import Database.Persist.TH
import Employment

share [mkPersist sqlSettings, mkMigrate "migrateAll"] [persistLowerCase|
Person
    name String
    employment Employment
|]

main :: IO ()
main = runSqlite ":memory:" $ do
    runMigration migrateAll

    insert $ Person "Bruce Wayne" Retired
    insert $ Person "Peter Parker" Unemployed
    insert $ Person "Michael" Employed

    return ()
```

derivePersistField stores the data in the database using a string field, and performs marshaling using the Show and Read instances of the data type. This may not be as efficient as storing via an integer, but it is much more future-proof: even if you add extra constructors in the future, your data will still be valid.

 We split our definition into two separate modules in this case. This is necessary due to the GHC stage restriction, which essentially means that, in many cases, Template Haskell generated code cannot be used in the same module it was created in.

Persistent: Raw SQL

The Persistent package provides a type-safe interface to data stores. It tries to be backend-agnostic (e.g., by not relying on relational features of SQL). My experience has been that you can easily perform 95% of what you need to do with the high-level interface (in fact, most of my web apps use the high-level interface exclusively).

But occasionally you'll want to use a feature that's specific to a backend. One feature I've used in the past is full-text search. In this case, we'll use the SQL LIKE operator, which is not modeled in Persistent. We'll get all people with the last name "Snoyman" and print the records out:

```
{-# LANGUAGE EmptyDataDecls            #-}
{-# LANGUAGE FlexibleContexts          #-}
{-# LANGUAGE GADTs                     #-}
{-# LANGUAGE GeneralizedNewtypeDeriving #-}
{-# LANGUAGE MultiParamTypeClasses     #-}
{-# LANGUAGE OverloadedStrings         #-}
{-# LANGUAGE QuasiQuotes               #-}
{-# LANGUAGE TemplateHaskell           #-}
{-# LANGUAGE TypeFamilies              #-}
import Database.Persist.TH
import Data.Text (Text)
import Database.Persist.Sqlite
import Control.Monad.IO.Class (liftIO)
import Data.Conduit
import qualified Data.Conduit.List as CL

share [mkPersist sqlSettings, mkMigrate "migrateAll"] [persistLowerCase|
Person
    name Text
|]

main :: IO ()
main = runSqlite ":memory:" $ do
    runMigration migrateAll
    insert $ Person "Michael Snoyman"
    insert $ Person "Miriam Snoyman"
    insert $ Person "Eliezer Snoyman"
    insert $ Person "Gavriella Snoyman"
    insert $ Person "Greg Weber"
    insert $ Person "Rick Richardson"

    -- Persistent does not provide the LIKE keyword, but we'd like to get the
    -- whole Snoyman family...
    let sql = "SELECT name FROM Person WHERE name LIKE '%Snoyman'"
    rawQuery sql [] $$ CL.mapM_ (liftIO . print)
```

There is also higher-level support that allows for automated data marshaling. Refer to the Haddock API docs (*http://www.stackage.org/package/persistent*) for more details.

Actually, you *can* express a LIKE operator directly in the normal syntax due to a feature added in Persistent 0.6, which allows backend-specific operators. But this is still a good example, so let's roll with it.

Integration with Yesod

So you've been convinced of the power of Persistent. How do you integrate it with your Yesod application? If you use the scaffolding, most of the work is done for you already. But as we normally do, we'll build up everything manually here to point out how it works under the surface.

The yesod-persistent package provides the meeting point between Persistent and Yesod. It provides the YesodPersist typeclass, which standardizes access to the database via the runDB method. Let's see this in action:

```haskell
{-# LANGUAGE EmptyDataDecls            #-}
{-# LANGUAGE FlexibleContexts          #-}
{-# LANGUAGE GADTs                     #-}
{-# LANGUAGE GeneralizedNewtypeDeriving #-}
{-# LANGUAGE MultiParamTypeClasses     #-}
{-# LANGUAGE OverloadedStrings         #-}
{-# LANGUAGE QuasiQuotes               #-}
{-# LANGUAGE TemplateHaskell           #-}
{-# LANGUAGE TypeFamilies              #-}
{-# LANGUAGE ViewPatterns              #-}
import Yesod
import Database.Persist.Sqlite
import Control.Monad.Trans.Resource (runResourceT)
import Control.Monad.Logger (runStderrLoggingT)

-- Define our entities as usual
share [mkPersist sqlSettings, mkMigrate "migrateAll"] [persistLowerCase|
Person
    firstName String
    lastName String
    age Int
    deriving Show
|]

-- We keep our connection pool in the foundation. At program initialization, we
-- create our initial pool, and each time we need to perform an action we check
-- out a single connection from the pool.
data PersistTest = PersistTest ConnectionPool

-- We'll create a single route, to access a person. It's a very common
-- occurrence to use an Id type in routes.
mkYesod "PersistTest" [parseRoutes|
/ HomeR GET
/person/#PersonId PersonR GET
|]

-- Nothing special here
instance Yesod PersistTest

-- Now we need to define a YesodPersist instance, which will keep track of
```

```
-- which backend we're using and how to run an action.
instance YesodPersist PersistTest where
    type YesodPersistBackend PersistTest = SqlBackend

    runDB action = do
        PersistTest pool <- getYesod
        runSqlPool action pool

-- List all people in the database
getHomeR :: Handler Html
getHomeR = do
    people <- runDB $ selectList [] [Asc PersonAge]
    defaultLayout
        [whamlet|
            <ul>
                $forall Entity personid person <- people
                    <li>
                        <a href=@{PersonR personid}>#{personFirstName person}
        |]

-- We'll just return the show value of a person, or a 404 if the Person doesn't
-- exist.
getPersonR :: PersonId -> Handler String
getPersonR personId = do
    person <- runDB $ get404 personId
    return $ show person

openConnectionCount :: Int
openConnectionCount = 10

main :: IO ()
main = runStderrLoggingT $ withSqlitePool "test.db3" openConnectionCount
  $ \pool -> liftIO $ do
    runResourceT $ flip runSqlPool pool $ do
        runMigration migrateAll
        insert $ Person "Michael" "Snoyman" 26
    warp 3000 $ PersistTest pool
```

There are two important pieces here for general use. runDB is used to run a DB action from within a Handler. Within the runDB, you can use any of the functions we've spoken about so far, such as insert and selectList.

The type of runDB is YesodDB site a -> HandlerT site IO a. YesodDB is defined as:

```
type YesodDB site =
    YesodPersistBackend site (HandlerT site IO)
```

Because it is built on top of the YesodPersistBackend associated type, it uses the appropriate database backend based on the current site.

The other new feature is get404. It works just like get, but instead of returning a Nothing when a result can't be found, it returns a 404 message page. The getPersonR function is a very common approach used in real-world Yesod applications: get404 a value and then return a response based on it.

More Complex SQL

Persistent strives to be backend-agnostic. The advantage of this approach is code that easily moves between different backend types. The downside is that you lose out on some backend-specific features. Probably the biggest casualty is SQL join support.

Fortunately, thanks to Felipe Lessa, you can have your cake and eat it too. The Esqueleto (*http://hackage.haskell.org/package/esqueleto*) library provides support for writing type-safe SQL queries, using the existing Persistent infrastructure. The Haddocks for that package provide a good introduction to its usage. And because it uses many Persistent concepts, most of your existing Persistent knowledge should transfer over easily.

For a simple example of using Esqueleto, see Chapter 19.

Something Besides SQLite

To keep the examples in this chapter simple, we've used the SQLite backend. Just to round things out, here's our original code rewritten to work with PostgreSQL:

```
{-# LANGUAGE EmptyDataDecls          #-}
{-# LANGUAGE FlexibleContexts        #-}
{-# LANGUAGE GADTs                   #-}
{-# LANGUAGE GeneralizedNewtypeDeriving #-}
{-# LANGUAGE MultiParamTypeClasses   #-}
{-# LANGUAGE OverloadedStrings       #-}
{-# LANGUAGE QuasiQuotes             #-}
{-# LANGUAGE TemplateHaskell         #-}
{-# LANGUAGE TypeFamilies            #-}
import           Control.Monad.IO.Class  (liftIO)
import           Control.Monad.Logger    (runStderrLoggingT)
import           Database.Persist
import           Database.Persist.Postgresql
import           Database.Persist.TH

share [mkPersist sqlSettings, mkMigrate "migrateAll"] [persistLowerCase|
Person
    name String
    age Int Maybe
    deriving Show
BlogPost
    title String
    authorId PersonId
```

```
        deriving Show
|]

connStr = "host=localhost dbname=test user=test password=test port=5432"

main :: IO ()
main = runStderrLoggingT $ withPostgresqlPool connStr 10 $ \pool -> liftIO $ do
    flip runSqlPersistMPool pool $ do
        runMigration migrateAll

        johnId <- insert $ Person "John Doe" $ Just 35
        janeId <- insert $ Person "Jane Doe" Nothing

        insert $ BlogPost "My fr1st p0st" johnId
        insert $ BlogPost "One more for good measure" johnId

        oneJohnPost <- selectList [BlogPostAuthorId ==. johnId] [LimitTo 1]
        liftIO $ print (oneJohnPost :: [Entity BlogPost])

        john <- get johnId
        liftIO $ print (john :: Maybe Person)

        delete janeId
        deleteWhere [BlogPostAuthorId ==. johnId]
```

Summary

Persistent brings the type safety of Haskell to your data access layer. Instead of writing error-prone untyped data access code, or manually writing boilerplate marshal code, you can rely on Persistent to automate the process for you.

The goal is to provide everything you need, *most* of the time. For the times when you need something a bit more powerful, Persistent gives you direct access to the underlying data store, so you can write whatever five-way joins you want.

Persistent integrates directly into the general Yesod workflow. Not only do helper packages like yesod-persistent provide a nice layer, but packages like yesod-form and yesod-auth also leverage Persistent's features.

CHAPTER 11

Deploying Your Web App

I can't speak for others, but I personally prefer programming to system administration. But the fact is that eventually you'll need to serve your app somehow, and odds are that you'll need to be the one to set it up.

There are some promising initiatives in the Haskell web community toward making deployment easier. In the future, we may even have a service that allows you to deploy your app with a single command.

But we're not there yet. And even if we were, such a solution will never work for everyone. This chapter covers the different deployment options, and gives some general recommendations on what you should choose in different situations.

Keter

The Yesod scaffolding comes with some built-in support for the Keter deployment engine, which is also written in Haskell and uses many of the same underlying technologies, like WAI and `http-client`. Keter works as a reverse proxy to your applications, as well as a system for starting, monitoring, and redeploying running apps. If you'd like to deploy with Keter, follow these steps:

1. Edit the *config/keter.yaml* file in your scaffolded application as necessary.

2. Set up some kind of server for hosting your apps. I recommend trying Ubuntu on Amazon EC2.

3. Install Keter on that machine (follow the instructions on the Keter website (*https://github.com/snoyberg/keter/*), as they will be the most up to date).

4. Run `yesod keter` to generate a Keter bundle (e.g., *myapp.keter*).

5. Copy *myapp.keter* to the */opt/keter/incoming* directory on your server.

If you've gotten things configured correctly, you should now be able to view your website, running in a production environment! In the future, upgrades can be handled by simply rerunning `yesod keter` and recopying the *myapp.keter* bundle to the server. Note that Keter will automatically detect the presence of the new file and reload your application.

The rest of this chapter will provide some more details about various steps, and present some alternatives in case you'd prefer not to use the scaffolding or Keter.

Compiling

The biggest advice I can give is this: don't compile on your server. It's tempting to do so, as you just have to transfer source code around and you avoid confusing dependency issues. However, compiling a Yesod application takes significiant memory and CPU resources, which means:

- While you're recompiling your app, your existing applications will suffer performance-wise.
- You will need to get a much larger machine to handle compilation, and that capacity will likely sit idle most of the time, as Yesod applications tend to require far less CPU and memory than GHC itself.

Once you're ready to compile, you should always make sure to run `cabal clean` before a new production build, to make sure no old files are lying around. Then, you can run `cabal configure && cabal build` to get an executable, which will be located at *dist/build/myapp/myapp*. (The `yesod keter` command does `cabal clean` for you automatically.)

Files to Deploy

With a Yesod scaffolded application, there are essentially three sets of files that need to be deployed:

- Your executable
- The *config/* folder
- The *static/* folder

Everything else (e.g., Shakespearean templates), gets compiled into the executable itself.

There is one caveat, however, regarding the *config/client_session_key.aes* file. This file controls the server-side encryption used for securing client-side session cookies. Yesod will automatically generate a new one of these keys if none is present. In practice, this means that, if you do not include this file in your deployment, all of your users will have to log in again when you redeploy. If you follow this advice and include the *config/* folder, this issue will be partially resolved. Another approach is to put your session key in an environment variable.

The other half of the resolution is to ensure that once you generate a *config/client_session_key.aes* file, you keep the same one for all future deployments. The simplest way to ensure this is to keep that file in your version control. However, if your version control is open source, this will be dangerous: anyone with access to your repository will be able to spoof login credentials!

The problem described here is essentially one of system administration, not programming. Yesod does not provide any built-in approach for securely storing client session keys. If you have an open source repository, or do not trust everyone who has access to your source code repository, it's vital to figure out a safe storage solution for the client session key.

SSL and Static Files

There are two commonly used features in the Yesod world: serving your site over HTTPS, and placing your static files in a separate domain name. Both of these are good practices, but used together they can lead to problems if you're not careful. In particular, most web browsers will not load up JavaScript files from a non-HTTPS domain name if your HTML is served from an HTTPS domain name. In this situation, you'll need to do one of two things:

- Serve your static files over HTTPS as well.
- Serve your static files from the same domain name as your main site.

Note that if you go for the first option (which is the better one), you'll need either two separate SSL certificates or a wildcard certificate.

Warp

As we have mentioned before, Yesod is built on the Web Application Interface (WAI), allowing it to run on any WAI backend. At the time of writing, the following backends are available:

- Warp
- FastCGI

- SCGI
- CGI
- WebKit
- Development server

The last two are not intended for production deployments. Of the remaining four, all can be used for production deployment in theory. In practice, a CGI backend will likely be horribly inefficient, because a new process must be spawned for each connection. And SCGI is not nearly as well supported by frontend web servers as Warp (via reverse proxying) or FastCGI.

Between the two remaining choices, Warp gets a very strong recommendation, for the following reasons:

- It is significantly faster.
- Like FastCGI, it can run behind a frontend server like Nginx, using a reverse HTTP proxy.
- It is a fully capable server of its own accord, and can therefore be used without any frontend server.

So that leaves one last question: should Warp run on its own, or via a reverse proxy behind a frontend server? For most use cases I recommend the latter, because:

- Having a reverse proxy in front of your app makes it easier to deploy new versions.
- If you have a bug in your application, a reverse proxy can give slightly nicer error messages to users.
- You can host multiple applications from a single host via virtual hosting.
- Your reverse proxy can function as a load balancer or SSL proxy as well, simplifying your application.

As already discussed, Keter is a great way to get started. If you have an existing web server running, like Nginx, Yesod will work just fine sitting behind it instead.

Nginx Configuration

Keter configuration is trivial, as it is designed to work with Yesod applications. But if you want to instead use Nginx, how do you set it up?

In general, Nginx will listen on port 80 and your Yesod/Warp app will listen on some unprivileged port (let's say 4321). You will then need to provide an *nginx.conf* file, such as the following:

```
daemon off; # Don't run nginx in the background, good for monitoring apps
events {
    worker_connections 4096;
}

http {
    server {
        listen 80; # Incoming port for Nginx
        server_name www.myserver.com;
        location / {
            proxy_pass http://127.0.0.1:4321; # Reverse proxy to your Yesod app
        }
    }
}
```

You can add as many server blocks as you like. A common addition is to ensure users always access your pages with the *www* prefix on the domain name, guaranteeing the RESTful principle of canonical URLs. (You could just as easily do the opposite and always strip the *www*; just make sure that your choice is reflected in both the Nginx config and the approot of your site.) In this case, we would add the block:

```
server {
    listen 80;
    server_name myserver.com;
    rewrite ^/(.*) http://www.myserver.com/$1 permanent;
}
```

A highly recommended optimization is to serve static files from a separate domain name, thereby bypassing the cookie transfer overhead. Assuming that our static files are stored in the *static/* folder within our site folder, and the site folder is located at */home/michael/sites/mysite*, this would look like:

```
server {
    listen 80;
    server_name static.myserver.com;
    root /home/michael/sites/mysite/static;
    # Because yesod-static appends a content hash in the query string,
    # we are free to set expiration dates far in the future without
    # concerns of stale content.
    expires max;
}
```

In order for this to work, your site must properly rewrite static URLs to this alternative domain name. The scaffolded site is set up to make this fairly simple via the Set tings.staticRoot function and the definition of urlRenderOverride. However, if you just want to get the benefit of Nginx's faster static file serving without dealing with separate domain names, you can instead modify your original server block like so:

```
server {
    listen 80; # Incoming port for Nginx
```

```
    server_name www.myserver.com;
    location / {
        proxy_pass http://127.0.0.1:4321; # Reverse proxy to your Yesod app
    }
    location /static {
        root /home/michael/sites/mysite; # Notice we do *not* include /static
        expires max;
    }
}
```

Server Process

Many people are familiar with an Apache/mod_php or Lighttpd/FastCGI kind of setup, where the web server automatically spawns the web application. With Nginx, either for reverse proxying or with FastCGI, this is not the case: you are responsible for running your own process. I strongly recommend using a monitoring utility that will automatically restart your application in case it crashes. There are many great options out there, such as angel or daemontools.

To give a concrete example, here is an Upstart config file. The file must be placed in */etc/init/mysite.conf*:

```
description "My awesome Yesod application"
start on runlevel [2345];
stop on runlevel [!2345];
respawn
chdir /home/michael/sites/mysite
exec /home/michael/sites/mysite/dist/build/mysite/mysite
```

Once this is in place, bringing up your application is as simple as sudo start mysite.

Nginx + FastCGI

Some people may prefer using FastCGI for deployment. In this case, you'll need to add an extra tool to the mix. FastCGI works by receiving new connections from a file descriptor. The C library assumes that this file descriptor will be 0 (standard input), so you need to use the spawn-fcgi program to bind your application's standard input to the correct socket.

It can be very convenient to use Unix named sockets for this instead of binding to a port, especially when hosting multiple applications on a single host. A possible script to load up your app could be:

```
spawn-fcgi \
    -d /home/michael/sites/mysite \
    -s /tmp/mysite.socket \
    -n \
    -M 511 \
```

```
    -u michael \
    -- /home/michael/sites/mysite/dist/build/mysite-fastcgi/mysite-fastcgi
```

You will also need to configure your frontend server to speak to your app over FastCGI. This is relatively painless in Nginx:

```
server {
    listen 80;
    server_name www.myserver.com;
    location / {
        fastcgi_pass unix:/tmp/mysite.socket;
    }
}
```

That should look pretty familiar. The only last trick is that, with Nginx, you need to manually specify all of the FastCGI variables. It is recommended to store these in a separate file (say, *fastcgi.conf*) and then add include fastcgi.conf; to the end of your http block. The contents of the file, to work with WAI, should be:

```
fastcgi_param   QUERY_STRING        $query_string;
fastcgi_param   REQUEST_METHOD      $request_method;
fastcgi_param   CONTENT_TYPE        $content_type;
fastcgi_param   CONTENT_LENGTH      $content_length;
fastcgi_param   PATH_INFO           $fastcgi_script_name;
fastcgi_param   SERVER_PROTOCOL     $server_protocol;
fastcgi_param   GATEWAY_INTERFACE   CGI/1.1;
fastcgi_param   SERVER_SOFTWARE     nginx/$nginx_version;
fastcgi_param   REMOTE_ADDR         $remote_addr;
fastcgi_param   SERVER_ADDR         $server_addr;
fastcgi_param   SERVER_PORT         $server_port;
fastcgi_param   SERVER_NAME         $server_name;
```

Desktop

Another nifty backend is wai-handler-webkit. This backend combines Warp and QtWebKit to create an executable that a user simply double-clicks. This can be a convenient way to provide an offline version of your application.

One of the very nice conveniences of Yesod for this is that your templates are all compiled into the executable, and thus do not need to be distributed with your application. Static files do, however.

> There's actually support for embedding your static files directly in the executable as well. See the yesod-static docs (*http://www.stackage.org/package/yesod-static*) for more details.

A similar approach, without requiring the QtWebKit library, is using `wai-handler-launch`, which launches a Warp server and then opens up the user's default web browser. There's a little trickery involved here: in order to know that the user is still using the site, `wai-handler-launch` inserts a "ping" JavaScript snippet to every HTML page it serves. If `wai-handler-launch` doesn't receive a ping for two minutes, it shuts down.

CGI on Apache

CGI and FastCGI work almost identically on Apache, so it should be fairly straightforward to port this configuration. You essentially need to accomplish two goals:

1. Get the server to serve your file as (Fast)CGI.
2. Rewrite all requests to your site to go through the (Fast)CGI executable.

Here is a configuration file for serving a blog application, with an executable named *bloggy.cgi*, living in a subfolder named *blog/* of the document root. This example was taken from an application living in the path */f5/snoyman/public/blog*:

```
Options +ExecCGI
AddHandler cgi-script .cgi
Options +FollowSymlinks

RewriteEngine On
RewriteRule ^/f5/snoyman/public/blog$ /blog/ [R=301,S=1]
RewriteCond $1 !^bloggy.cgi
RewriteCond $1 !^static/
RewriteRule ^(.*) bloggy.cgi/$1 [L]
```

The first `RewriteRule` is to deal with subfolders. In particular, it redirects a request for */blog* to */blog/*. The first `RewriteCond` prevents directly requesting the executable, the second allows Apache to serve the static files, and the last line does the actual rewriting.

FastCGI on lighttpd

For this example, I've left off some of the basic FastCGI settings like MIME types. I also have a more complex file in production that prepends *www* when absent and serves static files from a separate domain. However, this should serve to show the basics.

Here, */home/michael/fastcgi* is the FastCGI application. The idea is to rewrite all requests to start with */app*, and then serve everything beginning with */app* via the FastCGI executable:

```
server.port = 3000
server.document-root = "/home/michael"
server.modules = ("mod_fastcgi", "mod_rewrite")

url.rewrite-once = (
  "(.*)" => "/app/$1"
)

fastcgi.server = (
    "/app" => ((
        "socket" => "/tmp/test.fastcgi.socket",
        "check-local" => "disable",
        "bin-path" => "/home/michael/fastcgi", # full path to executable
        "min-procs" => 1,
        "max-procs" => 30,
        "idle-timeout" => 30
    ))
)
```

CGI on lighttpd

This is basically the same as the FastCGI version, but tells lighttpd to run a file ending in *.cgi* as a CGI executable. In this case, the file lives at */home/michael/myapp.cgi*:

```
server.port = 3000
server.document-root = "/home/michael"
server.modules = ("mod_cgi", "mod_rewrite")

url.rewrite-once = (
    "(.*)" => "/myapp.cgi/$1"
)

cgi.assign = (".cgi" => "")
```

PART II

Advanced

CHAPTER 12

RESTful Content

One of the stories from the early days of the Web is how search engines wiped out entire websites. When dynamic websites were still a new concept, developers didn't appreciate the difference between a GET and POST request. As a result, they created pages—accessed with the GET method—that would delete pages. When search engines started crawling these sites, they could wipe out all the content.

If these web developers had followed the HTTP spec properly, this would not have happened. A GET request is supposed to cause no side effects (you know, like wiping out a site). Recently, there has been a move in web development to properly embrace representational state transfer (a.k.a. REST). This chapter describes the RESTful features in Yesod and how you can use them to create more robust web applications.

Request Methods

In many web frameworks, you write one handler function per resource. In Yesod, the default is to have a separate handler function for each request method. The two most common request methods you will deal with in creating websites are GET and POST. These are the most well supported methods in HTML, as they are the only ones supported by web forms. However, when creating RESTful APIs, the other methods are very useful.

Technically speaking, you can create whichever request methods you like, but it is strongly recommended to stick to the ones spelled out in the HTTP spec. The most common of these are the following:

GET

> Used for read-only requests. Assuming no other changes occur on the server, calling a GET request multiple times should result in the same response, barring such things as "current time" or randomly assigned results.

POST

> Used for general mutating requests. A POST request should never be submitted twice by the user. A common example of this would be to transfer funds from one bank account to another.

PUT

> Creates a new resource on the server, or replaces an existing one. It *is* safe to call this method multiple times.

DELETE

> Just like it sounds: wipes out a resource on the server. Calling multiple times should be OK.

To a certain extent, this fits in very well with Haskell philosophy: a GET request is similar to a pure function, which cannot have side effects. In practice, your GET functions will probably perform IO, such as reading information from a database, logging user actions, and so on.

See Chapter 7 for more information on the syntax of defining handler functions for each request method.

Representations

Suppose we have a Haskell data type and value:

```
data Person = Person { name :: String, age :: Int }
michael = Person "Michael" 25
```

We could represent that data as HTML:

```
<table>
    <tr>
        <th>Name</th>
        <td>Michael</td>
    </tr>
    <tr>
        <th>Age</th>
        <td>25</td>
    </tr>
</table>
```

or we could represent it as JSON:

```
{"name":"Michael","age":25}
```

or as XML:

```
<person>
    <name>Michael</name>
    <age>25</age>
</person>
```

Web applications often use a different URL to get each of these representations—perhaps */person/michael.html*, */person/michael.json*, and so on. But Yesod follows the RESTful principle of a single URL for each resource, so in Yesod, all of these would be accessed from */person/michael*.

Then the question becomes how we determine *which* representation to serve. The answer is the HTTP Accept header: it gives a prioritized list of content types the client is expecting. Yesod provides a pair of functions to abstract away the details of parsing that header directly, and instead allows you to talk at a much higher level of representations. Let's make that last sentence a bit more concrete with some code:

```
{-# LANGUAGE OverloadedStrings #-}
{-# LANGUAGE QuasiQuotes       #-}
{-# LANGUAGE TemplateHaskell   #-}
{-# LANGUAGE TypeFamilies      #-}
import            Data.Text (Text)
import            Yesod

data App = App

mkYesod "App" [parseRoutes|
/ HomeR GET
|]

instance Yesod App

getHomeR :: Handler TypedContent
getHomeR = selectRep $ do
    provideRep $ return
        [shamlet|
            <p>Hello, my name is #{name} and I am #{age} years old.
        |]
    provideRep $ return $ object
        [ "name" .= name
        , "age" .= age
        ]
  where
    name = "Michael" :: Text
    age = 28 :: Int

main :: IO ()
main = warp 3000 App
```

The selectRep function says, "I'm about to give you some possible representations." Each provideRep call provides an alternative representation. Yesod uses the Haskell types to determine the MIME type for each representation. Because shamlet (a.k.a., simple Hamlet) produces an Html value, Yesod can determine that the relevant MIME type is text/html. Similarly, object generates a JSON value, which implies the MIME type application/json. TypedContent is a data type provided by Yesod for some raw content with an attached MIME type. We'll cover it in more detail in a little bit.

To test this, start up the server and try running each of the following `curl` commands:

```
curl http://localhost:3000 --header "accept: application/json"
curl http://localhost:3000 --header "accept: text/html"
curl http://localhost:3000
```

Notice how the response changes based on the `Accept` header value. Also, when you leave off the header, the HTML response is displayed by default. The rule here is that if there is no `Accept` header, the first representation is displayed. If an `Accept` header is present, but we have no matches, then a 406 Not Acceptable response is returned.

By default, Yesod provides a convenience middleware that lets you set the `Accept` header via a query string parameter. This can make it easier to test from your browser. To try this out, you can visit *http://localhost:3000/?_accept=application/json*.

JSON Conveniences

Because JSON is such a commonly used data format in web applications today, we have some built-in helper functions for providing JSON representations. These are built off of the wonderful `aeson` library, so let's start off with a quick explanation of how that library works.

`aeson` has a core data type, `Value`, which represents any valid JSON value. It also provides two typeclasses—`ToJSON` and `FromJSON`—to automate marshaling to and from JSON values, respectively. For our purposes, we're currently interested in `ToJSON`. Let's look at a quick example of creating a `ToJSON` instance for our ever-recurring `Person` data type examples:

```
{-# LANGUAGE OverloadedStrings #-}
{-# LANGUAGE RecordWildCards   #-}
import           Data.Aeson
import qualified Data.ByteString.Lazy.Char8 as L
import           Data.Text                  (Text)

data Person = Person
    { name :: Text
    , age  :: Int
    }

instance ToJSON Person where
    toJSON Person {..} = object
        [ "name" .= name
        , "age"  .= age
        ]
```

```
main :: IO ()
main = L.putStrLn $ encode $ Person "Michael" 28
```

I won't go into further detail on **aeson**, as the Haddock documentation (*https://www.fpcomplete.com/haddocks/aeson*) already provides a great introduction to the library. What I've described so far is enough to understand our convenience functions.

Let's suppose that you have such a Person data type, with a corresponding value, and you'd like to use it as the representation for your current page. For that, you can use the returnJson function:

```
{-# LANGUAGE OverloadedStrings #-}
{-# LANGUAGE QuasiQuotes       #-}
{-# LANGUAGE RecordWildCards   #-}
{-# LANGUAGE TemplateHaskell   #-}
{-# LANGUAGE TypeFamilies      #-}
import           Data.Text (Text)
import           Yesod

data Person = Person
    { name :: Text
    , age  :: Int
    }

instance ToJSON Person where
    toJSON Person {..} = object
        [ "name" .= name
        , "age"  .= age
        ]

data App = App

mkYesod "App" [parseRoutes|
/ HomeR GET
|]

instance Yesod App

getHomeR :: Handler Value
getHomeR = returnJson $ Person "Michael" 28

main :: IO ()
main = warp 3000 App
```

returnJson is actually a trivial function—it is implemented as return . toJSON—but, it makes things just a bit more convenient. Similarly, if you would like to provide a JSON value as a representation inside a selectRep, you can use provideJson:

```
{-# LANGUAGE OverloadedStrings #-}
{-# LANGUAGE QuasiQuotes       #-}
{-# LANGUAGE RecordWildCards   #-}
```

```
{-# LANGUAGE TemplateHaskell   #-}
{-# LANGUAGE TypeFamilies      #-}
import         Data.Text (Text)
import         Yesod

data Person = Person
    { name :: Text
    , age  :: Int
    }

instance ToJSON Person where
    toJSON Person {..} = object
        [ "name" .= name
        , "age"  .= age
        ]

data App = App

mkYesod "App" [parseRoutes|
/ HomeR GET
|]

instance Yesod App

getHomeR :: Handler TypedContent
getHomeR = selectRep $ do
    provideRep $ return
        [shamlet|
            <p>Hello, my name is #{name} and I am #{age} years old.
        |]
    provideJson person
  where
    person@Person {..} = Person "Michael" 28

main :: IO ()
main = warp 3000 App
```

provideJson is similarly trivial; in this case, it is implemented as provideRep .
returnJson.

New Data Types

Let's say I've come up with some new data format based on using Haskell's Show
instance; I'll call it "Haskell Show," and give it a MIME type of text/haskell-show.
And let's say that I decide to include this representation from my web app. How do I
do it? For a first attempt, let's use the TypedContent data type directly:

```
{-# LANGUAGE OverloadedStrings #-}
{-# LANGUAGE QuasiQuotes       #-}
{-# LANGUAGE TemplateHaskell   #-}
{-# LANGUAGE TypeFamilies      #-}
```

```
import            Data.Text (Text)
import            Yesod

data Person = Person
    { name :: Text
    , age  :: Int
    }
    deriving Show

data App = App

mkYesod "App" [parseRoutes|
/ HomeR GET
|]

instance Yesod App

mimeType :: ContentType
mimeType = "text/haskell-show"

getHomeR :: Handler TypedContent
getHomeR =
    return $ TypedContent mimeType $ toContent $ show person
  where
    person = Person "Michael" 28

main :: IO ()
main = warp 3000 App
```

There are a few important things to note here:

- We've used the toContent function. This is a typeclass function that can convert a number of data types to raw data ready to be sent over the wire. In this case, we've used the instance for String, which uses UTF8 encoding. Other common data types with instances are Text, ByteString, Html, and the aeson library's Value.

- We're using the TypedContent constructor directly. It takes two arguments: a MIME type and the raw content. Note that ContentType is simply a type alias for a strict ByteString.

That's all well and good, but it bothers me that the type signature for getHomeR is so uninformative. Also, the implementation of getHomeR looks pretty boilerplate. I'd rather just have a data type representing "Haskell Show" data, and provide some simple means of creating such values. Let's try this on for size:

```
{-# LANGUAGE ExistentialQuantification #-}
{-# LANGUAGE OverloadedStrings         #-}
{-# LANGUAGE QuasiQuotes               #-}
{-# LANGUAGE TemplateHaskell           #-}
```

```
{-# LANGUAGE TypeFamilies                 #-}
import            Data.Text (Text)
import            Yesod

data Person = Person
    { name :: Text
    , age  :: Int
    }
    deriving Show

data App = App

mkYesod "App" [parseRoutes|
/ HomeR GET
|]

instance Yesod App

mimeType :: ContentType
mimeType = "text/haskell-show"

data HaskellShow = forall a. Show a => HaskellShow a

instance ToContent HaskellShow where
    toContent (HaskellShow x) = toContent $ show x
instance ToTypedContent HaskellShow where
    toTypedContent = TypedContent mimeType . toContent

getHomeR :: Handler HaskellShow
getHomeR =
    return $ HaskellShow person
  where
    person = Person "Michael" 28

main :: IO ()
main = warp 3000 App
```

The magic here lies in two typeclasses. As we mentioned before, `ToContent` tells how to convert a value into a raw response. In our case, we would like to `show` the original value to get a `String`, and then convert that `String` into the raw content. Oftentimes, instances of `ToContent` will build on each other in this way.

`ToTypedContent` is used internally by Yesod and is called on the result of all handler functions. As you can see, the implementation is fairly trivial, simply stating the MIME type and then calling out to `toContent`.

Finally, let's make this a bit more complicated and get it to play well with `selectRep`:

```
{-# LANGUAGE ExistentialQuantification #-}
{-# LANGUAGE OverloadedStrings         #-}
{-# LANGUAGE QuasiQuotes               #-}
{-# LANGUAGE RecordWildCards           #-}
```

```
{-# LANGUAGE TemplateHaskell        #-}
{-# LANGUAGE TypeFamilies           #-}
import            Data.Text (Text)
import            Yesod

data Person = Person
    { name :: Text
    , age  :: Int
    }
    deriving Show

instance ToJSON Person where
    toJSON Person {..} = object
        [ "name" .= name
        , "age"  .= age
        ]

data App = App

mkYesod "App" [parseRoutes|
/ HomeR GET
|]

instance Yesod App

mimeType :: ContentType
mimeType = "text/haskell-show"

data HaskellShow = forall a. Show a => HaskellShow a

instance ToContent HaskellShow where
    toContent (HaskellShow x) = toContent $ show x
instance ToTypedContent HaskellShow where
    toTypedContent = TypedContent mimeType . toContent
instance HasContentType HaskellShow where
    getContentType _ = mimeType

getHomeR :: Handler TypedContent
getHomeR = selectRep $ do
    provideRep $ return $ HaskellShow person
    provideJson person
  where
    person = Person "Michael" 28

main :: IO ()
main = warp 3000 App
```

The important addition here is the `HasContentType` instance. This may seem redundant, but it serves an important role. We need to be able to determine the MIME type of a possible representation *before creating that representation*. `ToTypedContent` only works on a concrete value, and therefore can't be used before creating the value.

getContentType instead takes a proxy value, indicating the type without providing anything concrete.

 If you want to provide a representation for a value that doesn't have a HasContentType instance, you can use the provideRepType function, which requires you to explicitly state the MIME type present.

Other Request Headers

There are a great deal of other request headers available. Some of them only affect the transfer of data between the server and client, and should not affect the application at all. For example, Accept-Encoding informs the server which compression schemes the client understands, and Host informs the server which virtual host to serve up.

Other headers *do* affect the application, but are automatically read by Yesod. For example, the Accept-Language header specifies which human language (English, Spanish, German, Swiss-German) the client prefers. See Chapter 22 for details on how this header is used.

Summary

Yesod adheres to the following tenets of REST:

- Use the correct request method.
- Each resource should have precisely one URL.
- Allow multiple representations of data on the same URL.
- Inspect request headers to determine extra information about what the client wants.

This makes it easy to use Yesod not just for building websites, but for building APIs. In fact, using techniques such as selectRep/provideRep, you can serve both a user-friendly HTML page and a machine-friendly JSON page from the same URL.

CHAPTER 13

Yesod's Monads

As you've progressed through this book so far, a number of monads have appeared: `Handler`, `Widget`, and `YesodDB` (for Persistent). As with most monads, each one provides some specific functionality: `Handler` gives access to the request and allows you to send responses; a `Widget` contains HTML, CSS, and JavaScript; and `YesodDB` lets you make database queries. In model-view-controller (MVC) terms, we could consider `YesodDB` to be the model, `Widget` to be the view, and `Handler` to be the controller.

So far, we've presented some very straightforward ways to use these monads: your main handler will run in `Handler`, using `runDB` to execute a `YesodDB` query and `defaultLayout` to return a `Widget`, which in turn was created by calls to `toWidget`.

However, if we have a deeper understanding of these types, we can achieve some fancier results.

Monad Transformers

> Monads are like onions. Monads are *not* like cakes.
>
> —Variation on a quote from *Shrek*

Before we get into the heart of Yesod's monads, we need to understand a bit about monad transformers. (If you already know all about monad transformers, you can likely skip this section.) Different monads provide different functionality: `Reader` allows read-only access to some piece of data throughout a computation, `Error` allows you to short-circuit computations, and so on.

Oftentimes, however, you'll want to be able to combine a few of these features together. After all, why not have a computation with read-only access to some settings variable, that could error out at any time? One approach to this would be to write a new monad like ReaderError, but this has the obvious downside of exponential complexity: you'll need to write a new monad for every single possible combination.

Instead, we have monad transformers. For example, in addition to Reader, we have ReaderT, which adds reader functionality to any other monad. So, conceptually, we could represent our ReaderError as follows:

```
type ReaderError = ReaderT Error
```

In order to access our settings variable, we can use the ask function. But what about short-circuiting a computation? We'd like to use throwError, but that won't exactly work. Instead, we need to lift our call into the next monad up. In other words:

```
throwError :: errValue -> Error
lift . throwError :: errValue -> ReaderT Error
```

There are a few things you should pick up here:

- A transformer can be used to add functionality to an existing monad.
- A transformer must always wrap around an existing monad.
- The functionality available in a wrapped monad will be dependent not only on the monad transformer, but also on the inner monad that is being wrapped.

A great example of that last point is the IO monad. No matter how many layers of transformers you have around an IO, there's still an IO at the core, meaning you can perform I/O in any of these monad transformer stacks. You'll often see code that looks like `liftIO $ putStrLn "Hello There!"`.

The Three Transformers

We've already discussed two of our transformers: Handler and Widget. Remember that these are each application-specific synonyms for the more generic HandlerT and WidgetT. Each of those transformers takes two type parameters: your foundation data type, and a base monad. The most commonly used base monad is IO.

In earlier versions of Yesod, Handler and Widget were far more magical and scary. Since version 1.2, things are much simplified. So, if you remember reading some scary stuff about fake transformers and subsite parameters, rest assured: you haven't gone crazy, things have actually changed a bit. The story with Persistent is likewise much simpler.

In Persistent, we have a typeclass called PersistStore. This typeclass defines all of the primitive operations you can perform on a database, like get. There are instances of this typeclass for each database backend supported by Persistent. For example, for

SQL databases, there is a data type called `SqlBackend`. We then use a standard `Read erT` transformer to provide that `SqlBackend` value to all of our operations. This means that we can run a SQL database with any underlying monad that is an instance of `MonadIO`. The takeaway here is that we can layer our Persistent transformer on top of `Handler` or `Widget`.

In order to make it simpler to refer to the relevant Persistent transformer, the `yesod-persistent` package defines the `YesodPersistBackend` associated type. For example, if I have a site called `MyApp` and it uses SQL, I would define something like `type instance YesodPersistBackend MyApp = SqlBackend`. And for more convenience, we have a type synonym called `YesodDB`, which is defined as:

```
type YesodDB site = ReaderT (YesodPersistBackend site) (HandlerT site IO)
```

Our database actions will then have types that look like `YesodDB MyApp SomeResult`. In order to run these, we can use the standard Persistent unwrap functions (like `run SqlPool`) to run the action and get back a normal `Handler`. To automate this, we provide the `runDB` function. Putting it all together, we can now run database actions inside our handlers.

Most of the time in Yesod code, and especially thus far in this book, widgets have been treated as actionless containers that simply combine HTML, CSS, and Java-Script. But in reality, a `Widget` can do anything that a `Handler` can do, by using the `handlerToWidget` function. So, for example, you can run database queries inside a `Widget` by using something like `handlerToWidget . runDB`.

Example: Database-Driven Navbar

Let's put some of this new knowledge into action. We want to create a `Widget` that generates its output based on the contents of the database. Previously, our approach would have been to load up the data in a `Handler`, and then pass that data into a `Widget`. Now, we'll do the loading of data in the `Widget` itself. This is a boon for modularity, as this `Widget` can be used in any `Handler` we want, without any need to pass in the database contents:

```
{-# LANGUAGE FlexibleContexts           #-}
{-# LANGUAGE GADTs                      #-}
{-# LANGUAGE GeneralizedNewtypeDeriving #-}
{-# LANGUAGE MultiParamTypeClasses      #-}
{-# LANGUAGE OverloadedStrings          #-}
{-# LANGUAGE QuasiQuotes                #-}
{-# LANGUAGE TemplateHaskell            #-}
{-# LANGUAGE TypeFamilies               #-}
import           Control.Monad.Logger    (runNoLoggingT)
import           Data.Text               (Text)
import           Data.Time
```

```
import            Database.Persist.Sqlite
import            Yesod

share [mkPersist sqlSettings, mkMigrate "migrateAll"] [persistLowerCase|
Link
    title Text
    url Text
    added UTCTime
|]

data App = App ConnectionPool

mkYesod "App" [parseRoutes|
/           HomeR       GET
/add-link AddLinkR POST
|]

instance Yesod App

instance RenderMessage App FormMessage where
    renderMessage _ _ = defaultFormMessage

instance YesodPersist App where
    type YesodPersistBackend App = SqlBackend
    runDB db = do
        App pool <- getYesod
        runSqlPool db pool

getHomeR :: Handler Html
getHomeR = defaultLayout
    [whamlet|
        <form method=post action=@{AddLinkR}>
            <p>
                Add a new link to
                <input type=url name=url value=http://>
                titled
                <input type=text name=title>
                <input type=submit value="Add link">
        <h2>Existing links
        ^{existingLinks}
    |]

existingLinks :: Widget
existingLinks = do
    links <- handlerToWidget $ runDB $ selectList [] [LimitTo 5, Desc LinkAdded]
    [whamlet|
        <ul>
            $forall Entity _ link <- links
                <li>
                    <a href=#{linkUrl link}>#{linkTitle link}
    |]
```

```
postAddLinkR :: Handler ()
postAddLinkR = do
    url <- runInputPost $ ireq urlField "url"
    title <- runInputPost $ ireq textField "title"
    now <- liftIO getCurrentTime
    runDB $ insert $ Link title url now
    setMessage "Link added"
    redirect HomeR

main :: IO ()
main = runNoLoggingT $ withSqlitePool "links.db3" 10 $ \pool -> liftIO $ do
    runSqlPersistMPool (runMigration migrateAll) pool
    warp 3000 $ App pool
```

Pay attention in particular to the existingLinks function. Notice how all we needed to do was apply handlerToWidget . runDB to a normal database action. And from within getHomeR, we treated existingLinks like any ordinary Widget, with no special parameters at all. Figure 13-1 shows the output of this app.

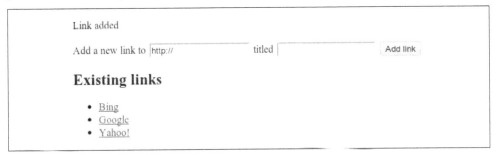

Figure 13-1. Screenshot of the navbar

Example: Request Information

Likewise, you can get request information inside a Widget. Here we can determine the sort order of a list based on a GET parameter:

```
{-# LANGUAGE MultiParamTypeClasses #-}
{-# LANGUAGE OverloadedStrings     #-}
{-# LANGUAGE QuasiQuotes           #-}
{-# LANGUAGE TemplateHaskell       #-}
{-# LANGUAGE TypeFamilies          #-}
import           Data.List (sortBy)
import           Data.Ord  (comparing)
import           Data.Text (Text)
import           Yesod

data Person = Person
    { personName :: Text
    , personAge  :: Int
    }
```

```haskell
people :: [Person]
people =
    [ Person "Miriam" 25
    , Person "Eliezer" 3
    , Person "Michael" 26
    , Person "Gavriella" 1
    ]

data App = App

mkYesod "App" [parseRoutes|
/ HomeR GET
|]

instance Yesod App

instance RenderMessage App FormMessage where
    renderMessage _ _ = defaultFormMessage


getHomeR :: Handler Html
getHomeR = defaultLayout
    [whamlet|
        <p>
            <a href="?sort=name">Sort by name
            |
            <a href="?sort=age">Sort by age
            |
            <a href="?">No sort
        ^{showPeople}
    |]

showPeople :: Widget
showPeople = do
    msort <- runInputGet $ iopt textField "sort"
    let people' =
            case msort of
                Just "name" -> sortBy (comparing personName) people
                Just "age"  -> sortBy (comparing personAge)  people
                _                    -> people
    [whamlet|
        <dl>
            $forall person <- people'
                <dt>#{personName person}
                <dd>#{show $ personAge person}
    |]

main :: IO ()
main = warp 3000 App
```

Notice that in this case, we didn't even have to call handlerToWidget. The reason is that a number of the functions included in Yesod automatically work for both Handler and Widget, by means of the MonadHandler typeclass. In fact, MonadHandler will allow these functions to be "autolifted" through many common monad transformers.

But if you want to, you can wrap up the call to runInputGet using handlerToWidget, and everything will work the same.

Performance and Error Messages

At this point, you may be just a bit confused. As I already mentioned, the Widget synonym uses IO as its base monad, not Handler. So how can Widget perform Handler actions? And why *not* just make Widget a transformer on top of Handler, and then use lift instead of this special handlerToWidget? And finally, I mentioned that Widget and Handler were both instances of MonadResource. If you're familiar with MonadResource, you may be wondering why ResourceT doesn't appear in the monad transformer stack.

 You can consider this section extra credit. It gets into some of the design motivation behind Yesod, which isn't necessary for usage of Yesod.

The fact of the matter is that there's a much simpler (in terms of implementation) approach we could take for all of these monad transformers. Handler could be a transformer on top of ResourceT IO instead of just IO, which would be a bit more accurate. And Widget could be layered on top of Handler. The end result would look something like this:

```
type Handler = HandlerT App (ResourceT IO)
type Widget  = WidgetT  App (HandlerT App (ResourceT IO))
```

Doesn't look too bad, especially considering you mostly deal with the friendlier type synonyms instead of directly with the transformer types. The problem is that any time those underlying transformers leak out, these larger type signatures can be incredibly confusing. And the most common time for them to leak out is in error messages, when you're probably already pretty confused! (Another time is when working on subsites, which happens to be confusing too.)

One other concern is that each monad transformer layer does add some amount of performance penalty. This will probably be negligible compared to the I/O you'll be performing, but the overhead is there.

So, instead of having properly layered transformers, we flatten out each of `HandlerT` and `WidgetT` into a one-level transformer. Here's a high-level overview of the approach we use:

- `HandlerT` is really just a `ReaderT` monad. (We give it a different name to make error messages clearer.) This is a reader for the `HandlerData` type, which contains request information and some other immutable contents.

- In addition, `HandlerData` holds an `IORef` to a `GHState` (badly named for historical reasons), which holds some data that can be mutated during the course of a handler (e.g., session variables). The reason we use an `IORef` instead of a `StateT` kind of approach is that `IORef` will maintain the mutated state even if a runtime exception is thrown.

- The `ResourceT` monad transformer is essentially a `ReaderT` holding onto an `IORef`. This `IORef` contains the information on all cleanup actions that must be performed. (This is called `InternalState`.) Instead of having a separate transformer layer to hold onto that reference, we hold onto the reference ourselves in `HandlerData`. (And yes, the reason for an `IORef` here is also for runtime exceptions.)

- A `WidgetT` is essentially just a `WriterT` on top of everything that a `HandlerT` does. But because `HandlerT` is just a `ReaderT`, we can easily compress the two aspects into a single transformer, which looks something like `newtype WidgetT site m a = WidgetT (HandlerData -> m (a, WidgetData))`.

The definitions of `HandlerT` and `WidgetT` in `Yesod.Core.Types` are useful if you want to better understand this.

Adding a New Monad Transformer

At times, you'll want to add your own monad transformer in part of your application. As a motivating example, let's consider the `monadcryptorandom` (*http://hackage.haskell.org/package/monadcryptorandom*) package from Hackage, which defines both a `MonadCRandom` typeclass for monads that allow generating cryptographically secure random values, and `CRandT` as a concrete instance of that typeclass. Say we want to write some code that generates a random `Bytestring` such as the following:

```
import Control.Monad.CryptoRandom
import Data.ByteString.Base16 (encode)
import Data.Text.Encoding (decodeUtf8)

getHomeR = do
    randomBS <- getBytes 128
    defaultLayout
        [whamlet|
```

```
<p>Here's some random data: #{decodeUtf8 $ encode randomBS}
|]
```

However, this results in an error message along the lines of:

```
No instance for (MonadCRandom e0 (HandlerT App IO))
    arising from a use of 'getBytes'
In a stmt of a 'do' block: randomBS <- getBytes 128
```

How do we get such an instance? One approach is to simply use the CRandT monad transformer when we call getBytes. A complete example of doing so would be:

```
{-# LANGUAGE OverloadedStrings, QuasiQuotes, TemplateHaskell, TypeFamilies #-}
import Yesod
import Crypto.Random (SystemRandom, newGenIO)
import Control.Monad.CryptoRandom
import Data.ByteString.Base16 (encode)
import Data.Text.Encoding (decodeUtf8)

data App = App

mkYesod "App" [parseRoutes|
/ HomeR GET
|]

instance Yesod App

getHomeR :: Handler Html
getHomeR = do
    gen <- liftIO newGenIO
    eres <- evalCRandT (getBytes 16) (gen :: SystemRandom)
    randomBS <-
        case eres of
            Left e -> error $ show (e :: GenError)
            Right gen -> return gen
    defaultLayout
        [whamlet|
            <p>Here's some random data: #{decodeUtf8 $ encode randomBS}
        |]

main :: IO ()
main = warp 3000 App
```

Note that what we're doing is layering the CRandT transformer on *top* of the HandlerT transformer. It does not work to do things the other way around: Yesod itself would ultimately have to unwrap the CRandT transformer, and it has no knowledge of how to do so. Notice that this is the same approach we take with Persistent: its transformer goes on top of HandlerT.

But there are two downsides to this approach:

- It requires you to jump into this alternative monad each time you want to work with random values.

- It's inefficient: you need to create a new random seed each time you enter this other monad.

The second point could be worked around by storing the random seed in the foundation data type, in a mutable reference like an IORef, and then atomically sampling it each time we enter the CRandT transformer. But we can even go a step further, and use this trick to make our Handler monad itself an instance of MonadCRandom! Let's look at the code, which is in fact a bit involved:

```haskell
{-# LANGUAGE FlexibleInstances     #-}
{-# LANGUAGE MultiParamTypeClasses #-}
{-# LANGUAGE OverloadedStrings     #-}
{-# LANGUAGE QuasiQuotes           #-}
{-# LANGUAGE TemplateHaskell       #-}
{-# LANGUAGE TypeFamilies          #-}
{-# LANGUAGE TypeSynonymInstances  #-}
import           Control.Monad            (join)
import           Control.Monad.Catch      (catch, throwM)
import           Control.Monad.CryptoRandom
import           Control.Monad.Error.Class (MonadError (..))
import           Crypto.Random            (SystemRandom, newGenIO)
import           Data.ByteString.Base16   (encode)
import           Data.IORef
import           Data.Text.Encoding       (decodeUtf8)
import           Yesod

data App = App
    { randGen :: IORef SystemRandom
    }

mkYesod "App" [parseRoutes|
/ HomeR GET
|]

instance Yesod App

getHomeR :: Handler Html
getHomeR = do
    randomBS <- getBytes 16
    defaultLayout
        [whamlet|
            <p>Here's some random data: #{decodeUtf8 $ encode randomBS}
        |]

instance MonadError GenError Handler where
    throwError = throwM
    catchError = catch
instance MonadCRandom GenError Handler where
```

```
getCRandom  = wrap crandom
{-# INLINE getCRandom #-}
getBytes i = wrap (genBytes i)
{-# INLINE getBytes #-}
getBytesWithEntropy i e = wrap (genBytesWithEntropy i e)
{-# INLINE getBytesWithEntropy #-}
doReseed bs = do
    genRef <- fmap randGen getYesod
    join $ liftIO $ atomicModifyIORef genRef $ \gen ->
        case reseed bs gen of
            Left e -> (gen, throwM e)
            Right gen' -> (gen', return ())
{-# INLINE doReseed #-}

wrap :: (SystemRandom -> Either GenError (a, SystemRandom)) -> Handler a
wrap f = do
    genRef <- fmap randGen getYesod
    join $ liftIO $ atomicModifyIORef genRef $ \gen ->
        case f gen of
            Left e -> (gen, throwM e)
            Right (x, gen') -> (gen', return x)

main :: IO ()
main = do
    gen <- newGenIO
    genRef <- newIORef gen
    warp 3000 App
        { randGen = genRef
        }
```

This really comes down to a few different concepts:

1. We modify the App data type to have a field for an IORef SystemRandom.

2. Similarly, we modify the main function to generate an IORef SystemRandom.

3. Our getHomeR function has become a lot simpler: we can now simply call get Bytes without playing with transformers.

4. However, we *have* gained some complexity in needing a MonadCRandom instance. This is a book about Yesod, not monadcryptorandom, so I'm not going to go into details on this instance, but I encourage you to inspect it and, if you're interested, compare it to the instance for CRandT.

Hopefully, this helps get across an important point: the power of the HandlerT transformer. As it provides you with a readable environment, you're able to re-create a StateT transformer by relying on mutable references. In fact, if you rely on the underlying IO monad for runtime exceptions, you can implement most cases of Read erT, WriterT, StateT, and ErrorT with this abstraction.

Summary

If you completely ignore this chapter, you'll still be able to use Yesod to great benefit. The advantage of understanding how Yesod's monads interact that it enables you to produce cleaner, more modular code. Being able to perform arbitrary actions in a Widget can be a powerful tool, and understanding how Persistent and your Handler code interact can help you make more informed design decisions in your app.

CHAPTER 14

Authentication and Authorization

Authentication and authorization are conceptually related, but they are not one and the same. The former deals with identifying a user, whereas the latter determines what a user is allowed to do. Unfortunately, because both terms are frequently abbreviated as "auth," the concepts are often conflated.

Yesod provides built-in support for a number of third-party authentication systems, such as OpenID, BrowserID, and OAuth. These are systems where your application trusts some external system for validating a user's credentials. Additionally, there is support for more commonly used username/password and email/password systems. The former route ensures simplicity for users (no new passwords to remember) and implementors (no need to deal with an entire security architecture), and the latter gives the developer more control.

On the authorization side, we are able to take advantage of REST and type-safe URLs to create simple, declarative systems. Additionally, because all authorization code is written in Haskell, you have the full flexibility of the language at your disposal.

This chapter will cover how to set up an "auth" solution in Yesod and discuss some trade-offs in the different authentication options.

Overview

The yesod-auth package provides a unified interface for a number of different authentication plug-ins. The only real requirement for these backends is that they identify a user based on some unique string. In OpenID, for instance, this would be the actual OpenID value. In BrowserID, it's the email address. For HashDB (which uses a database of hashed passwords), it's the username.

Each authentication plug-in provides its own system for logging in, whether it be via passing tokens with an external site or a email/password form. After a successful login, the plug-in sets a value in the user's session to indicate his `AuthId`. This `AuthId` is usually a Persistent ID from a table used for keeping track of users.

There are a few functions available for querying a user's `AuthId`—most commonly `maybeAuthId`, `requireAuthId`, `maybeAuth`, and `requireAuth`. The "require" versions will redirect to a login page if the user is not logged in, while the second set of functions (the ones *not* ending in Id) give both the table ID *and* entity value.

All of the storage of `AuthId` is built on top of sessions, so the same rules from there apply. In particular, the data is stored in an encrypted, HMACed client cookie, which automatically times out after a certain configurable period of inactivity. Additionally, because there is no server-side component to sessions, logging out simply deletes the data from the session cookie; if a user reuses an older cookie value, the session will still be valid.

You can replace the default client-side sessions with server-side sessions to provide a forced logout capability, if this is desired.

On the flip side, authorization is handled by a few methods inside the `Yesod` typeclass. For every request, these methods are run to determine if access should be allowed or denied, or if the user needs to be authenticated. By default, these methods allow access for every request. Alternatively, you can implement authorization in a more adhoc way by adding calls to `requireAuth` and the like within individual handler functions, though this undermines many of the benefits of a declarative authorization system.

Authenticate Me

Let's jump right in with an example of authentication:

```
{-# LANGUAGE MultiParamTypeClasses #-}
{-# LANGUAGE OverloadedStrings     #-}
{-# LANGUAGE QuasiQuotes           #-}
{-# LANGUAGE TemplateHaskell       #-}
{-# LANGUAGE TypeFamilies          #-}
import           Data.Default              (def)
import           Data.Text                 (Text)
import           Network.HTTP.Client.Conduit (Manager, newManager)
import           Yesod
import           Yesod.Auth
import           Yesod.Auth.BrowserId
```

```haskell
import             Yesod.Auth.GoogleEmail

data App = App
    { httpManager :: Manager
    }

mkYesod "App" [parseRoutes|
/ HomeR GET
/auth AuthR Auth getAuth
|]

instance Yesod App where
    -- Note: In order to log in with BrowserID, you must correctly
    -- set your hostname here.
    approot = ApprootStatic "http://localhost:3000"

instance YesodAuth App where
    type AuthId App = Text
    getAuthId = return . Just . credsIdent

    loginDest _ = HomeR
    logoutDest _ = HomeR

    authPlugins _ =
        [ authBrowserId def
        , authGoogleEmail
        ]

    authHttpManager = httpManager

    -- The default maybeAuthId assumes a Persistent database. We're going for a
    -- simpler AuthId, so we'll just do a direct lookup in the session.
    maybeAuthId = lookupSession "_ID"

instance RenderMessage App FormMessage where
    renderMessage _ _ = defaultFormMessage

getHomeR :: Handler Html
getHomeR = do
    maid <- maybeAuthId
    defaultLayout
        [whamlet|
            <p>Your current auth ID: #{show maid}
            $maybe _ <- maid
                <p>
                    <a href=@{AuthR LogoutR}>Logout
            $nothing
                <p>
                    <a href=@{AuthR LoginR}>Go to the login page
        |]

main :: IO ()
```

```
main = do
    man <- newManager
    warp 3000 $ App man
```

We'll start with the route declarations. First we declare our standard `HomeR` route, and then we set up the authentication subsite. Remember that a subsite needs four parameters: the path to the subsite, the route name, the subsite name, and a function to get the subsite value. In other words, based on the line:

```
/auth AuthR Auth getAuth
```

we need to have `getAuth :: MyAuthSite -> Auth`. Although we haven't written that function ourselves, `yesod-auth` provides it automatically. With other subsites (like static files), we provide configuration settings in the subsite value, and therefore need to specify the `get` function. In the auth subsite, we specify these settings in a separate typeclass, `YesodAuth`.

 Why not use the subsite value? There are a number of settings we would like to give for an auth subsite, and doing so from a record type would be inconvenient. Also, we want to have an `AuthId` associated type, so a typeclass is more natural. Why not use a typeclass for all subsites? It comes with a downside: you can then only have a single instance per site, disallowing serving different sets of static files from different routes. Also, the subsite value works better when we want to load data at app initialization.

So what exactly goes in this `YesodAuth` instance? There are six required declarations:

- `AuthId` is an associated type. This is the value `yesod-auth` will give you when you ask if a user is logged in (via `maybeAuthId` or `requireAuthId`). In the example, we'll simply use `Text` to store the raw identifier (email address, in this case).

- `getAuthId` gets the actual `AuthId` from the `Creds` (credentials) data type. This type has three pieces of information: the authentication backend used (BrowserID or Google Email, in our case), the actual identifier, and an associated list of arbitrary extra information. Each backend provides different extra information; see their docs for more information.

- `loginDest` gives the route to redirect to after a successful login.

- Likewise, `logoutDest` gives the route to redirect to after a logout.

- `authPlugins` is a list of individual authentication backends to use. In our example we're using BrowserID, which logs in via Mozilla's BrowserID system, and Google Email, which authenticates a user's email address using the user's Google account. The nice thing about these two backends is:

— They require no setup, as opposed to Facebook or OAuth, which require setting up credentials.

— They use email addresses as identifiers, which people are comfortable with, as opposed to OpenID, which uses a URL.

- `authHttpManager` gets an HTTP connection manager from the foundation type. This allow authentication backends that use HTTP connections (i.e., almost all third-party login systems) to share connections, avoiding the cost of restarting a TCP connection for each request.

In addition to these six methods, there are other methods available to control other behavior of the authentication system, such as what the login page looks like. For more information, see the API documentation (*http://haddocks.fpcomplete.com/fp/ 7.8/20140916-162/yesod-auth/Yesod-Auth.html*).

In our `HomeR` handler, we have some simple links to the login and logout pages, depending on whether or not the user is logged in. Notice how we construct these subsite links: first we give the subsite route name (`AuthR`), followed by the route within the subsite (`LoginR` and `LogoutR`).

Figures 14-1 through 14-3 show what the login process looks like from a user's perspective.

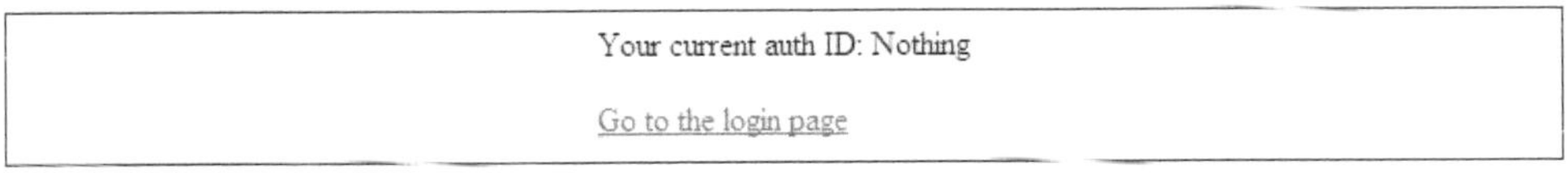

Your current auth ID: Nothing

Go to the login page

Figure 14-1. Initial page load

Figure 14-2. BrowserID login screen

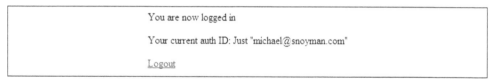

Figure 14-3. Homepage after logging in

Email

For many use cases, third-party authentication using email will be sufficient. Occasionally, however, you'll want users to create passwords on your site. The scaffolded site does not include this setup, because:

- In order to securely accept passwords, you need to be running over SSL. Many users are not serving their sites over SSL.

- Although the email backend properly salts and hashes passwords, a compromised database could still be problematic. Again, we make no assumptions that Yesod users are following secure deployment practices.

- You need to have a working system for sending email. Many web servers these days are not equipped to deal with all of the spam protection measures used by mail servers.

The following example will use the system's built-in *sendmail* executable. If you would like to avoid the hassle of dealing with an email server yourself, you can use Amazon SES. There is a package called `mime-mail-ses` (*http://hackage.haskell.org/package/mime-mail-ses*) that provides a drop-in replacement for the *sendmail* code, which we'll use. This is the approach I generally recommend, and it's what I use on most of my sites, including FP Haskell Center (*http://bit.ly/fp-center*) and *haskellers.com*.

But assuming you are able to meet these demands, and you want to have a separate password login specifically for your site, Yesod offers a built-in backend. It requires quite a bit of code to set up, because it needs to store passwords securely in the database and send a number of different emails to users (for account verification, password retrieval, etc.).

Let's have a look at a site that provides email authentication, storing passwords in a Persistent SQLite database:

```haskell
{-# LANGUAGE DeriveDataTypeable        #-}
{-# LANGUAGE FlexibleContexts          #-}
{-# LANGUAGE GADTs                     #-}
{-# LANGUAGE GeneralizedNewtypeDeriving #-}
{-# LANGUAGE MultiParamTypeClasses     #-}
{-# LANGUAGE OverloadedStrings         #-}
{-# LANGUAGE QuasiQuotes               #-}
{-# LANGUAGE TemplateHaskell           #-}
{-# LANGUAGE TypeFamilies              #-}
import           Control.Monad          (join)
import           Control.Monad.Logger   (runNoLoggingT)
import           Data.Maybe             (isJust)
import           Data.Text              (Text)
import qualified Data.Text.Lazy.Encoding
import           Data.Typeable          (Typeable)
import           Database.Persist.Sqlite
import           Database.Persist.TH
import           Network.Mail.Mime
import           Text.Blaze.Html.Renderer.Utf8 (renderHtml)
import           Text.Hamlet            (shamlet)
import           Text.Shakespeare.Text  (stext)
import           Yesod
import           Yesod.Auth
import           Yesod.Auth.Email

share [mkPersist sqlSettings { mpsGeneric = False }, mkMigrate "migrateAll"]
    [persistLowerCase|
User
    email Text
    password Text Maybe -- Password may not be set yet
    verkey Text Maybe -- Used for resetting passwords
    verified Bool
```

```
        UniqueUser email
        deriving Typeable
|]

data App = App SqlBackend

mkYesod "App" [parseRoutes|
/ HomeR GET
/auth AuthR Auth getAuth
|]

instance Yesod App where
    -- Emails will include links, so be sure to include an approot so that
    -- the links are valid!
    approot = ApprootStatic "http://localhost:3000"

instance RenderMessage App FormMessage where
    renderMessage _ _ = defaultFormMessage

-- Set up Persistent
instance YesodPersist App where
    type YesodPersistBackend App = SqlBackend
    runDB f = do
        App conn <- getYesod
        runSqlConn f conn

instance YesodAuth App where
    type AuthId App = UserId

    loginDest _ = HomeR
    logoutDest _ = HomeR
    authPlugins _ = [authEmail]

    -- Need to find the UserId for the given email address.
    getAuthId creds = runDB $ do
        x <- insertBy $ User (credsIdent creds) Nothing Nothing False
        return $ Just $
            case x of
                Left (Entity userid _) -> userid -- newly added user
                Right userid -> userid -- existing user

    authHttpManager = error "Email doesn't need an HTTP manager"

instance YesodAuthPersist App

-- Here's all of the email-specific code
instance YesodAuthEmail App where
    type AuthEmailId App = UserId

    afterPasswordRoute _ = HomeR

    addUnverified email verkey =
```

```
        runDB $ insert $ User email Nothing (Just verkey) False

sendVerifyEmail email _ verurl =
    liftIO $ renderSendMail (emptyMail $ Address Nothing "noreply")
        { mailTo = [Address Nothing email]
        , mailHeaders =
            [ ("Subject", "Verify your email address")
            ]
        , mailParts = [[textPart, htmlPart]]
        }
  where
    textPart = Part
        { partType = "text/plain; charset=utf-8"
        , partEncoding = None
        , partFilename = Nothing
        , partContent = Data.Text.Lazy.Encoding.encodeUtf8
            [stext|
                Please confirm your email address
                by clicking on the link below.

                #{verurl}

                Thank you
            |]
        , partHeaders = []
        }
    htmlPart = Part
        { partType = "text/html; charset=utf-8"
        , partEncoding = None
        , partFilename = Nothing
        , partContent = renderHtml
            [shamlet|
                <p>Please confirm your email address
                    by clicking on the link below.
                <p>
                    <a href=#{verurl}>#{verurl}
                <p>Thank you
            |]
        , partHeaders = []
        }
getVerifyKey = runDB . fmap (join . fmap userVerkey) . get
setVerifyKey uid key = runDB $ update uid [UserVerkey =. Just key]
verifyAccount uid = runDB $ do
    mu <- get uid
    case mu of
        Nothing -> return Nothing
        Just u -> do
            update uid [UserVerified =. True]
            return $ Just uid
getPassword = runDB . fmap (join . fmap userPassword) . get
setPassword uid pass = runDB $ update uid [UserPassword =. Just pass]
getEmailCreds email = runDB $ do
```

```
        mu <- getBy $ UniqueUser email
        case mu of
            Nothing -> return Nothing
            Just (Entity uid u) -> return $ Just EmailCreds
                { emailCredsId = uid
                , emailCredsAuthId = Just uid
                , emailCredsStatus = isJust $ userPassword u
                , emailCredsVerkey = userVerkey u
                , emailCredsEmail = email
                }
    getEmail = runDB . fmap (fmap userEmail) . get

getHomeR :: Handler Html
getHomeR = do
    maid <- maybeAuthId
    defaultLayout
        [whamlet|
            <p>Your current auth ID: #{show maid}
            $maybe _ <- maid
                <p>
                    <a href=@{AuthR LogoutR}>Logout
            $nothing
                <p>
                    <a href=@{AuthR LoginR}>Go to the login page
        |]

main :: IO ()
main = runNoLoggingT $ withSqliteConn "email.db3" $ \conn -> liftIO $ do
    runSqlConn (runMigration migrateAll) conn
    warp 3000 $ App conn
```

Authorization

Once you can authenticate your users, you can use their credentials to *authorize* requests. Authorization in Yesod is simple and declarative: most of the time, you just need to add the `authRoute` and `isAuthorized` methods to your `Yesod` typeclass instance. Let's look at an example:

```
{-# LANGUAGE MultiParamTypeClasses #-}
{-# LANGUAGE OverloadedStrings     #-}
{-# LANGUAGE QuasiQuotes           #-}
{-# LANGUAGE TemplateHaskell       #-}
{-# LANGUAGE TypeFamilies          #-}
import           Data.Default        (def)
import           Data.Text           (Text)
import           Network.HTTP.Conduit (Manager, conduitManagerSettings,
                                       newManager)
import           Yesod
import           Yesod.Auth
import           Yesod.Auth.Dummy -- just for testing; don't use in real life!
```

```
data App = App
    { httpManager :: Manager
    }

mkYesod "App" [parseRoutes|
/       HomeR   GET POST
/admin AdminR GET
/auth   AuthR   Auth getAuth
|]

instance Yesod App where
    authRoute _ = Just $ AuthR LoginR

    -- route name, then a Boolean indicating if it's a write request
    isAuthorized HomeR True = isAdmin
    isAuthorized AdminR _ = isAdmin

    -- anyone can access other pages
    isAuthorized _ _ = return Authorized

isAdmin = do
    mu <- maybeAuthId
    return $ case mu of
        Nothing -> AuthenticationRequired
        Just "admin" -> Authorized
        Just _ -> Unauthorized "You must be an admin"

instance YesodAuth App where
    type AuthId App = Text
    getAuthId = return . Just . credsIdent

    loginDest _ = HomeR
    logoutDest _ = HomeR

    authPlugins _ = [authDummy]

    authHttpManager = httpManager

    maybeAuthId = lookupSession "_ID"

instance RenderMessage App FormMessage where
    renderMessage _ _ = defaultFormMessage

getHomeR :: Handler Html
getHomeR = do
    maid <- maybeAuthId
    defaultLayout
        [whamlet|
            <p>Note: Log in as "admin" to be an administrator.
            <p>Your current auth ID: #{show maid}
            $maybe _ <- maid
                <p>
```

```
                    <a href=@{AuthR LogoutR}>Logout
            <p>
                <a href=@{AdminR}>Go to admin page
            <form method=post>
                Make a change (admins only)
                \ #
                <input type=submit>
        |]

postHomeR :: Handler ()
postHomeR = do
    setMessage "You made some change to the page"
    redirect HomeR

getAdminR :: Handler Html
getAdminR = defaultLayout
    [whamlet|
        <p>I guess you're an admin!
        <p>
            <a href=@{HomeR}>Return to homepage
    |]

main :: IO ()
main = do
    manager <- newManager conduitManagerSettings
    warp 3000 $ App manager
```

authRoute should be your login page, almost always AuthR LoginR. isAuthorized is a function that takes two parameters: the requested route, and whether or not the request was a "write" request. You can actually change the meaning of what a write request is using the isWriteRequest method, but the out-of-the-box version follows RESTful principles: anything but a GET, HEAD, OPTIONS, or TRACE request is a write request.

What's convenient about the body of isAuthorized is that you can run any Handler code you want in it. This means you can:

- Access the filesystem (normal I/O).
- Look up values in the database.
- Pull any session or request values you want.

Using these techniques, you can develop as sophisticated an authorization system as you like, or even tie into existing systems used by your organization.

Summary

This chapter covered the basics of setting up user authentication, as well as how the built-in authorization functions provide a simple, declarative approach for users.

Although these are complicated concepts, with many approaches, Yesod should provide you with the building blocks you need to create your own customized auth solution.

CHAPTER 15

Scaffolding and the Site Template

So you're tired of running small examples, and ready to write a real site? Then you've arrived at the right chapter. Even with the entire Yesod library at your fingertips, there are still a lot of steps you need to go through to get a production-quality site set up. Considerations include:

- Config file parsing
- Signal handling (*nix)
- More efficient static file serving
- A good file layout

The scaffolded site is a combination of many Yesoders' best practices, rolled into a ready-to-use skeleton for your sites. It is highly recommended for all sites. This chapter will explain the overall structure of the scaffolding, how to use it, and some of its less-than-obvious features.

For the most part, this chapter will not contain code samples. It is recommended that you follow along with an actual scaffolded site.

 Due to the nature of the scaffolded site, it is the most fluid component of Yesod, and can change from version to version. It is possible that the information in this chapter will be slightly outdated by the time you are reading it.

How to Scaffold

The `yesod-bin` package installs an executable (conveniently named *yesod* as well). This executable provides a few commands (run `yesod` by itself to get a list). In order to generate a scaffolding, the command is `yesod init`. This will start a question-and-answer process where you get to provide basic details. After answering the questions, you will have a site template in a subfolder with the name of your project.

The most important of these questions concerns the database backend. You get a few choices here, including SQL and MongoDB backends, or you can select the simple option and skip database support. This last option also turns off a few extra dependencies, giving you a leaner overall site. The remainder of this chapter will focus on the scaffoldings for one of the database backends. There will be minor differences for the simple backend.

After creating your files, the scaffolder will print a message about getting started. You should follow those instructions to ensure a reliable installation. In particular, the commands provided will ensure that any missing dependencies are built and installed. Even if you've installed the `yesod` package, you most likely do not yet have in place all the dependencies needed by your site. For example, none of the database backends (or the JavaScript minifier, `hjsmin`) are installed when installing the `yesod` package.

Finally, to launch your development site, you'll use `yesod devel`. This site will automatically be rebuilt and reloaded whenever you change your code.

File Structure

The scaffolded site is built as a fully cabalized Haskell package. In addition to source files, config files, templates, and static files are produced.

Cabal File

Whether directly using `cabal` or indirectly using `yesod devel`, building your code will always go through the cabal file. If you open the file, you'll see that there are both library and executable blocks. If the `library-only` flag is turned on, then the executable block is not built. This is how `yesod devel` calls your app. Otherwise, the executable is built.

The `library-only` flag should only be used by `yesod devel`; you should never be explicitly passing it into `cabal`. There is an additional flag, dev, that allows Cabal to build an executable but turns on some of the same features as the `library-only` flag —i.e., no optimizations and reload versions of the Shakespearean template functions.

In general, you will build as follows:

- When developing, use `yesod devel` exclusively.

- When building a production build, perform `cabal clean && cabal configure && cabal build`. This will produce an optimized executable in your *dist* folder. (You can also use the `yesod keter` command for this.)

You might be surprised to see the `NoImplicitPrelude` extension. We turn this on because the site includes its own module, `Import`, with a few changes to `Prelude` that make working with Yesod a little more convenient.

The last thing to note is the `exported-modules` list. If you add any modules to your application, you *must* update this list to get `yesod devel` to work correctly. Unfortunately, neither Cabal nor GHC will give you a warning if you forget to make this update, and instead you'll get a very scary-looking error message from `yesod devel`.

Routes and Entities

Multiple times in this book, you've seen comments stating that while we're declaring our routes/entities with quasiquotes for convenience, "in a production site, you should use an external file." The scaffolding uses such an external file.

Routes are defined in *config/routes*, and entities in *config/models*. They have the exact same syntax as the quasiquoting you've seen throughout the book, and `yesod devel` knows to automatically recompile the appropriate modules when these files change.

The *models* file is referenced by *Model.hs*. You are free to declare whatever you like in this file, but here are some guidelines:

- Any data types used in entities *must* be imported/declared in *Model.hs*, above the `persistFile` call.
- Helper utilities should be declared either in *Import.hs* or, if very model-centric, in a file within the *Model/* folder and imported into *Import.hs*.

Foundation and Application Modules

The `mkYesod` function that we have used throughout the book declares a few things:

- Route type
- Route render function
- Dispatch function

The dispatch function refers to all of the handler functions, and therefore all of those must either be defined in the same file as the dispatch function, or be imported into the module containing the dispatch function.

Meanwhile, the handler functions will almost certainly refer to the route type. Therefore, *they* either must be in the same file where the route type is defined, or must import that file. If you follow the logic here, your entire application must essentially live in a single file!

Clearly this isn't what we want. So, instead of using mkYesod, the scaffolded site uses a decomposed version of the function. Foundation calls mkYesodData, which declares the route type and render function. It does not declare the dispatch function, so the handler functions need not be in scope. The *Import.hs* file imports *Foundation.hs*, and all the handler modules import *Import.hs*.

In *Application.hs*, we call mkYesodDispatch, which creates our dispatch function. For this to work, all handler functions must be in scope, so be sure to add an import statement for any new handler modules you create.

Other than that, *Application.hs* is pretty simple. It provides two primary functions: getApplicationDev is used by yesod devel to launch your app, and makeApplication is used by the executable to launch.

Foundation.hs is much more exciting because it does the following:

- It declares your foundation data type and a number of instances, such as Yesod, YesodAuth, and YesodPersist.

- It imports the message files. If you look for the line starting with mkMessage, you will see that it specifies the folder containing the messages (*messages/*) and the default language (en, for English).

This is the right file for adding extra instances for your foundation, such as YesodAuthEmail or YesodBreadcrumbs.

We'll be referring back to this file later, as we discuss some of the special implementations of Yesod typeclass methods.

Import

The Import module was born out of a few commonly recurring patterns:

- I want to define some helper functions (maybe the <> = mappend operator) to be used by all handlers.

- I'm always adding the same five import statements (e.g., Data.Text, Control.Applicative, etc.) to every handler module.

- I want to make sure I never use some evil function (head, readFile, etc.) from Prelude.

Yes, "evil" is hyperbole. If you're wondering why I listed those functions as bad, head is partial and throws exceptions on an empty list, and readFile uses lazy I/O, which doesn't close file handles quickly enough. Also, readFile uses String instead of Text.

The solution is to turn on the NoImplicitPrelude language extension, re-export the parts of Prelude we want, add in all the other stuff we want, define our own functions as well, and then import this file in all handlers.

It is likely that, at some point after publishing this chapter, the scaffolded site will switch to an alternative prelude, such as classy-prelude-yesod. Don't be surprised if Import looks quite different than described here.

Handler Modules

Handler modules should go inside the *Handler/* folder. The site template includes one module: *Handler/Home.hs.* How you split up your handler functions into individual modules is your decision, but a good rule of thumb is:

- Different methods for the same route should go in the same file (e.g., getBlogR and postBlogR).
- Related routes should also go in the same file (e.g., getPeopleR and getPersonR).

Of course, it's entirely up to you. When you add a new handler file, make sure you do the following:

1. Add it to version control (you *are* using version control, right?).
2. Add it to the cabal file.
3. Add it to the *Application.hs* file.
4. Put a module statement at the top, and an import Import line below it.

You can use the yesod add-handler command to automate the last three steps.

widgetFile

It's very common to want to include CSS and JavaScript specific to a page. You don't want to have to include those Lucius and Julius files manually every time you refer to a Hamlet file. For this, the site template provides the widgetFile function.

If you have a handler function:

```
getHomeR = defaultLayout $(widgetFile "homepage")
```
Yesod will look for the following files:

- *templates/homepage.hamlet*
- *templates/homepage.lucius*
- *templates/homepage.cassius*
- *templates/homepage.julius*

If any of those files are present, they will be automatically included in the output.

 Due to the nature of how this works, if you launch your app with yesod devel and then create a new file (e.g., *templates/home-page.julius*), the contents will *not* be included until the file calling widgetFile is recompiled. In such a case, you may need to force a save of that file to get yesod devel to recompile.

defaultLayout

One of the first things you'll want to customize is the look of your site. The layout is actually broken up into two files:

templates/default-layout-wrapper.hamlet
This contains just the basic shell of a page. This file is interpreted as plain Hamlet, not as a Widget, and therefore cannot refer to other widgets, embed i18n strings, or add extra CSS/JS.

templates/default-layout.hamlet
This is where you would put the bulk of your page. You *must* remember to include the widget value in the page, as that contains the per-page contents. This file is interpreted as a Widget.

Also, because *default-layout* is included via the widgetFile function, any Lucius, Cassius, or Julius files named *default-layout.** will automatically be included as well.

Static Files

The scaffolded site automatically includes the static file subsite, optimized for serving files that will not change over the lifetime of the current build. What this means is that:

- When your static file identifiers are generated (e.g., *static/mylogo.png* becomes *mylogo_png*), a query string parameter is added to it with a hash of the contents of the file. All of this happens at compile time.

- When `yesod-static` serves your static files, it sets expiration headers far in the future and includes an etag based on a hash of your content.
- Whenever you embed a link to `mylogo_png`, the rendering includes the query string parameter. If you change the logo, recompile, and launch your new app, the query string will have changed, causing users to ignore the cached copy and download a new version.

Additionally, you can set a specific static root in your *Settings.hs* file to serve from a different domain name. This has the advantage of not requiring transmission of cookies for static file requests, and also lets you offload static file hosting to a CDN or a service like Amazon S3. See the comments in the file for more details.

Another optimization is that CSS and JavaScript included in your widgets will not be included inside your HTML. Instead, their contents will be written to an external file, and a link given. This file will be named based on a hash of the contents as well, meaning:

- Caching works properly.
- Yesod can avoid an expensive disk write of the CSS/JavaScript file contents if a file with the same hash already exists.

Finally, all of your JavaScript is automatically minified via `hjsmin`.

Summary

The purpose of this chapter was not to explain every line that exists in the scaffolded site, but instead to give a general overview of how it works. The best way to become more familiar with it is to jump right in and start writing a Yesod site with it.

CHAPTER 16

Internationalization

Users expect our software to speak their language. Unfortunately for us, there will likely be more than one language involved. While doing simple string replacement isn't too involved, correctly dealing with all the grammar issues can be tricky. After all, who wants to see "List 1 file(s)" from a program output?

But a real i18n solution needs to do more than just provide a means of achieving the correct output. It needs to make this process relatively error-proof, and easy for both the programmer and the translator. Yesod's answer to the problem gives you:

- Intelligent guessing of the user's desired language based on request headers, with the ability to override.
- A simple syntax for giving translations that requires no Haskell knowledge. (After all, most translators aren't programmers.)
- The ability to bring in the full power of Haskell for tricky grammar issues as necessary, along with a default selection of helper functions to cover most needs.
- Absolutely no issues at all with word order.

Synopsis

```
-- @messages/en.msg
Hello: Hello
EnterItemCount: I would like to buy:
Purchase: Purchase
ItemCount count@Int: You have purchased #{showInt count}
                     #{plural count "item" "items"}.
SwitchLanguage: Switch language to:
Switch: Switch
```

```
-- @messages/he.msg
Hello: שלום
EnterItemCount: אני רוצה לקנות:
Purchase: קנה
ItemCount count: קנית #{showInt count} #{plural count "דבר" "דברים"}.
SwitchLanguage: החלף שפה ל:
Switch: החלף

{-# LANGUAGE MultiParamTypeClasses #-}
{-# LANGUAGE OverloadedStrings     #-}
{-# LANGUAGE QuasiQuotes           #-}
{-# LANGUAGE TemplateHaskell       #-}
{-# LANGUAGE TypeFamilies          #-}
import          Yesod

data App = App

mkMessage "App" "messages" "en"

plural :: Int -> String -> String -> String
plural 1 x _ = x
plural _ _ y = y

showInt :: Int -> String
showInt = show

instance Yesod App

instance RenderMessage App FormMessage where
    renderMessage _ _ = defaultFormMessage

mkYesod "App" [parseRoutes|
/     HomeR GET
/buy  BuyR  GET
/lang LangR POST
|]

getHomeR :: Handler Html
getHomeR = defaultLayout
    [whamlet|
        <h1>_{MsgHello}
        <form action=@{BuyR}>
            _{MsgEnterItemCount}
            <input type=text name=count>
            <input type=submit value=_{MsgPurchase}>
        <form action=@{LangR} method=post>
            _{MsgSwitchLanguage}
            <select name=lang>
                <option value=en>English
                <option value=he>Hebrew
            <input type=submit value=_{MsgSwitch}>
    |]
```

```
getBuyR :: Handler Html
getBuyR = do
    count <- runInputGet $ ireq intField "count"
    defaultLayout [whamlet|<p>_{MsgItemCount count}|]

postLangR :: Handler ()
postLangR = do
    lang <- runInputPost $ ireq textField "lang"
    setLanguage lang
    redirect HomeR

main :: IO ()
main = warp 3000 App
```

Overview

Most existing i18n solutions out there, like `gettext` or Java message bundles, work on the principle of string lookups. Usually some form of `printf` interpolation is used to interpolate variables into the strings. In Yesod, as you might guess, we instead rely on types. This gives us all of our normal advantages, such as the compiler automatically catching mistakes.

Let's take a concrete example. Suppose our application needs to accomplish two simple tasks: saying "hello," and stating how many users are logged into the system. This can be modeled with a sum type:

```
data MyMessage = MsgHello | MsgUsersLoggedIn Int
```

We can also write a function to turn this data type into an English representation:

```
toEnglish :: MyMessage -> String
toEnglish MsgHello = "Hello there!"
toEnglish (MsgUsersLoggedIn 1) = "There is 1 user logged in."
toEnglish (MsgUsersLoggedIn i) = "There are " ++ show i ++ " users logged in."
```

We can write similar functions for other languages, too. The advantage to this inside-Haskell approach is that we have the full power of Haskell for addressing tricky grammar issues, especially pluralization.

The downside, however, is that you have to write all of this inside of Haskell, which won't be very translator-friendly. To solve this problem, Yesod introduces the concept of message files. We'll cover those in the next section.

 You may think pluralization isn't so complicated: you have one version for one item, and another for any other count. That might be true in English, but it's not true for every language. Russian, for example, has six different forms, and you need to use some modulus logic to determine which one to use.

Assuming we have this full set of translation functions, how do we go about using them? What we need is a new function to wrap them all up together, and then choose the appropriate translation function based on the user's selected language. Once we have that, Yesod can automatically choose the most relevant render function and call it on the values provided.

As we'll see shortly, in order to simplify things a bit Hamlet has a special interpolation syntax, _{…}, which handles all the calls to the render functions. To associate a render function with your application, you use the YesodMessage typeclass.

Message Files

The simplest approach to creating translations is via message files. The setup is simple: there is a single folder containing all of your translation files, with a single file for each language. Each file is named based on its language code (e.g., *en.msg*), and each line in a file handles one phrase, which correlates to a single constructor in your message data type.

 The scaffolded site already includes a fully configured message folder.

So first, a word about language codes. There are really two choices available: using a two-letter language code or a **language-LOCALE** code. For example, when I load up a page in my web browser, it sends two language codes: en-US and en. What my browser is saying is, "If you have American English, I like that the most. If you have English, I'll take that instead."

So which format should you use in your application? Most likely two-letter codes, unless you are actually creating separate translations by locale. This ensures that someone asking for Canadian English will still see your English. Behind the scenes, Yesod will add the two-letter codes where relevant. For example, suppose a user has the following language list:

    pt-BR, es, he

What this means is "I like Brazilian Portuguese, then Spanish, and then Hebrew." Suppose your application provides the languages pt (general Portuguese) and en (English), with English as the default. Strictly following the user's language list would result in the user being served English. Instead, Yesod translates that list into:

    pt-BR, es, he, pt

In other words, unless you're giving different translations based on locale, just stick to the two-letter language codes.

Now what about these message files? The syntax should be very familiar after your work with Hamlet and Persistent. The line starts off with the name of the message. Because this is a data constructor, it must start with a capital letter. Next, you can have individual parameters, which must be given as lowercase. These will be arguments to the data constructor.

The argument list is terminated by a colon, and then followed by the translated string, which allows usage of our typical variable interpolation syntax #{myVar}. By referring to the parameters defined before the colon, and using translation helper functions to deal with issues like pluralization, you can create all the translated messages you need.

Specifying Types

We will be creating a data type out of our message specifications, so each parameter to a data constructor must be given a data type. We use @ syntax for this. For example, to create the data type data MyMessage = MsgHello | MsgSayAge Int, we would write:

```
Hello: Hi there!
SayAge age@Int: Your age is: #{show age}
```

But there are two problems with this:

- It's not very DRY (Don't Repeat Yourself) to specify this data type in every file.

- Translators will be confused by having to specify these data types.

So instead, the type specification is only required in the main language file. This is specified as the third argument in the mkMessage function. This also specifies what the backup language will be, to be used when none of the languages provided by your application match the user's language list.

RenderMessage typeclass

Your call to mkMessage creates an instance of the RenderMessage typeclass, which is the core of Yesod's i18n. It is defined as:

```
class RenderMessage master message where
    renderMessage :: master
                  -> [Text] -- ^ languages
                  -> message
                  -> Text
```

Notice that there are two parameters to the `RenderMessage` class: the master site and the message type. In theory, we could skip the master type here, but that would mean that every site would need to have the same set of translations for each message type. When it comes to shared libraries like forms, that would not be a workable solution.

The `renderMessage` function takes a parameter for each of the class's type parameters: `master` and `message`. The extra parameter is a list of languages the user will accept, in descending order of priority. The method then returns a user-ready `Text` that can be displayed.

A simple instance of `RenderMessage` may involve no actual translation of strings; instead, it will just display the same value for every language. For example:

```
data MyMessage = Hello | Greet Text
instance RenderMessage MyApp MyMessage where
    renderMessage _ _ Hello = "Hello"
    renderMessage _ _ (Greet name) = "Welcome, " <> name <> "!"
```

Notice how we ignore the first two parameters to `renderMessage`. We can now extend this to support multiple languages:

```
renderEn Hello = "Hello"
renderEn (Greet name) = "Welcome, " <> name <> "!"
renderHe Hello = "שלום"
renderHe (Greet name) = "ברוכים הבאים, " <> name <> "!"
instance RenderMessage MyApp MyMessage where
    renderMessage _ ("en":_) = renderEn
    renderMessage _ ("he":_) = renderHe
    renderMessage master (_:langs) = renderMessage master langs
    renderMessage _ [] = renderEn
```

The idea here is fairly straightforward: we define helper functions to support each language. We then add a clause to catch each of those languages in the `renderMessage` definition. We then have two final cases: if no languages matched, continue checking with the next language in the user's priority list; or, if we've exhausted all languages the user specified, then use the default language (in our case, English).

Odds are that you will never need to worry about writing this stuff manually, as the message file interface does all this for you. But it's always a good idea to have an understanding of what's going on under the surface.

Interpolation

One way to use your new `RenderMessage` instance would be to directly call the `renderMessage` function. This would work, but it's a bit tedious: you need to pass in the foundation value and the language list manually. Instead, Hamlet provides a specialized i18n interpolation, which looks like _{...}.

Why the underscore? The underscore is already a well-established character for i18n, as it is used in the gettext library.

Hamlet will then automatically translate that to a call to renderMessage. Once Hamlet gets the output Text value, it uses the toHtml function to produce an Html value, meaning that any special characters (e.g., <, &, >) will be automatically escaped.

Phrases, Not Words

As a final note, I'd just like to give some general i18n advice. Let's say you have an application for selling turtles. You're going to use the word "turtle" in multiple places, like "You have added 4 turtles to your cart." and "You have purchased 4 turtles, congratulations!" As a programmer, you'll immediately notice the code reuse potential: we have the phrase "4 turtles" twice. So, you might structure your message file as:

```
AddStart: You have added
AddEnd: to your cart.
PurchaseStart: You have purchased
PurchaseEnd: , congratulations!
Turtles count@Int: #{show count} #{plural count "turtle" "turtles"}
```

Stop right there! This is all well and good from a programming perspective, but translations are *not* programming. There are a many things that could go wrong with this, such as:

- Some languages might put "to your cart." before "You have added".
- Maybe "added" will be constructed differently depending on whether the user added one or more turtles.
- There are a bunch of whitespace issues.

So the general rule is: translate entire phrases, not just words.

CHAPTER 17

Creating a Subsite

How many sites provide authentication systems? Or need to provide create, read, update, and delete (CRUD) management of some objects? Or a blog? Or a wiki?

The theme here is that many websites include common components that can be reused throughout multiple sites. However, it is often quite difficult to get code to be modular enough to be truly plug and play: a component will require hooks into the routing system, usually for multiple routes, and will need some way of sharing styling information with the master site.

In Yesod, the solution is *subsites*. A subsite is a collection of routes and their handlers that can be easily inserted into a master site. The use of typeclasses makes it easy to ensure that the master site provides certain capabilities, and to access the default site layout. And with type-safe URLs, it's easy to link from the master site to subsites.

Hello, World

Perhaps the trickiest part of writing subsites is getting started. Let's dive in with a simple Hello, World subsite. We need to create one module to contain our subsite's data types, another for the subsite's dispatch code, and then a final module for an application that uses the subsite.

 The reason for the breakdown between the data and dispatch code is due to the GHC stage restriction. This requirement makes smaller demos a bit more verbose, but in practice, this splitting up into multiple modules is a good practice to adhere to.

```
-- @HelloSub/Data.hs
{-# LANGUAGE QuasiQuotes     #-}
{-# LANGUAGE TemplateHaskell #-}
```

```
{-# LANGUAGE TypeFamilies     #-}
module HelloSub.Data where

import          Yesod

-- Subsites have foundations just like master sites.
data HelloSub = HelloSub

-- We have a familiar analogue from mkYesod, with just one extra parameter.
-- We'll discuss that later.
mkYesodSubData "HelloSub" [parseRoutes|
/ SubHomeR GET
|]

-- @HelloSub.hs
{-# LANGUAGE FlexibleInstances     #-}
{-# LANGUAGE MultiParamTypeClasses #-}
{-# LANGUAGE OverloadedStrings     #-}
{-# LANGUAGE QuasiQuotes           #-}
{-# LANGUAGE TemplateHaskell       #-}
module HelloSub
    ( module HelloSub.Data
    , module HelloSub
    ) where

import          HelloSub.Data
import          Yesod

-- We'll spell out the handler type signature.
getSubHomeR :: Yesod master => HandlerT HelloSub (HandlerT master IO) Html
getSubHomeR = lift $ defaultLayout [whamlet|Welcome to the subsite!|]

instance Yesod master => YesodSubDispatch HelloSub (HandlerT master IO) where
    yesodSubDispatch = $(mkYesodSubDispatch resourcesHelloSub)

{-# LANGUAGE OverloadedStrings #-}
{-# LANGUAGE QuasiQuotes       #-}
{-# LANGUAGE TemplateHaskell   #-}
{-# LANGUAGE TypeFamilies      #-}
import          HelloSub
import          Yesod

-- And let's create a master site that calls it.
data Master = Master
    { getHelloSub :: HelloSub
    }

mkYesod "Master" [parseRoutes|
/ HomeR GET
/subsite SubsiteR HelloSub getHelloSub
|]

instance Yesod Master
```

```
-- Spelling out type signature again.
getHomeR :: HandlerT Master IO Html
getHomeR = defaultLayout
    [whamlet|
        <h1>Welcome to the homepage
        <p>
            Feel free to visit the #
            <a href=@{SubsiteR SubHomeR}>subsite
            \ as well.
    |]

main = warp 3000 $ Master HelloSub
```

This simple example actually shows most of the complications involved in creating a subsite. Like in a normal Yesod application, everything in a subsite is centered around a foundation data type (HelloSub, in our case). We then use mkYesodSubData to generate our subsite route data type and associated parse and render functions.

On the dispatch side, we start off by defining our handler function for the SubHomeR route. You should pay special attention to the type signature on this function:

```
getSubHomeR :: Yesod master
            => HandlerT HelloSub (HandlerT master IO) Html
```

This is the heart and soul of what a subsite is all about. All of our actions live in this layered monad, where we have our subsite wrapping around our main site. Given this monadic layering, it should come as no surprise that we end up calling lift. In this case, our subsite is using the master site's defaultLayout function to render a widget.

The defaultLayout function is part of the Yesod typeclass. Therefore, in order to call it, the master type argument must be an instance of Yesod. The advantage of this approach is that any modifications to the master site's defaultLayout method will automatically be reflected in subsites.

When we embed a subsite in our master site route definition, we need to specify four pieces of information: the route to use as the base of the subsite (*/subsite*, in this case), the constructor for the subsite routes (SubsiteR), the subsite foundation data type (HelloSub), and a function that takes a master foundation value and returns a subsite foundation value (getHelloSub).

In the definition of getHomeR, we can see how the route constructor gets used. In a sense, SubsiteR promotes any subsite route to a master site route, making it possible to safely link to it from any master site template.

CHAPTER 18

Understanding a Request

You can oftentimes get away with using Yesod for quite a while without needing to understand its internal workings. However, developing an understanding of its ins and outs is advantageous. This chapter will walk you through the request handling process for a fairly typical Yesod application. Note that a fair amount of this discussion involves code changes in Yesod 1.2. Most of the concepts are the same in previous versions, though the data types involved were a bit messier.

Yesod's usage of Template Haskell to bypass boilerplate code can make it a bit difficult to understand this process sometimes. If you wish to go beyond the information in this chapter, it can be useful to view GHC's generated code using -ddump-splices.

A lot of this information was originally published as a blog series on the 1.2 release. You can see the blog posts at:

- Yesod 1.2's cleaner internals (*http://bit.ly/12-cleaner*)
- Big Subsite Rewrite (*http://bit.ly/subsite-write*)
- Yesod dispatch, version 1.2 (*http://bit.ly/12-dispatch*)

Handlers

When trying to understand Yesod request handling, we need to look at two components: how a request is dispatched to the appropriate handler code, and how handler functions are processed. We'll start off with the latter, and then circle back to understanding the dispatch process itself.

Layers

Yesod builds itself on top of WAI, which provides a protocol for web servers (or, more generally, handlers) and applications to communicate with each other. This is expressed through two data types: `Request` and `Response`. Then, an `Application` is defined as:

```
type Application = Request
                -> (Response -> IO ResponseReceived)
                -> IO ResponseReceived
```

A WAI handler will take an application and run it.

> The structure of `Application` looks a bit complicated. It uses continuation passing style to allow an application to safely acquire resources, similar to the `bracket` function. See the WAI API documentation for more details.

`Request` and `Response` are both very low level, trying to represent the HTTP protocol without too much embellishment. This keeps WAI as a generic tool, but also leaves out a lot of the information we need in order to implement a web framework. For example, WAI will provide us with the raw data for all request headers. But Yesod needs to parse that to get cookie information, and then parse the cookies in order to extract session information.

To deal with this dichotomy, Yesod introduces two new data types: `YesodRequest` and `YesodResponse`. `YesodRequest` contains a WAI `Request`, and also adds in such request information as cookies and session variables. On the response side can either be a standard WAI `Response` or a higher-level representation of such a response including such things as updated session information and extra response headers. To parallel WAI's `Application`, we have:

```
type YesodApp = YesodRequest -> ResourceT IO YesodResponse
```

> Yesod uses `ResourceT` for exception safety, instead of continuation passing style. This makes it much easier to write exception-safe code in Yesod.

But as a Yesod user, you never really see `YesodApp`. There's another layer on top of that, which you are used to dealing with: `HandlerT`. When you write handler functions, you need to have access to three different things:

- The `YesodRequest` value for the current request.

- Some basic environment information, like how to log messages or handle error conditions. This is provided by the data type RunHandlerEnv.

- A mutable variable to keep track of updateable information, such as the headers to be returned and the user session state. This is called GHState. (I know that's not a great name, but it's there for historical reasons.)

So when you're writing a handler function, you're essentially just writing a ReaderT transformer that has access to all of this information. The runHandler function will turn a HandlerT into a YesodApp. yesodRunner takes this a step further and converts it to a WAI Application.

Content

The preceding example, and many others you've already seen, gives a handler with a type of Handler Html. We've just described what the Handler means, but how does Yesod know how to deal with Html? The answer lies in the ToTypedContent typeclass. The relevant bit of code are:

```
data Content = ContentBuilder !BBuilder.Builder !(Maybe Int)
                 -- ^ The content and optional content length.
             | ContentSource !(Source (ResourceT IO) (Flush BBuilder.Builder))
             | ContentFile !FilePath !(Maybe FilePart)
             | ContentDontEvaluate !Content
data TypedContent = TypedContent !ContentType !Content

class ToContent a where
    toContent :: a -> Content
class ToContent a => ToTypedContent a where
    toTypedContent :: a -> TypedContent
```

The Content data type represents the different ways you can provide a response body. The first three mirror WAI's representation directly. The fourth option (ContentDontEvaluate) is used to indicate to Yesod whether response bodies should be fully evaluated before being returned to users. The advantage to fully evaluating is that we can provide meaningful error messages if an exception is thrown from pure code. The downside is possibly increased time and memory usage.

In any event, Yesod knows how to turn a Content into a response body. The ToContent typeclass provides a way to allow many different data types to be converted into response bodies. Many commonly used types are already instances of ToContent, including strict and lazy ByteString and Text, and of course Html.

TypedContent adds an extra piece of information: the content type of the value. As you might expect, there are ToTypedContent instances for a number of common data types, including Html, the aeson library's Value (for JSON), and Text (treated as plain text):

```
instance ToTypedContent J.Value where
    toTypedContent v = TypedContent typeJson (toContent v)
instance ToTypedContent Html where
    toTypedContent h = TypedContent typeHtml (toContent h)
instance ToTypedContent T.Text where
    toTypedContent t = TypedContent typePlain (toContent t)
```

Putting this all together, a `Handler` is able to return any value that is an instance of `ToTypedContent`, and Yesod will handle turning it into an appropriate representation and setting the `Content-Type` response header.

Short-Circuit Responses

One other oddity is how short-circuiting works. For example, you can call `redirect` in the middle of a handler function, and the rest of the function will not be called. The mechanism we use is standard Haskell exceptions. Calling `redirect` just throws an exception of type `HandlerContents`. The `runHandler` function will catch any exceptions thrown and produce an appropriate response. For `HandlerContents`, each constructor gives a clear action to perform, be it redirecting or sending a file. For all other exception types, an error message is displayed to the user.

Dispatch

Dispatch is the act of taking an incoming request and generating an appropriate response. We have a few different constraints, depending on how we want to handle dispatch:

- Dispatch based on path segments (or pieces).
- Optionally dispatch on request method.
- Support subsites: packaged collections of functionality providing multiple routes under a specific URL prefix.
- Support using `WAI Applications` as subsites, while introducing as little runtime overhead to the process as possible. In particular, we want to avoid performing any unnecessary parsing to generate a `YesodRequest` if it won't be used.

The lowest common denominator for this is to simply use a WAI `Application`. However, this doesn't provide quite enough information: we need access to the foundation data type, and the logger, and for subsites, we need to know how a subsite route is converted to a parent site route. To address this, we have two helper data types—`YesodRunnerEnv` and `YesodSubRunnerEnv`—providing this extra information for normal sites and subsites.

With those types, dispatch now becomes a relatively simple matter: give me an environment and a request, and I'll give you a response. This is represented by the typeclasses `YesodDispatch` and `YesodSubDispatch`:

```
class Yesod site => YesodDispatch site where
    yesodDispatch :: YesodRunnerEnv site -> W.Application

class YesodSubDispatch sub m where
    yesodSubDispatch :: YesodSubRunnerEnv sub (HandlerSite m) m
                        -> W.Application
```

We'll see a bit later how `YesodSubDispatch` is used. Let's first understand how `Yesod Dispatch` comes into play.

toWaiApp, toWaiAppPlain, and warp

Let's assume for the moment that you have a data type that is an instance of `YesodDis patch`. You'll want to now actually run this thing somehow. To do this, you need to convert it into a WAI `Application` and pass it to some kind of WAI handler/server. To start this journey, we use `toWaiAppPlain`. It performs any app-wide initialization necessary. At the time of writing, this means allocating a logger and setting up the session backend, but more functionality may be added in the future. Using this data, we can create a `YesodRunnerEnv`. And when that value is passed to `yesodDispatch`, we get a WAI `Application`.

We're almost done. The final remaining modification is path segment cleanup. The `Yesod` typeclass includes a member function named `cleanPath` that can be used to create canonical URLs. For example, the default implementation would remove double slashes and redirect a user from */foo//bar* to */foo/bar*. `toWaiAppPlain` adds in some preprocessing to the normal WAI request by analyzing the requested path and performing cleanup/redirects as necessary.

At this point, we have a fully functional WAI `Application`. There are two other helper functions included. `toWaiApp` wraps `toWaiAppPlain` and additionally includes some commonly used WAI middlewares, including request logging and gzip compression (see the Haddocks for an up-to-date list). Finally, we have the `warp` function, which as you might guess, runs your application with Warp.

 There's also the `warpEnv` function, which reads the port number information from the `PORT` environment variable. This is used for interacting with certain tools, including the Keter deployment manager and FP Haskell Center.

Generated Code

The last remaining black box is the Template Haskell generated code. This generated code is responsible for handling some of the tedious, error-prone pieces of your site. If you want to, you can write these all by hand instead. We'll demonstrate what that translation would look like, and in the process elucidate how YesodDispatch and YesodSubDispatch work. Let's start with a fairly typical Yesod application:

```haskell
{-# LANGUAGE OverloadedStrings #-}
{-# LANGUAGE QuasiQuotes       #-}
{-# LANGUAGE TemplateHaskell   #-}
{-# LANGUAGE TypeFamilies      #-}
{-# LANGUAGE ViewPatterns      #-}
import qualified Data.ByteString.Lazy.Char8 as L8
import           Network.HTTP.Types    (status200)
import           Network.Wai           (pathInfo, rawPathInfo,
                                        requestMethod, responseLBS)
import           Yesod

data App = App

mkYesod "App" [parseRoutes|
/only-get       OnlyGetR    GET
/any-method     AnyMethodR
/has-param/#Int HasParamR   GET
/my-subsite     MySubsiteR WaiSubsite getMySubsite
|]

instance Yesod App

getOnlyGetR :: Handler Html
getOnlyGetR = defaultLayout
    [whamlet|
        <p>Accessed via GET method
        <form method=post action=@{AnyMethodR}>
            <button>POST to /any-method
    |]

handleAnyMethodR :: Handler Html
handleAnyMethodR = do
    req <- waiRequest
    defaultLayout
        [whamlet|
            <p>In any-method, method == #{show $ requestMethod req}
        |]

getHasParamR :: Int -> Handler String
getHasParamR i = return $ show i

getMySubsite :: App -> WaiSubsite
getMySubsite _ =
```

```
        WaiSubsite app
    where
        app req sendResponse = sendResponse $ responseLBS
            status200
            [("Content-Type", "text/plain")]
            $ L8.pack $ concat
                [ "pathInfo == "
                , show $ pathInfo req
                , ", rawPathInfo == "
                , show $ rawPathInfo req
                ]

main :: IO ()
main = warp 3000 App
```

For completeness, we've provided a full listing, but let's focus on just the Template Haskell portion:

```
mkYesod "App" [parseRoutes|
/only-get        OnlyGetR    GET
/any-method      AnyMethodR
/has-param/#Int  HasParamR   GET
/my-subsite      MySubsiteR WaiSubsite getMySubsite
|]
```

Although this generates a few pieces of code, we only need to replicate three components to make our site work. Let's start with the simplest—the Handler type synonym:

```
type Handler = HandlerT App IO
```

Next is the type-safe URL and its rendering function. The rendering function is allowed to generate both path segments and query string parameters. Standard Yesod sites never generate query string parameters, but it is technically possible. And in the case of subsites, this often does happen. Notice how we handle the qs parameter for the MySubsiteR case:

```
instance RenderRoute App where
    data Route App = OnlyGetR
                   | AnyMethodR
                   | HasParamR Int
                   | MySubsiteR (Route WaiSubsite)
        deriving (Show, Read, Eq)

    renderRoute OnlyGetR = (["only-get"], [])
    renderRoute AnyMethodR = (["any-method"], [])
    renderRoute (HasParamR i) = (["has-param", toPathPiece i], [])
    renderRoute (MySubsiteR subRoute) =
        let (ps, qs) = renderRoute subRoute
         in ("my-subsite" : ps, qs)
```

You can see that there's a fairly simple mapping from the higher-level route syntax and the RenderRoute instance. Each route becomes a constructor, each URL parameter becomes an argument to its constructor, we embed a route for the subsite, and we use toPathPiece to render parameters to text.

The final component is the YesodDispatch instance. Let's look at this in a few pieces:

```
instance YesodDispatch App where
    yesodDispatch env req =
        case pathInfo req of
            ["only-get"] ->
                case requestMethod req of
                    "GET" -> yesodRunner
                        getOnlyGetR
                        env
                        (Just OnlyGetR)
                        req
                    _ -> yesodRunner
                        (badMethod >> return ())
                        env
                        (Just OnlyGetR)
                        req
```

As just described, yesodDispatch is handed both an environment and a WAI Request value. We can now perform dispatch based on the requested path, or, in WAI terms, the pathInfo. Referring back to our original high-level route syntax, we can see that our first route is going to be the single piece only-get, which we pattern match for.

Once that match has succeeded, we additionally pattern match on the request method. If it's GET, we use the handler function getOnlyGetR. Otherwise, we want to return a 405 Bad Method response, and therefore use the badMethod handler. At this point, we've come full circle to our original handler discussion. You can see that we're using yesodRunner to execute our handler function. As a reminder, this will take our environment and WAI Request, convert it to a YesodRequest, construct a RunHand lerEnv, hand that to the handler function, and then convert the resulting YesodRes ponse into a WAI Response.

Wonderful; one down, three to go. The next one is even easier:

```
["any-method"] ->
    yesodRunner handleAnyMethodR env (Just AnyMethodR) req
```

Unlike OnlyGetR, AnyMethodR will work for any request method, so we don't need to perform any further pattern matching:

```
["has-param", t] | Just i <- fromPathPiece t ->
    case requestMethod req of
        "GET" -> yesodRunner
            (getHasParamR i)
            env
            (Just $ HasParamR i)
```

```
            req
     _ -> yesodRunner
            (badMethod >> return ())
            env
            (Just $ HasParamR i)
            req
```

We add in one extra complication here: a dynamic parameter. While we used toPath Piece to render to a textual value earlier, we now use fromPathPiece to perform the parsing. Assuming the parse succeeds, we then follow a very similar dispatch system as was used for OnlyGetR. The prime difference is that our parameter needs to be passed to both the handler function and the route data constructor.

Next, we'll look at the subsite, which is quite different:

```
("my-subsite":rest) -> yesodSubDispatch
    YesodSubRunnerEnv
        { ysreGetSub = getMySubsite
        , ysreParentRunner = yesodRunner
        , ysreToParentRoute = MySubsiteR
        , ysreParentEnv = env
        }
    req { pathInfo = rest }
```

Unlike the other pattern matches, here we just look to see if our pattern prefix matches. Any route beginning with */my-subsite* should be passed off to the subsite for processing. This is where we finally get to use yesodSubDispatch. This function closely mirrors yesodDispatch. We need to construct a new environment to be passed to it. Let's discuss the four fields:

- ysreGetSub demonstrates how to get the subsite foundation type from the master site. We provide getMySubsite, which is the function we provided in the high-level route syntax.

- ysreParentRunner provides a means of running a handler function. It may seem a bit boring to just provide yesodRunner, but by having a separate parameter we allow the construction of deeply nested subsites, which will wrap and unwrap many layers of interleaving subsites. (This is a more advanced concept, and we won't be covering it in this chapter.)

- ysreToParentRoute will convert a route for the subsite into a route for the parent site. This is the purpose of the MySubsiteR constructor. This allows subsites to use functions such as getRouteToParent.

- ysreParentEnv simply passes on the initial environment, which contains a number of things the subsite may need (such as the logger).

The other interesting thing is how we modify the `pathInfo`. This allows subsites to *continue dispatching* from where the parent site left off. Figure 18-1 shows screenshots of a few requests.

```
localhost:3000/my-subsite/foo/bar

pathInfo == ["foo","bar"], rawPathInfo == "/my-subsite/foo/bar"

localhost:3000/my-subsite

pathInfo == [], rawPathInfo == "/my-subsite"
```

Figure 18-1. Path info in subsite

And finally, not all requests will be valid routes. For those cases, we just want to respond with a 404 Not Found:

```
_ -> yesodRunner (notFound >> return ()) env Nothing req
```

Complete Code

Here is the full code for the non-Template Haskell approach:

```haskell
{-# LANGUAGE OverloadedStrings #-}
{-# LANGUAGE QuasiQuotes       #-}
{-# LANGUAGE TemplateHaskell   #-}
{-# LANGUAGE TypeFamilies      #-}
{-# LANGUAGE ViewPatterns      #-}
import qualified Data.ByteString.Lazy.Char8 as L8
import           Network.HTTP.Types      (status200)
import           Network.Wai             (pathInfo, rawPathInfo,
                                          requestMethod, responseLBS)
import           Yesod
import           Yesod.Core.Types        (YesodSubRunnerEnv (..))

data App = App

instance RenderRoute App where
    data Route App = OnlyGetR
                   | AnyMethodR
                   | HasParamR Int
                   | MySubsiteR (Route WaiSubsite)
        deriving (Show, Read, Eq)

    renderRoute OnlyGetR = (["only-get"], [])
    renderRoute AnyMethodR = (["any-method"], [])
    renderRoute (HasParamR i) = (["has-param", toPathPiece i], [])
    renderRoute (MySubsiteR subRoute) =
        let (ps, qs) = renderRoute subRoute
        in ("my-subsite" : ps, qs)
```

```
type Handler = HandlerT App IO

instance Yesod App

instance YesodDispatch App where
    yesodDispatch env req =
        case pathInfo req of
            ["only-get"] ->
                case requestMethod req of
                    "GET" -> yesodRunner
                        getOnlyGetR
                        env
                        (Just OnlyGetR)
                        req
                    _ -> yesodRunner
                        (badMethod >> return ())
                        env
                        (Just OnlyGetR)
                        req
            ["any-method"] ->
                yesodRunner handleAnyMethodR env (Just AnyMethodR) req
            ["has-param", t] | Just i <- fromPathPiece t ->
                case requestMethod req of
                    "GET" -> yesodRunner
                        (getHasParamR i)
                        env
                        (Just $ HasParamR i)
                        req
                    _ -> yesodRunner
                        (badMethod >> return ())
                        env
                        (Just $ HasParamR i)
                        req
            ("my-subsite":rest) -> yesodSubDispatch
                YesodSubRunnerEnv
                    { ysreGetSub = getMySubsite
                    , ysreParentRunner = yesodRunner
                    , ysreToParentRoute = MySubsiteR
                    , ysreParentEnv = env
                    }
                req { pathInfo = rest }
            _ -> yesodRunner (notFound >> return ()) env Nothing req

getOnlyGetR :: Handler Html
getOnlyGetR = defaultLayout
    [whamlet|
        <p>Accessed via GET method
        <form method=post action=@{AnyMethodR}>
            <button>POST to /any-method
    |]

handleAnyMethodR :: Handler Html
```

```
handleAnyMethodR = do
    req <- waiRequest
    defaultLayout
        [whamlet|
            <p>In any-method, method == #{show $ requestMethod req}
        |]

getHasParamR :: Int -> Handler String
getHasParamR i = return $ show i

getMySubsite :: App -> WaiSubsite
getMySubsite _ =
    WaiSubsite app
  where
    app req sendResponse = sendResponse $ responseLBS
        status200
        [("Content-Type", "text/plain")]
        $ L8.pack $ concat
            [ "pathInfo == "
            , show $ pathInfo req
            , ", rawPathInfo == "
            , show $ rawPathInfo req
            ]

main :: IO ()
main = warp 3000 App
```

Summary

Yesod abstracts away quite a bit of the plumbing from you as a developer. Most of this is boilerplate code that you'll be happy to ignore. But it can be empowering to understand exactly what's going on under the surface. At this point, you should hopefully be able—with help from the Haddocks—to write a site without any of the autogenerated Template Haskell code. Not that I'd recommend it; I think using the generated code is easier and safer.

One particular advantage of understanding this material is seeing where Yesod sits in the world of WAI. This makes it easier to see how Yesod will interact with WAI middleware, or how to include code from other WAI frameworks in a Yesod application (or vice versa!).

CHAPTER 19

SQL Joins

Persistent touts itself as a database-agnostic interface. How, then, are you supposed to do things that are inherently backend-specific? This most often comes up in Yesod when you want to join two tables together. There are some pure-Haskell solutions that are completely backend-agonistic, but there are also more efficient methods at our disposal. In this chapter, we'll introduce a common problem you might want to solve, and then build up more sophisticated solutions.

Multiauthor Blog

Blogs are a well-understood problem domain, so let's use that for our problem setup. Consider a blog engine that allows for multiple authors in the database, but supports blog posts that have a single author. In Persistent, we may model this as:

```
Author
    name Text
Blog
    author AuthorId
    title Text
    content Html
```

Let's set up our initial Yesod application to show a blog post index indicating the blog title and the author:

```
{-# LANGUAGE EmptyDataDecls             #-}
{-# LANGUAGE FlexibleContexts           #-}
{-# LANGUAGE GADTs                      #-}
{-# LANGUAGE GeneralizedNewtypeDeriving #-}
{-# LANGUAGE MultiParamTypeClasses      #-}
{-# LANGUAGE OverloadedStrings          #-}
{-# LANGUAGE QuasiQuotes                #-}
{-# LANGUAGE TemplateHaskell            #-}
{-# LANGUAGE TypeFamilies               #-}
```

```
{-# LANGUAGE ViewPatterns              #-}
import          Control.Monad.Logger
import          Data.Text              (Text)
import          Database.Persist.Sqlite
import          Yesod

share [mkPersist sqlSettings, mkMigrate "migrateAll"] [persistLowerCase|
Author
    name Text
Blog
    author AuthorId
    title Text
    content Html
|]

data App = App
    { persistConfig :: SqliteConf
    , connPool      :: ConnectionPool
    }
instance Yesod App
instance YesodPersist App where
    type YesodPersistBackend App = SqlBackend
    runDB = defaultRunDB persistConfig connPool
instance YesodPersistRunner App where
    getDBRunner = defaultGetDBRunner connPool

mkYesod "App" [parseRoutes|
/ HomeR GET
/blog/#BlogId BlogR GET
|]

getHomeR :: Handler Html
getHomeR = do
    blogs <- runDB $ selectList [] []

    defaultLayout $ do
        setTitle "Blog posts"
        [whamlet|
            <ul>
                $forall Entity blogid blog <- blogs
                    <li>
                        <a href=@{BlogR blogid}>
                            #{blogTitle blog} by #{show $ blogAuthor blog}
        |]

getBlogR :: BlogId -> Handler Html
getBlogR _ = error "Implementation left as exercise to reader"

main :: IO ()
main = do
    -- Use an in-memory database with 1 connection. Terrible for production,
    -- but useful for testing.
```

```
let conf = SqliteConf ":memory:" 1
pool <- createPoolConfig conf
flip runSqlPersistMPool pool $ do
    runMigration migrateAll

    -- Fill in some testing data
    alice <- insert $ Author "Alice"
    bob   <- insert $ Author "Bob"

    insert_ $ Blog alice "Alice's first post" "Hello, World!"
    insert_ $ Blog bob "Bob's first post" "Hello, World!!!"
    insert_ $ Blog alice "Alice's second post" "Goodbye, World!"

warp 3000 App
    { persistConfig = conf
    , connPool      = pool
    }
```

That's all well and good, but let's look at the output, shown in Figure 19-1.

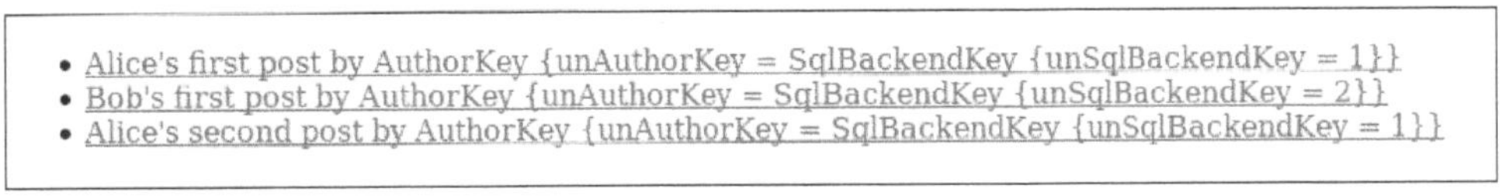

- Alice's first post by AuthorKey {unAuthorKey = SqlBackendKey {unSqlBackendKey = 1}}
- Bob's first post by AuthorKey {unAuthorKey = SqlBackendKey {unSqlBackendKey = 2}}
- Alice's second post by AuthorKey {unAuthorKey = SqlBackendKey {unSqlBackendKey = 1}}

Figure 19-1. Authors appear as numeric identifiers

All we're doing is displaying the numeric identifier of each author, instead of the author's name. In order to fix this, we need to pull extra information from the Author table as well. Let's dive into getting that done.

Database Queries in Widgets

I'll address this one right off the bat, as it catches many users by surprise. You might think that you can solve the problem of database queries in the Hamlet template itself. For example:

```
<ul>
    $forall Entity blogid blog <- blogs
        $with author <- runDB $ get404 $ blogAuthor
            <li>
                <a href=@{BlogR blogid}>
                    #{blogTitle blog} by #{authorName author}
```

However, this isn't allowed, because Hamlet will *not* allow you to run database actions inside of it. One of the goals of Shakespearean templates is to help you keep your pure and impure code separated, with the idea being that all impure code needs to stay in Haskell.

But we can actually tweak the preceding code to work in Yesod. The idea is to separate out the code for each blog entry into a `Widget` function, and then perform the database action in the Haskell portion of the function:

```
getHomeR :: Handler Html
getHomeR = do
    blogs <- runDB $ selectList [] []

    defaultLayout $ do
        setTitle "Blog posts"
        [whamlet|
            <ul>
                $forall blogEntity <- blogs
                    ^{showBlogLink blogEntity}
        |]

showBlogLink :: Entity Blog -> Widget
showBlogLink (Entity blogid blog) = do
    author <- handlerToWidget $ runDB $ get404 $ blogAuthor blog
    [whamlet|
        <li>
            <a href=@{BlogR blogid}>
                #{blogTitle blog} by #{authorName author}
    |]
```

We need to use `handlerToWidget` to turn our `Handler` action into a `Widget` action, but otherwise the code is straightforward. And furthermore, we now get exactly the output we wanted, as shown in Figure 19-2.

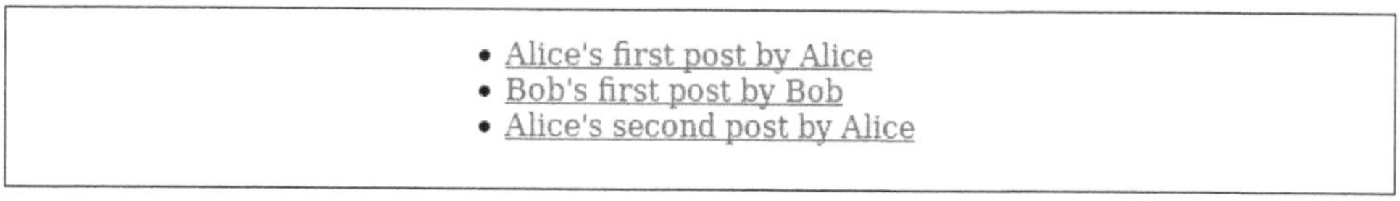

- Alice's first post by Alice
- Bob's first post by Bob
- Alice's second post by Alice

Figure 19-2. Authors appear as names

Joins

If we have the exact result we're looking for, why isn't this chapter over? The problem is that this technique is highly inefficient. We're performing one database query to load up all of the blog posts, then a separate query for each blog post to get the author names. This is far less efficient than simply using a SQL join. The question is: how do we do a join in Persistent? We'll start off by writing some raw SQL:

```
getHomeR :: Handler Html
getHomeR = do
    blogs <- runDB $ rawSql
        "SELECT ??, ?? \
        \FROM blog INNER JOIN author \
        \ON blog.author=author.id"
```

```
        []

    defaultLayout $ do
        setTitle "Blog posts"
        [whamlet|
            <ul>
                $forall (Entity blogid blog, Entity _ author) <- blogs
                    <li>
                        <a href=@{BlogR blogid}>
                            #{blogTitle blog} by #{authorName author}
        |]
```

We pass the `rawSql` function two parameters: a SQL query, and a list of additional parameters to replace placeholders in the query. That list is empty, because we're not using any placeholders. However, note that we're using ?? in our SELECT statement. This is a form of type inspection: `rawSql` will detect the type of entities being demanded and automatically fill in the fields that are necessary to make the query.

`rawSql` is certainly powerful, but it's also unsafe. There's no syntax checking on your SQL query string, so you can get runtime errors. Also, it's easy to end up querying for the wrong type, resulting in some very confusing runtime error messages.

Esqueleto

Persistent has a companion library called Esqueleto (*http://hackage.haskell.org/pack age/esqueleto*) that provides an expressive, type-safe DSL for writing SQL queries. It takes advantage of the Persistent types to ensure it generates valid SQL queries and produces the results requested by the program. In order to use Esqueleto, we're going to add some imports:

```
import qualified Database.Esqueleto    as E
import           Database.Esqueleto    ((^.))
```

We can then write our query using Esqueleto as follows:

```
getHomeR :: Handler Html
getHomeR = do
    blogs <- runDB
            $ E.select
            $ E.from $ \(blog `E.InnerJoin` author) -> do
                E.on $ blog ^. BlogAuthor E.==. author ^. AuthorId
                return
                    ( blog    ^. BlogId
                    , blog    ^. BlogTitle
                    , author ^. AuthorName
                    )

    defaultLayout $ do
        setTitle "Blog posts"
        [whamlet|
```

```
<ul>
    $forall (E.Value blogid, E.Value title, E.Value name) <- blogs
        <li>
            <a href=@{BlogR blogid}>#{title} by #{name}
|]
```

Notice how similar the query looks to the SQL we wrote previously. One thing of particular interest is the \^. operator, which is a *projection*. blog ^. BlogAuthor, for example, means "take the author column of the blog table." And thanks to the type safety of Esqueleto, you could never accidentally project AuthorName from blog: the type system will stop you!

In addition to safety, there's also a performance advantage to Esqueleto. Notice the returned tuple; it explicitly lists the three columns that we need to generate our listing. This can provide a huge performance boost: unlike all other examples we've had, this one does not require transferring the (potentially quite large) content column of the blog post to generate the listing.

 For the record, it's possible to achieve this with rawSql as well (it's just a bit trickier).

Esqueleto is really the gold standard in writing SQL queries in Persistent. The rule of thumb should be: if you're doing something that fits naturally into Persistent's query syntax, use Persistent, as it's database-agnostic and a bit easier to use. But if you're doing something that would be more efficient with a SQL-specific feature, you should strongly consider Esqueleto.

Streaming

There's still a problem with our Esqueleto approach. If there are thousands of blog posts, then the workflow will be:

1. Read thousands of blog posts into memory on the server.
2. Render out the entire HTML page.
3. Send the HTML page to the client.

This has two downsides: it uses a lot of memory, and it results in high latency for the user. If this is a bad approach, why does Yesod gear you toward it out of the box, instead of following a streaming approach? Two reasons:

Correctness

Imagine if there was an error reading the 243rd record from the database. By sending a non-streaming response, Yesod can catch the exception and send a meaningful 500 error response. If we were already streaming, the streaming body would simply stop in the middle of a misleading 200 OK response.

Ease of use

It's usually easier to work with non-streaming bodies.

The standard recommendation I'd give someone who wants to generate listings that may be large is to use pagination. This allows you to do less work on the server, write simple code, get the correctness guarantees Yesod provides out of the box, and reduce user latency. However, there are times when you'll really want to generate a streaming response, so let's cover that here.

Switching Esqueleto to a streaming response is easy: replace select with select Source. The Esqueleto query itself remains unchanged. Then we'll use the respond SourceDB function to generate a streaming database response, and manually construct our HTML to wrap up the listing:

```
getHomeR :: Handler TypedContent
getHomeR = do
    let blogsSrc =
            E.selectSource
        $ E.from $ \(blog `E.InnerJoin` author) -> do
            E.on $ blog ^. BlogAuthor E.==. author ^. AuthorId
            return
                ( blog    ^. BlogId
                , blog    ^. BlogTitle
                , author ^. AuthorName
                )

    render <- getUrlRenderParams
    respondSourceDB typeHtml $ do
        sendChunkText "<html><head><title>Blog posts</title></head><body><ul>"
        blogsSrc $= CL.map (\(E.Value blogid, E.Value title, E.Value name) ->
            toFlushBuilder $
            [hamlet|
                <li>
                    <a href=@{BlogR blogid}>#{title} by #{name}
            |] render
            )
        sendChunkText "</ul></body></html>"
```

Notice the usage of sendChunkText, which sends some raw Text values over the network. We then take each of our blog tuples and use conduit's map function to create a streaming value. We use hamlet to get templating, and then pass in our render function to convert the type-safe URLs into their textual versions. Finally, toFlush

Builder converts our `Html` value into a `Flush Builder` value, as needed by Yesod's streaming framework.

Unfortunately, we're no longer able to take advantage of Hamlet to do our overall page layout, as we need to explicitly generate start and end tags separately. This introduces another point for possible bugs, if we accidentally create unbalanced tags. We also lose the ability to use `defaultLayout`, for exactly the same reason.

Streaming HTML responses are a powerful tool, and are sometimes necessary. But generally speaking, I'd recommend sticking to safer options.

Summary

This chapter covered a number of ways of doing a SQL join:

- Avoid the join entirely, and manually grab the associated data in Haskell. This is also known as an application-level join.

- Write the SQL explicitly with `rawSql`. This is somewhat convenient, but it loses a lot of Persistent's type safety.

- Use Esqueleto's DSL functionality to create a type-safe SQL query.

- If you need it, you can even generate a streaming response from Esqueleto.

  For completeness, here's the entire body of the final, streaming example:

```
{-# LANGUAGE EmptyDataDecls            #-}
{-# LANGUAGE FlexibleContexts          #-}
{-# LANGUAGE GADTs                     #-}
{-# LANGUAGE GeneralizedNewtypeDeriving #-}
{-# LANGUAGE MultiParamTypeClasses     #-}
{-# LANGUAGE OverloadedStrings         #-}
{-# LANGUAGE QuasiQuotes               #-}
{-# LANGUAGE TemplateHaskell           #-}
{-# LANGUAGE TypeFamilies              #-}
{-# LANGUAGE ViewPatterns              #-}
import                Control.Monad.Logger
import                Data.Text           (Text)
import qualified Database.Esqueleto     as E
import                Database.Esqueleto  ((^.))
import                Database.Persist.Sqlite
import                Yesod
import qualified Data.Conduit.List as CL
import Data.Conduit (($=))

share [mkPersist sqlSettings, mkMigrate "migrateAll"] [persistLowerCase|
Author
    name Text
Blog
    author AuthorId
```

```
    title Text
    content Html
|]

data App = App
    { persistConfig :: SqliteConf
    , connPool      :: ConnectionPool
    }
instance Yesod App
instance YesodPersist App where
    type YesodPersistBackend App = SqlBackend
    runDB = defaultRunDB persistConfig connPool
instance YesodPersistRunner App where
    getDBRunner = defaultGetDBRunner connPool

mkYesod "App" [parseRoutes|
/ HomeR GET
/blog/#BlogId BlogR GET
|]

getHomeR :: Handler TypedContent
getHomeR = do
    let blogsSrc =
            E.selectSource
          $ E.from $ \(blog `E.InnerJoin` author) -> do
                E.on $ blog ^. BlogAuthor E.==. author ^. AuthorId
                return
                    ( blog   ^. BlogId
                    , blog   ^. BlogTitle
                    , author ^. AuthorName
                    )

    render <- getUrlRenderParams
    respondSourceDB typeHtml $ do
        sendChunkText "<html><head><title>Blog posts</title></head><body><ul>"
        blogsSrc $= CL.map (\(E.Value blogid, E.Value title, E.Value name) ->
            toFlushBuilder $
            [hamlet|
                <li>
                    <a href=@{BlogR blogid}>#{title} by #{name}
            |] render
            )
        sendChunkText "</ul></body></html>"

getBlogR :: BlogId -> Handler Html
getBlogR _ = error "Implementation left as exercise to reader"

main :: IO ()
main = do
    -- Use an in-memory database with 1 connection. Terrible for production,
    -- but useful for testing.
    let conf = SqliteConf ":memory:" 1
```

```
    pool <- createPoolConfig conf
    flip runSqlPersistMPool pool $ do
        runMigration migrateAll

        -- Fill in some testing data
        alice <- insert $ Author "Alice"
        bob   <- insert $ Author "Bob"

        insert_ $ Blog alice "Alice's first post" "Hello, World!"
        insert_ $ Blog bob "Bob's first post" "Hello, World!!!"
        insert_ $ Blog alice "Alice's second post" "Goodbye, World!"

    warp 3000 App
        { persistConfig = conf
        , connPool      = pool
        }
```

CHAPTER 20

Yesod for Haskellers

The majority of this book is built around giving practical information on how to get common tasks done, without drilling too much into the details of what's going on under the surface. This book presumes knowledge of Haskell, but it does not follow the typical style of many introductions to Haskell libraries. Many seasoned Haskellers may be put off by this hiding of implementation details. The purpose of this chapter is to address those concerns. We'll start off with a bare-minimum web application and build up to more complicated examples, explaining the components and their types along the way.

Hello, Warp

Let's start off with the most bare-minimum application I can think of:

```
{-# LANGUAGE OverloadedStrings #-}
import         Network.HTTP.Types         (status200)
import         Network.Wai                (Application, responseLBS)
import         Network.Wai.Handler.Warp   (run)

main :: IO ()
main = run 3000 app

app :: Application
app _req sendResponse = sendResponse $ responseLBS
    status200
    [("Content-Type", "text/plain")]
    "Hello, Warp!"
```

Wait a minute, there's no Yesod in there! Don't worry, we'll get there. Remember, we're building from the ground up, and in Yesod the ground floor is WAI, the Web Application Interface. WAI sits between a web *handler*, such as a web server or a test framework, and a web *application*. In our case, the handler is Warp, a high-performance web server, and our application is the app function.

What's this mysterious Application type? It's a type synonym defined as:

```
type Application = Request
                -> (Response -> IO ResponseReceived)
                -> IO ResponseReceived
```

The Request value contains information such as the requested path, query string, request headers, request body, and the IP address of the client. The second argument is the "send response" function. Instead of simply having the application return an IO Response, WAI uses continuation passing style (CPS) to allow for full exception safety, similar to how the bracket function works.

We can use this to do some simple dispatching:

```
{-# LANGUAGE OverloadedStrings #-}
import            Network.HTTP.Types       (status200)
import            Network.Wai              (Application, pathInfo, responseLBS)
import            Network.Wai.Handler.Warp (run)

main :: IO ()
main = run 3000 app

app :: Application
app req sendResponse =
    case pathInfo req of
        ["foo", "bar"] -> sendResponse $ responseLBS
            status200
            [("Content-Type", "text/plain")]
            "You requested /foo/bar"
        _ -> sendResponse $ responseLBS
            status200
            [("Content-Type", "text/plain")]
            "You requested something else"
```

WAI mandates that the path be split into individual fragments (the stuff between forward slashes) and converted into text. This allows for easy pattern matching. If you need the original, unmodified ByteString, you can use rawPathInfo. For more information on the available fields, see the WAI Haddocks.

That addresses the request side; what about responses? We've already seen responseLBS, which is a convenient way of creating a response from a lazy ByteString. That function takes three arguments: the status code, a list of response headers (as key/value pairs), and the body itself. But responseLBS is just a convenience wrapper. Under the surface, WAI uses blaze-builder's Builder data type to represent the raw bytes. Let's dig down another level and use that directly:

```
{-# LANGUAGE OverloadedStrings #-}
import            Blaze.ByteString.Builder (Builder, fromByteString)
```

```
import          Network.HTTP.Types       (status200)
import          Network.Wai              (Application, responseBuilder)
import          Network.Wai.Handler.Warp (run)

main :: IO ()
main = run 3000 app

app :: Application
app _req sendResponse = sendResponse $ responseBuilder
    status200
    [("Content-Type", "text/plain")]
    (fromByteString "Hello from blaze-builder!" :: Builder)
```

This opens up some nice opportunities for efficiently building up response bodies, as Builder allows for O(1) append operations. We're also able to take advantage of blaze-html, which sits on top of blaze-builder. Let's take a look at our first HTML application:

```
{-# LANGUAGE OverloadedStrings #-}
import          Network.HTTP.Types               (status200)
import          Network.Wai                      (Application, responseBuilder)
import          Network.Wai.Handler.Warp         (run)
import          Text.Blaze.Html.Renderer.Utf8    (renderHtmlBuilder)
import          Text.Blaze.Html5                 (Html, docTypeHtml)
import qualified Text.Blaze.Html5                as H

main :: IO ()
main = run 3000 app

app :: Application
app _req sendResponse = sendResponse $ responseBuilder
    status200
    [("Content-Type", "text/html")] -- yay!
    (renderHtmlBuilder myPage)

myPage :: Html
myPage = docTypeHtml $ do
    H.head $ do
        H.title "Hello from blaze-html and Warp"
    H.body $ do
        H.h1 "Hello from blaze-html and Warp"
```

There's a limitation with using a pure Builder value: we need to create the entire response body before returning the Response value. With lazy evaluation, that's not as bad as it sounds, because not all of the body will live in memory at once. However, if we need to perform some I/O to generate our response body (such as reading data from a database), we'll be in trouble.

To deal with that situation, WAI provides a means for generating streaming response bodies. It also allows explicit control of flushing the stream. Let's see how this works:

```
{-# LANGUAGE OverloadedStrings #-}
import          Blaze.ByteString.Builder          (Builder, fromByteString)
import          Blaze.ByteString.Builder.Char.Utf8 (fromShow)
import          Control.Concurrent                (threadDelay)
import          Control.Monad                     (forM_)
import          Control.Monad.Trans.Class         (lift)
import          Data.Monoid                       ((<>))
import          Network.HTTP.Types                (status200)
import          Network.Wai                       (Application,
                                                   responseStream)
import          Network.Wai.Handler.Warp          (run)

main :: IO ()
main = run 3000 app

app :: Application
app _req sendResponse = sendResponse $ responseStream
    status200
    [("Content-Type", "text/plain")]
    myStream

myStream :: (Builder -> IO ()) -> IO () -> IO ()
myStream send flush = do
    send $ fromByteString "Starting streaming response.\n"
    send $ fromByteString "Performing some I/O.\n"
    flush
    -- pretend we're performing some I/O
    threadDelay 1000000
    send $ fromByteString "I/O performed, here are some results.\n"
    forM_ [1..50 :: Int] $ \i -> do
        send $ fromByteString "Got the value: " <>
               fromShow i <>
               fromByteString "\n"
```

 WAI previously relied on the conduit library for its streaming data abstraction, but has since gotten rid of that dependency. However, conduit is still well supported in the WAI ecosystem, via the wai-conduit helper package.

Another common requirement when dealing with a streaming response is safely allocating a scarce resource, such as a file handle. By *safely*, I mean ensuring that the response will be released, even in the case of some exception. This is where the continuation passing style mentioned earlier comes into play:

```
{-# LANGUAGE OverloadedStrings #-}
import          Blaze.ByteString.Builder  (fromByteString)
import qualified Data.ByteString           as S
import          Data.Conduit              (Flush (Chunk), ($=))
import          Data.Conduit.Binary       (sourceHandle)
import qualified Data.Conduit.List         as CL
```

```
import          Network.HTTP.Types      (status200)
import          Network.Wai             (Application, responseStream)
import          Network.Wai.Handler.Warp (run)
import          System.IO               (IOMode (ReadMode), withFile)

main :: IO ()
main = run 3000 app

app :: Application
app _req sendResponse = withFile "index.html" ReadMode $ \handle ->
    sendResponse $ responseStream
        status200
        [("Content-Type", "text/html")]
        $ \send _flush ->
            let loop = do
                    bs <- S.hGet handle 4096
                    if S.null bs
                        then return ()
                        else send (fromByteString bs) >> loop
            in loop
```

Notice how we're able to take advantage of existing exception-safe functions like withFile to deal with exceptions properly.

But in the case of serving files, it's more efficient to use responseFile, which can use the sendfile system call to avoid unnecessary buffer copies:

```
{-# LANGUAGE OverloadedStrings #-}
import          Network.HTTP.Types      (status200)
import          Network.Wai             (Application, responseFile)
import          Network.Wai.Handler.Warp (run)

main :: IO ()
main = run 3000 app

app :: Application
app _req sendResponse = sendResponse $ responseFile
    status200
    [("Content-Type", "text/html")]
    "index.html"
    Nothing -- means "serve whole file"
            -- you can also serve specific ranges in the file
```

There are many aspects of WAI we haven't covered here. One important topic is WAI middlewares. We also haven't inspected request bodies at all. But for the purposes of understanding Yesod, we've covered enough for the moment.

What About Yesod?

In all our excitement about WAI and Warp, we still haven't seen anything about Yesod! We just learned all about WAI, so our first question should be: how does Yesod interact with WAI? The answer to that is one very important function:

```
toWaiApp :: YesodDispatch site => site -> IO Application
```

 There's an even more basic function in Yesod, called `toWaiApp Plain`. The distinction is that `toWaiAppPlain` doesn't install any additional WAI middlewares, while `toWaiApp` provides commonly used middlewares for logging, gzip compression, HEAD request method handling, etc.

This function takes some `site` value, which must be an instance of `YesodDispatch`, and creates an `Application`. The function lives in the `IO` monad, because it will likely perform actions like allocating a shared logging buffer. The more interesting question is what this `site` value is all about.

Yesod has a concept of a *foundation data type*. This is a data type at the core of each application, and is used in three important ways:

- It can hold onto values that are initialized and shared amongst all aspects of your application, such as an HTTP connection manager, a database connection pool, settings loaded from a file, or some shared mutable state like a counter or cache.

- Typeclass instances provide even more information about your application. The `Yesod` typeclass has various settings, such as what the default template of your app should be, or the maximum allowed request body size. The `YesodDispatch` class indicates how incoming requests should be dispatched to handler functions. And there are a number of typeclasses commonly used in Yesod helper libraries, such as `RenderMessage` for i18n support or `YesodJquery` for providing the shared location of the jQuery JavaScript library.

- Associated types (i.e., type families) are used to create a related *route data type* for each application. This is a simple algebraic data type that represents all legal routes in your application. By using this intermediate data type instead of dealing directly with strings, Yesod applications can take advantage of the compiler to prevent creating invalid links. This feature is known as *type-safe URLs*.

In keeping with the spirit of this chapter, we're going to create our first Yesod application the hard way, by writing everything manually. We'll progressively add more convenience helpers on top as we go along:

```
{-# LANGUAGE OverloadedStrings #-}
{-# LANGUAGE TypeFamilies      #-}
```

```
import              Network.HTTP.Types            (status200)
import              Network.Wai                   (responseBuilder)
import              Network.Wai.Handler.Warp      (run)
import              Text.Blaze.Html.Renderer.Utf8 (renderHtmlBuilder)
import qualified Text.Blaze.Html5              as H
import              Yesod.Core                    (Html, RenderRoute (..), Yesod,
                                                   YesodDispatch (..), toWaiApp)
import              Yesod.Core.Types              (YesodRunnerEnv (..))

-- | Our foundation data type
data App = App
    { welcomeMessage :: !Html
    }

instance Yesod App

instance RenderRoute App where
    data Route App = HomeR -- just one accepted URL
        deriving (Show, Read, Eq, Ord)

    renderRoute HomeR = ( [] -- empty path info, means "/"
                        , [] -- empty query string
                        )
instance YesodDispatch App where
    yesodDispatch
      (YesodRunnerEnv _logger site _sessionBackend _)
      _req
      sendResponse =
        sendResponse $ responseBuilder
            status200
            [("Content-Type", "text/html")]
            (renderHtmlBuilder $ welcomeMessage site)

main :: IO ()
main = do
    -- We could get this message from a file instead if we wanted.
    let welcome = H.p "Welcome to Yesod!"
    waiApp <- toWaiApp App
        { welcomeMessage = welcome
        }
    run 3000 waiApp
```

OK, we've added quite a few new pieces here, so let's attack them one at a time. First
we created a new data type, App. This is commonly used as the foundation data type
name for each application, though you're free to use whatever name you want. We've
added one field to this data type, welcomeMessage, which will hold the content for our
homepage.

Next, we declare our Yesod instance. We just use the default values for all of the
methods for this example. More interesting is the RenderRoute typeclass. This is the

heart of type-safe URLs. We create an associated data type for App that lists all of our app's accepted routes. In this case, we have just one: the homepage, which we call HomeR. It's yet another Yesod naming convention to append R to all of the route data constructors.

We also need to create a renderRoute method, which converts each type-safe route value into a tuple of path pieces and query string parameters. We'll get to more interesting examples later, but for now, our homepage has an empty list for both of those.

YesodDispatch determines how our application behaves. It has one method, yesod Dispatch, of type:

```
yesodDispatch :: YesodRunnerEnv site -> Application
```

YesodRunnerEnv provides three values: a Logger value for outputting log messages, the foundation data type value itself, and a session backend used for storing and retrieving information for the user's active session. In real Yesod applications, as you'll see shortly, you don't need to interact with these values directly, but it's informative to understand what's under the surface.

The return type of yesodDispatch is Application from WAI. But as we saw earlier, Application is simply a CPSed function from Request to Response. So, our implementation of yesodDispatch is able to use everything we've learned about WAI. Notice also how we accessed the welcomeMessage from our foundation data type.

Finally, we have the main function. The App value is easy to create, and as you can see, you could just as easily have performed some I/O to acquire the welcome message. We use toWaiApp to obtain a WAI application and then pass off our application to Warp, just like we did in the past.

Congratulations! You've now seen your first Yesod application (or at least, your first Yesod application in this chapter).

The HandlerT Monad Transformer

The preceding example was technically using Yesod, but it wasn't incredibly inspiring. In fact, Yesod did nothing more than get in our way relative to WAI. And that's because we haven't started taking advantage of any of Yesod's features. Let's address that, starting with the HandlerT monad transformer.

There are many common things you'll want to do when handling a single request, including the following:

- Return some HTML.
- Redirect to a different URL.
- Return a 404 Not Found response.

- Do some logging.

To encapsulate all of this common functionality, Yesod provides a `HandlerT` monad transformer. The vast majority of the code you write in Yesod will live in this transformer, so you should get acquainted with it. Let's start off by replacing our previous `YesodDispatch` instance with a new one that takes advantage of `HandlerT`:

```haskell
{-# LANGUAGE OverloadedStrings #-}
{-# LANGUAGE TypeFamilies      #-}
import           Network.Wai              (pathInfo)
import           Network.Wai.Handler.Warp (run)
import qualified Text.Blaze.Html5         as H
import           Yesod.Core               (HandlerT, Html, RenderRoute (..),
                                           Yesod, YesodDispatch (..), getYesod,
                                           notFound, toWaiApp, yesodRunner)

-- | Our foundation data type
data App = App
    { welcomeMessage :: !Html
    }

instance Yesod App

instance RenderRoute App where
    data Route App = HomeR -- just one accepted URL
        deriving (Show, Read, Eq, Ord)

    renderRoute HomeR = ( [] -- empty path info, means "/"
                        , [] -- empty query string
                        )

getHomeR :: HandlerT App IO Html
getHomeR = do
    site <- getYesod
    return $ welcomeMessage site

instance YesodDispatch App where
    yesodDispatch yesodRunnerEnv req sendResponse =
        let maybeRoute =
                case pathInfo req of
                    [] -> Just HomeR
                    _  -> Nothing
            handler =
                case maybeRoute of
                    Nothing -> notFound
                    Just HomeR -> getHomeR
         in yesodRunner handler yesodRunnerEnv maybeRoute req sendResponse

main :: IO ()
main = do
    -- We could get this message from a file instead if we wanted.
```

```
let welcome = H.p "Welcome to Yesod!"
waiApp <- toWaiApp App
    { welcomeMessage = welcome
    }
run 3000 waiApp
```

getHomeR is our first handler function. (That name is yet another naming convention in the Yesod world: the lowercase HTTP request method, followed by the route constructor name.) Notice its signature: HandlerT App IO Html. It's so common to have the monad stack HandlerT App IO that most applications have a type synonym for it, type Handler = HandlerT App IO. The function is returning some Html. You might be wondering if Yesod is hardcoded to only work with Html values. I'll explain that detail in a moment.

Our function body is short. We use the getYesod function to get the foundation data type value, and then return the welcomeMessage field. We'll build up more interesting handlers as we continue.

The implementation of yesodDispatch is now quite different. The key to it is the yesodRunner function, which is a low-level function for converting HandlerT stacks into WAI Applications. Let's look at its type signature:

```
yesodRunner :: (ToTypedContent res, Yesod site)
            => HandlerT site IO res
            -> YesodRunnerEnv site
            -> Maybe (Route site)
            -> Application
```

We're already familiar with YesodRunnerEnv from our previous example. As you can see in our call to yesodRunner, we pass that value in unchanged. The Maybe (Route site) is a bit interesting, and gives us more insight into how type-safe URLs work. Until now, we've only seen the rendering side of these URLs. But just as important is the *parsing* side: converting a requested path into a route value. In our example, this code is just a few lines, and we store the result in maybeRoute.

 It's true that our current parse function is small, but in a larger application it would need to be more complex, also dealing with issues like dynamic parameters. At that point, it becomes a nontrivial endeavor to ensure that our parsing and rendering functions remain in proper alignment. We'll discuss how Yesod deals with that later.

Coming back to the parameters to yesodRunner: we've now addressed the Maybe (Route site) and YesodRunerEnv site. To get our HandlerT site IO res value, we pattern match on maybeRoute. If it's Just HomeR, we use getHomeR. Otherwise, we use the notFound function, which is a built-in function that returns a 404 Not Found response, using your default site template. That template can be overridden in the Yesod typeclass; out of the box, it's just a boring HTML page.

This almost all makes sense, except for one issue: what's that `ToTypedContent` typeclass, and what does it have to do with our `Html` response? Let's start by answering that earlier question: no, Yesod does *not* in any way hardcode support for `Html`. A handler function can return any value that has an instance of `ToTypedContent`. This typeclass (which we will examine in a moment) provides both a MIME type and a representation of the data that WAI can consume. `yesodRunner` then converts that into a WAI response, setting the `Content-Type` response header to the MIME type, using a 200 OK status code, and sending the response body.

(To)Content, (To)TypedContent

At the very core of Yesod's content system are the following types:

```
data Content = ContentBuilder !Builder !(Maybe Int)
             -- ^ The content and optional content length.
           | ContentSource !(Source (ResourceT IO) (Flush Builder))
           | ContentFile !FilePath !(Maybe FilePart)
           | ContentDontEvaluate !Content

type ContentType = ByteString
data TypedContent = TypedContent !ContentType !Content
```

`Content` should remind you a bit of the WAI response types. `ContentBuilder` is similar to `responseBuilder`, `ContentSource` is like `responseStream` but specialized to conduit, and `ContentFile` is like `responseFile`. Unlike their WAI counterparts, none of these constructors contain information on the status code or response headers; that's handled orthogonally in Yesod.

The one completely new constructor is `ContentDontEvaluate`. By default, when you create a response body in Yesod, Yesod fully evaluates the body before generating the response. The reason for this is to ensure that there are no impure exceptions in your value. Yesod wants to make sure to catch any such exceptions before starting to send your response so that, if there *is* an exception, it can generate a proper 500 Internal Server Error response instead of simply dying in the middle of sending a non-error response. However, performing this evaluation can cause more memory usage. Therefore, Yesod provides a means of opting out of this protection.

`TypedContent` is then a minor addition to `Content`: it includes the `ContentType` as well. Together with a convention that an application returns a 200 OK status unless otherwise specified, we have everything we need from the `TypedContent` type to create a response.

Although Yesod *could* have required users to always return `TypedContent` from a handler function, that approach would have required manually converting to that

type. Instead, Yesod uses a pair of typeclasses for this, appropriately named ToCon
tent and ToTypedContent. They have exactly the definitions you'd expect:

```
class ToContent a where
    toContent :: a -> Content
class ToContent a => ToTypedContent a where
    toTypedContent :: a -> TypedContent
```

And Yesod provides instances for many common data types, including Text, Html,
and the aeson library's Value type (containing JSON data). That's how the getHomeR
function was able to return Html: Yesod knows how to convert it to TypedContent,
and from there it can be converted into a WAI response.

HasContentType and Representations

This typeclass approach allows for one other nice abstraction. For many types, the
type system itself lets us know what the content type for the content should be. For
example, Html will always be served with a text/html content type.

This isn't true for all instance of ToTypedContent. For a counterex-
ample, consider the ToTypedContent TypedContent instance.

Some requests to a web application can be displayed with various *representations*. For
example, a request for tabular data could be served with:

- An HTML table
- A CSV file
- XML
- JSON data to be consumed by some client-side JavaScript

The HTTP spec allows a client to specify its preference of representation via the
Accept request header. And Yesod allows a handler function to use the selectRep/
provideRep function combo to provide multiple representations, and have the framework automatically choose the appropriate one based on the client headers.

The last missing piece to make this all work is the HasContentType typeclass:

```
class ToTypedContent a => HasContentType a where
    getContentType :: Monad m => m a -> ContentType
```

The parameter m a is just a poor man's Proxy type. And, in hindsight, we should have
used Proxy, but that would now be a breaking change. There are instances for this

typeclass for most data types supported by ToTypedContent. Here is our previous example, tweaked just a bit to provide multiple representations of the data:

```haskell
{-# LANGUAGE OverloadedStrings #-}
{-# LANGUAGE TypeFamilies      #-}
import            Data.Text             (Text)
import            Network.Wai           (pathInfo)
import            Network.Wai.Handler.Warp (run)
import qualified  Text.Blaze.Html5      as H
import            Yesod.Core            (HandlerT, Html, RenderRoute (..),
                                         TypedContent, Value, Yesod,
                                         YesodDispatch (..), getYesod,
                                         notFound, object, provideRep,
                                         selectRep, toWaiApp, yesodRunner,
                                         (.=))

-- | Our foundation data type
data App = App
    { welcomeMessageHtml :: !Html
    , welcomeMessageText :: !Text
    , welcomeMessageJson :: !Value
    }

instance Yesod App

instance RenderRoute App where
    data Route App = HomeR -- just one accepted URL
        deriving (Show, Read, Eq, Ord)

    renderRoute HomeR = ( [] -- empty path info, means "/"
                        , [] -- empty query string
                        )

getHomeR :: HandlerT App IO TypedContent
getHomeR = do
    site <- getYesod
    selectRep $ do
        provideRep $ return $ welcomeMessageHtml site
        provideRep $ return $ welcomeMessageText site
        provideRep $ return $ welcomeMessageJson site

instance YesodDispatch App where
    yesodDispatch yesodRunnerEnv req sendResponse =
        let maybeRoute =
                case pathInfo req of
                    [] -> Just HomeR
                    _  -> Nothing
            handler =
                case maybeRoute of
                    Nothing -> notFound
                    Just HomeR -> getHomeR
        in yesodRunner handler yesodRunnerEnv maybeRoute req sendResponse
```

```
main :: IO ()
main = do
    waiApp <- toWaiApp App
        { welcomeMessageHtml = H.p "Welcome to Yesod!"
        , welcomeMessageText = "Welcome to Yesod!"
        , welcomeMessageJson = object ["msg" .= ("Welcome to Yesod!" :: Text)]
        }
    run 3000 waiApp
```

Convenience warp Function

One minor convenience you'll see quite a bit in the Yesod world: it's very common to call toWaiApp to create a WAI Application and then pass that to Warp's run function, so Yesod provides a convenience warp wrapper function. We can therefore replace our previous main function with the following:

```
main :: IO ()
main =
    warp 3000 App
        { welcomeMessageHtml = H.p "Welcome to Yesod!"
        , welcomeMessageText = "Welcome to Yesod!"
        , welcomeMessageJson = object ["msg" .= ("Welcome to Yesod!" :: Text)]
        }
```

There's also a warpEnv function that reads the port number from the PORT environment variable, which is useful for working with platforms such as FP Haskell Center or deployment tools like Keter.

Writing Handlers

The vast majority of your application will end up living in the HandlerT monad transformer, so it's not surprising that there are quite a few functions that work in that context. HandlerT is an instance of many common typeclasses, including MonadIO, MonadTrans, MonadBaseControl, MonadLogger, and MonadResource, and so can automatically take advantage of those functionalities.

In addition to that standard functionality, the following are some common categories of functions. The only requirement Yesod places on your handler functions is that, ultimately, they return a type that is an instance of ToTypedContent.

This section is just a short overview of functionality. For more information, you should either look through the Haddocks or read the rest of this book.

Getting Request Parameters

There are a few pieces of information provided by the client in a request:

- The requested path. This is usually handled by Yesod's routing framework, and is not directly queried in a handler function.

- Query string parameters. These can be queried using `lookupGetParam`.

- Request bodies. In the case of URL-encoded and multipart bodies, you can use `lookupPostParam` to get the request parameter. For multipart bodies, there's also `lookupFile` for file parameters.

- Request headers can be queried via `lookupHeader`. (And response headers can be set with `addHeader`.)

- Yesod parses cookies for you automatically, and they can be queried using `lookupCookie`. (Cookies can be set via the `setCookie` function.)

- Finally, Yesod provides a user session framework, where data can be set in a cryptographically secure session and associated with each user. This can be queried and set using the functions `lookupSession`, `setSession`, and `deleteSession`.

Although you can use these functions directly for such purposes as processing forms, you usually will want to use the `yesod-form` library, which provides a higher-level form abstraction based on applicative functors.

Short-Circuiting

In some cases, you'll want to short-circuit the handling of a request. Reasons for doing this would be:

- Sending an HTTP redirect via the `redirect` function. This will default to using the 303 status code. You can use `redirectWith` to get more control over this.

- Returning a 404 Not Found with `notFound`, or a 405 Bad Method via `badMethod`.

- Indicating some error in the request via `notAuthenticated`, `permissionDenied`, or `invalidArgs`.

- Sending a special response, such as with `sendFile` or `sendResponseStatus` (to override the status 200 response code)

- Using `sendWaiResponse` to drop down a level of abstraction, bypass some Yesod abstractions, and use WAI itself.

Streaming

So far, the examples of `ToTypedContent` instances we've seen have all involved non-streaming responses. `Html`, `Text`, and `Value` all get converted into a `ContentBuilder` constructor. As such, they cannot interleave I/O with sending data to the user. What happens if we want to perform such interleaving?

When we encountered this issue in WAI, we introduced the `responseSource` method of constructing a response. Using `sendWaiResponse`, we could reuse that same method for creating a streaming response in Yesod. But there's also a simpler API for doing this: `respondSource`. The `respondSource` API takes two parameters: the content type of the response, and a `Source` of `Flush Builder`. Yesod also provides a number of convenience functions for creating that `Source`, such as `sendChunk`, `sendChunkBS`, and `sendChunkText`.

Here's an example, which just converts our initial `responseSource` example from WAI to Yesod:

```
{-# LANGUAGE OverloadedStrings #-}
{-# LANGUAGE TypeFamilies      #-}
import          Blaze.ByteString.Builder            (fromByteString)
import          Blaze.ByteString.Builder.Char.Utf8  (fromShow)
import          Control.Concurrent                  (threadDelay)
import          Control.Monad                       (forM_)
import          Data.Monoid                         ((<>))
import          Network.Wai                         (pathInfo)
import          Yesod.Core                          (HandlerT, RenderRoute (..),
                                                     TypedContent, Yesod,
                                                     YesodDispatch (..), liftIO,
                                                     notFound, respondSource,
                                                     sendChunk, sendChunkBS,
                                                     sendChunkText, sendFlush,
                                                     warp, yesodRunner)

-- | Our foundation data type
data App = App

instance Yesod App

instance RenderRoute App where
    data Route App = HomeR -- just one accepted URL
        deriving (Show, Read, Eq, Ord)

    renderRoute HomeR = ( [] -- empty path info, means "/"
                        , [] -- empty query string
                        )

getHomeR :: HandlerT App IO TypedContent
getHomeR = respondSource "text/plain" $ do
    sendChunkBS "Starting streaming response.\n"
    sendChunkText "Performing some I/O.\n"
    sendFlush
    -- pretend we're performing some I/O
    liftIO $ threadDelay 1000000
    sendChunkBS "I/O performed, here are some results.\n"
    forM_ [1..50 :: Int] $ \i -> do
        sendChunk $ fromByteString "Got the value: " <>
                    fromShow i <>
```

```
                        fromByteString "\n"

    instance YesodDispatch App where
        yesodDispatch yesodRunnerEnv req sendResponse =
            let maybeRoute =
                    case pathInfo req of
                        [] -> Just HomeR
                        _  -> Nothing
                handler =
                    case maybeRoute of
                        Nothing -> notFound
                        Just HomeR -> getHomeR
             in yesodRunner handler yesodRunnerEnv maybeRoute req sendResponse

    main :: IO ()
    main = warp 3000 App
```

Dynamic Parameters

Now that we've finished our detour into the details of the HandlerT transformer, let's get back to higher-level Yesod request processing. So far, all of our examples have dealt with a single supported request route. Let's make this more interesting. We now want to have an application that serves Fibonacci numbers. If you make a request to */fib/5*, it will return the fifth Fibonacci number. And if you visit */*, it will automatically redirect you to */fib/1*.

In the Yesod world, the first question to ask is: how do we model our route data type? This is pretty straightforward: data Route App = HomeR | FibR Int. The next question is, how do we want to define our RenderRoute instance? We need to convert the Int to a Text. What function should we use?

Before you answer that, realize that we'll *also* need to be able to parse a Text back into an Int for dispatch purposes. So we need to make sure that we have a pair of functions with the property fromText . toText == Just. Show/Read could be a candidate for this, except that:

- We'd be required to convert through String.
- The Show/Read instances for Text and String both involve extra escaping, which we don't want to incur.

Instead, the approach taken by Yesod is to use the path-pieces package, and in particular the PathPiece typeclass, defined as:

```
    class PathPiece s where
        fromPathPiece :: Text -> Maybe s
        toPathPiece   :: s    -> Text
```

Using this typeclass, we can write parse and render functions for our route data type:

```
instance RenderRoute App where
    data Route App = HomeR | FibR Int
        deriving (Show, Read, Eq, Ord)

    renderRoute HomeR = ([], [])
    renderRoute (FibR i) = (["fib", toPathPiece i], [])

parseRoute' [] = Just HomeR
parseRoute' ["fib", i] = FibR <$> fromPathPiece i
parseRoute' _ = Nothing
```

And then we can write our YesodDispatch typeclass instance:

```
instance YesodDispatch App where
    yesodDispatch yesodRunnerEnv req sendResponse =
        let maybeRoute = parseRoute' (pathInfo req)
            handler =
                case maybeRoute of
                    Nothing -> notFound
                    Just HomeR -> getHomeR
                    Just (FibR i) -> getFibR i
         in yesodRunner handler yesodRunnerEnv maybeRoute req sendResponse

getHomeR = redirect (FibR 1)

fibs :: [Int]
fibs = 0 : scanl (+) 1 fibs

getFibR i = return $ show $ fibs !! i
```

Notice our call to redirect in getHomeR. We're able to use the route data type as the
parameter to redirect, and Yesod takes advantage of our renderRoute function to
create a textual link.

Routing with Template Haskell

Now let's suppose we want to add a new route to our previous application. We'd have
to make the following changes:

1. Modify the route data type itself.

2. Add a clause to renderRoute.

3. Add a clause to parseRoute, and make sure it corresponds correctly to render
   Route.

4. Add a clause to the case statement in yesodDispatch to call our handler function.

5. Write our handler function.

That's a lot of changes! And lots of manual, boilerplate changes means lots of potential for mistakes. Some of the mistakes can be caught by the compiler if you turn on warnings (forgetting to add a clause in renderRoute or a match in yesodDispatch's case statement), but others cannot (ensuring that renderRoute and parseRoute have the same logic, or adding the parseRoute clause).

This is where Template Haskell comes into the Yesod world. Instead of dealing with all of these changes manually, Yesod declares a high-level routing syntax. This syntax lets you specify your route syntax, dynamic parameters, constructor names, and accepted request methods, and automatically generates parse, render, and dispatch functions.

To get an idea of how much manual coding this saves, have a look at our previous example converted to the Template Haskell version:

```
{-# LANGUAGE OverloadedStrings #-}
{-# LANGUAGE QuasiQuotes       #-}
{-# LANGUAGE TemplateHaskell   #-}
{-# LANGUAGE TypeFamilies      #-}
{-# LANGUAGE ViewPatterns      #-}
import            Yesod.Core (RenderRoute (..), Yesod, mkYesod, parseRoutes,
                              redirect, warp)

-- | Our foundation data type
data App = App

instance Yesod App

mkYesod "App" [parseRoutes|
/         HomeR GET
/fib/#Int FibR  GET
|]

getHomeR :: Handler ()
getHomeR = redirect (FibR 1)

fibs :: [Int]
fibs = 0 : scanl (+) 1 fibs

getFibR :: Int -> Handler String
getFibR i = return $ show $ fibs !! i

main :: IO ()
main = warp 3000 App
```

What's wonderful about this is that, as the developer, you can now focus on the important part of your application and not get involved in the details of writing parsers and renderers. But there are of course some downsides to the usage of Template Haskell:

- Compile times are a bit slower.

- The details of what's going on behind the scenes aren't easily apparent. (Though you can use `cabal haddock` to see what identifiers have been generated for you.)

- You don't have as much fine-grained control. For example, in the Yesod route syntax, each dynamic parameter has to be a separate field in the route constructor, as opposed to bundling fields together. This is a conscious trade-off in Yesod between flexibility and complexity.

This usage of Template Haskell is likely the most controversial decision in Yesod. I personally think the benefits definitely justify its usage, but if you'd rather avoid Template Haskell, you're free to do so. Every example so far in this chapter has done so, and you can follow those techniques. We also have another, simpler approach in the Yesod world: `LiteApp`.

LiteApp

`LiteApp` allows you to throw away type-safe URLs and Template Haskell. It uses a simple routing DSL in pure Haskell. Once again, as a simple comparison, let's rewrite our Fibonacci example to use it:

```
import           Data.Text  (pack)
import           Yesod.Core (LiteHandler, dispatchTo, dispatchTo, liteApp,
                                  onStatic, redirect, warp, withDynamic)

getHomeR :: LiteHandler ()
getHomeR = redirect "/fib/1"

fibs :: [Int]
fibs = 0 : scanl (+) 1 fibs

getFibR :: Int -> LiteHandler String
getFibR i = return $ show $ fibs !! i

main :: IO ()
main = warp 3000 $ liteApp $ do
    dispatchTo getHomeR
    onStatic (pack "fib") $ withDynamic $ \i -> dispatchTo (getFibR i)
```

There you go: a simple Yesod app without any language extensions at all! However, even this application still demonstrates some type safety. Yesod will use `fromPath Piece` to convert the parameter for `getFibR` from `Text` to an `Int`, so any invalid parameter will be caught by Yesod itself. It's just one less piece of checking that you have to perform.

Shakespeare

Generating plain text pages can be fun, but it's hardly what one normally expects from a web framework. As you'd hope, Yesod comes with built-in support for generating HTML, CSS, and JavaScript as well.

Before we get into templating languages, let's do it the raw, low-level way, and then build up to something a bit more pleasant:

```
import          Data.Text  (pack)
import          Yesod.Core

getHomeR :: LiteHandler TypedContent
getHomeR = return $ TypedContent typeHtml $ toContent
    "<html><head><title>Hi There!</title>\
    \<link rel='stylesheet' href='/style.css'>\
    \<script src='/script.js'></script></head>\
    \<body><h1>Hello, World!</h1></body></html>"

getStyleR :: LiteHandler TypedContent
getStyleR = return $ TypedContent typeCss $ toContent
    "h1 { color: red }"

getScriptR :: LiteHandler TypedContent
getScriptR = return $ TypedContent typeJavascript $ toContent
    "alert('Yay, Javascript works too!');"

main :: IO ()
main = warp 3000 $ liteApp $ do
    dispatchTo getHomeR
    onStatic (pack "style.css") $ dispatchTo getStyleR
    onStatic (pack "script.js") $ dispatchTo getScriptR
```

We're just reusing all of the `TypedContent` stuff we've already learned. We now have three separate routes, providing HTML, CSS, and JavaScript. We write our content as `Strings`, convert them to `Content` using `toContent`, and then wrap them with a `TypedContent` constructor to give them the appropriate content type headers.

But as usual, we can do better. Dealing with `Strings` is not very efficient, and it's tedious to have to manually put in the content type all the time. We already know the solution to those problems: use the `Html` data type from `blaze-html`. Let's convert our `getHomeR` function to use it:

```
import          Data.Text               (pack)
import          Text.Blaze.Html5        (toValue, (!))
import qualified Text.Blaze.Html5        as H
import qualified Text.Blaze.Html5.Attributes as A
import          Yesod.Core

getHomeR :: LiteHandler Html
getHomeR = return $ H.docTypeHtml $ do
```

```
        H.head $ do
            H.title $ toHtml "Hi There!"
            H.link ! A.rel (toValue "stylesheet") ! A.href (toValue "/style.css")
            H.script ! A.src (toValue "/script.js") $ return ()
        H.body $ do
            H.h1 $ toHtml "Hello, World!"

    getStyleR :: LiteHandler TypedContent
    getStyleR = return $ TypedContent typeCss $ toContent
        "h1 { color: red }"

    getScriptR :: LiteHandler TypedContent
    getScriptR = return $ TypedContent typeJavascript $ toContent
        "alert('Yay, Javascript works too!');"

    main :: IO ()
    main = warp 3000 $ liteApp $ do
        dispatchTo getHomeR
        onStatic (pack "style.css") $ dispatchTo getStyleR
        onStatic (pack "script.js") $ dispatchTo getScriptR
```

Ahh, far nicer. `blaze-html` provides a convenient combinator library, and will execute far faster in most cases than whatever `String` concatenation you might attempt.

If you're happy with `blaze-html` combinators, by all means use them. However, many people like to use a more specialized templating language. Yesod's standard providers for this are the Shakespearean languages: Hamlet, Lucius, and Julius. You are by all means welcome to use a different system if so desired; the only requirement is that you can produce a `Content` value from the template.

Because Shakespearean templates are compile-time–checked, their usage requires either quasiquotation or Template Haskell. We'll use the former approach here (see Chapter 4 for more information):

```
{-# LANGUAGE QuasiQuotes #-}
import         Data.Text    (Text, pack)
import         Text.Julius  (Javascript)
import         Text.Lucius  (Css)
import         Yesod.Core

getHomeR :: LiteHandler Html
getHomeR = withUrlRenderer $
    [hamlet|
        $doctype 5
        <html>
            <head>
                <title>Hi There!
                <link rel=stylesheet href=/style.css>
                <script src=/script.js>
            <body>
                <h1>Hello, World!
```

```
    |]

getStyleR :: LiteHandler Css
getStyleR = withUrlRenderer [lucius|h1 { color: red }|]

getScriptR :: LiteHandler Javascript
getScriptR = withUrlRenderer [julius|alert('Yay, Javascript works too!');|]

main :: IO ()
main = warp 3000 $ liteApp $ do
    dispatchTo getHomeR
    onStatic (pack "style.css") $ dispatchTo getStyleR
    onStatic (pack "script.js") $ dispatchTo getScriptR
```

The URL Rendering Function

Likely the most confusing part of this is the `withUrlRenderer` calls. This gets into one of the most powerful features of Yesod: type-safe URLs. If you notice in our HTML, we're providing links to the CSS and JavaScript URLs via strings. This leads to a duplication of that information, as in our `main` function we have to provide those strings a second time. This is very fragile: our codebase is one refactor away from having broken links.

The recommended approach would be to use our type-safe URL data type in our template instead of including explicit strings. As mentioned earlier, `LiteApp` doesn't provide any meaningful type-safe URLs, so we don't have that option here. But if you use the Template Haskell generators, you get type-safe URLs for free.

In any event, the Shakespearean templates all expect to receive a function to handle the rendering of type-safe URLs. Because we don't actually use any type-safe URLs, just about any function would work here (the function will be ignored entirely), but `withUrlRenderer` is a convenient option.

As we'll see next, `withUrlRenderer` isn't really needed most of the time, as widgets end up providing the render function for us automatically.

Widgets

Dealing with HTML, CSS, and JavaScript as individual components can be nice in many cases. However, when you want to build up reusable components for a page, it can get in the way of composability. If you want more motivation for why widgets are useful, see Chapter 5. For now, let's just dig into using them:

```
{-# LANGUAGE QuasiQuotes #-}
import         Yesod.Core

getHomeR :: LiteHandler Html
getHomeR = defaultLayout $ do
```

```
    setTitle $ toHtml "Hi There!"
    [whamlet|<h1>Hello, World!|]
    toWidget [lucius|h1 { color: red }|]
    toWidget [julius|alert('Yay, Javascript works too!');|]

main :: IO ()
main = warp 3000 $ liteApp $ dispatchTo getHomeR
```

This is the same example as earlier, but we've now condensed it into a single handler. Yesod will automatically handle providing the CSS and JavaScript to the HTML. By default, it will place them in <style> and <script> tags in the <head> and <body> of the page, respectively, but Yesod provides many customization settings to do other things (such as automatically creating temporary static files and linking to them).

Widgets also have another advantage. The defaultLayout function is a member of the Yesod typeclass, and can be modified to provide a customized look and feel for your website. Many built-in pieces of Yesod, such as error messages, take advantage of the widget system, so by using widgets you get a consistent feel throughout your site.

Details We Won't Cover

Hopefully this chapter has pulled back enough of the "magic" in Yesod to let you understand what's going on under the surface. We could of course continue using this approach for analyzing the rest of the Yesod ecosystem, but that would be mostly redundant with the rest of this book. Hopefully you can now feel more informed as you read chapters on using Persistent, forms, subsites, and sessions.

PART III

Examples

CHAPTER 21

Initializing Data in the Foundation Data Type

This chapter demonstrates a relatively simple concept: performing some initialization of data to be kept in the foundation data type. There are various reasons to do this, though the two most important are:

Efficiency
> By initializing data once, at process startup, you can avoid having to recompute the same value in each request.

Persistence
> We want to store some information in a mutable location that will be persisted between individual requests. This is frequently done via an external database, but it can also be done via an in-memory mutable variable.

 Mutable variables can be a convenient storage mechanism, but remember that they have some downsides. If your process dies, you lose your data. Also, if you scale horizontally to more than one process, you'll need some way to synchronize the data between processes. We'll punt on both of those issues here, but the problems are real. This is one of the reasons Yesod puts such a strong emphasis on using an external database for persistence.

To demonstrate, we'll implement a very simple website. It will contain a single route and will serve content stored in a Markdown file. In addition to serving that content, we'll also display an old-school visitor counter indicating how many visitors have been to the site.

Step 1: Define Your Foundation

We've identified two pieces of information to be initialized: the Markdown content to be display on the homepage, and a mutable variable holding the visitor count. Remember that our goal is to perform as much of the work in the initialization phase as possible and thereby avoid performing the same work in the handlers themselves. Therefore, we want to preprocess the Markdown content into HTML. As for the visitor count, a simple `IORef` should be sufficient. So, our foundation data type is:

```
data App = App
    { homepageContent :: Html
    , visitorCount    :: IORef Int
    }
```

Step 2: Use the Foundation

For this trivial example, we only have one route: the homepage. All we need to do is:

1. Increment the visitor count.

2. Get the new visitor count.

3. Display the Markdown content together with the visitor count.

One trick we'll use to make the code a bit shorter is to utilize record wildcard syntax: `App {..}`. This is convenient when we want to deal with a number of different fields in a data type:

```
getHomeR :: Handler Html
getHomeR = do
    App {..} <- getYesod
    currentCount <- liftIO $ atomicModifyIORef visitorCount
        $ \i -> (i + 1, i + 1)
    defaultLayout $ do
        setTitle "Homepage"
        [whamlet|
            <article>#{homepageContent}
            <p>You are visitor number: #{currentCount}.
        |]
```

Step 3: Create the Foundation Value

When we initialize our application, we'll now need to provide values for the two fields we described previously. This is normal `IO` code and can perform any arbitrary actions needed. In our case, we need to:

1. Read the Markdown from the file.

2. Convert that Markdown to HTML.

3. Create the visitor counter variable.

The code ends up being just as simple as those steps imply:

```
go :: IO ()
go = do
    rawMarkdown <- TLIO.readFile "homepage.md"
    countRef <- newIORef 0
    warp 3000 App
        { homepageContent = markdown def rawMarkdown
        , visitorCount    = countRef
        }
```

Summary

There's no rocket science involved in this example—just very straightforward programming. The purpose of this chapter is to demonstrate the commonly used best practice, for achieving these often-needed objectives. In your own applications, the initialization steps will likely be much more complicated: setting up database connection pools, starting background jobs to batch-process large data, or anything else. After reading this chapter, you should now have a good idea of where to place your application-specific initialization code.

Here is the full source code for the example:

```
{-# LANGUAGE OverloadedStrings #-}
{-# LANGUAGE QuasiQuotes       #-}
{-# LANGUAGE RecordWildCards   # }
{-# LANGUAGE TemplateHaskell   #-}
{-# LANGUAGE TypeFamilies      #-}
import           Data.IORef
import qualified Data.Text.Lazy.IO as TLIO
import           Text.Markdown
import           Yesod

data App = App
    { homepageContent :: Html
    , visitorCount    :: IORef Int
    }

mkYesod "App" [parseRoutes|
/ HomeR GET
|]
instance Yesod App

getHomeR :: Handler Html
getHomeR = do
    App {..} <- getYesod
    currentCount <- liftIO $ atomicModifyIORef visitorCount
        $ \i -> (i + 1, i + 1)
    defaultLayout $ do
```

```
        setTitle "Homepage"
        [whamlet|
            <article>#{homepageContent}
            <p>You are visitor number: #{currentCount}.
        |]

main :: IO ()
main = do
    rawMarkdown <- TLIO.readFile "homepage.md"
    countRef <- newIORef 0
    warp 3000 App
        { homepageContent = markdown def rawMarkdown
        , visitorCount    = countRef
        }
```

CHAPTER 22

Blog: i18n, Authentication, Authorization, and Database

This chapter presents a simple blog app. It allows an admin to add blog posts via a rich text editor (nicedit), allows logged-in users to comment, and has full i18n support. It is also a good example of using a Persistent database, leveraging Yesod's authorization system, and using templates.

It is generally recommended to place templates, Persist entity definitions, and routing in separate files, but we'll keep it all in one file here for convenience. The one exception you'll see will be i18n messages.

We'll start off with our language extensions. In scaffolded code, the language extensions are specified in the cabal file, so you won't need to put this in your individual Haskell files:

```
{-# LANGUAGE OverloadedStrings, TypeFamilies, QuasiQuotes,
             TemplateHaskell, GADTs, FlexibleContexts,
             MultiParamTypeClasses, DeriveDataTypeable,
             GeneralizedNewtypeDeriving, ViewPatterns #-}
```

Now our imports:

```
import Yesod
import Yesod.Auth
import Yesod.Form.Nic (YesodNic, nicHtmlField)
import Yesod.Auth.BrowserId (authBrowserId, def)
import Data.Text (Text)
import Network.HTTP.Client.TLS (tlsManagerSettings)
import Network.HTTP.Conduit (Manager, newManager)
import Database.Persist.Sqlite
    ( ConnectionPool, SqlBackend, runSqlPool, runMigration
    , createSqlitePool, runSqlPersistMPool
    )
```

```
import Data.Time (UTCTime, getCurrentTime)
import Control.Applicative ((<$>), (<*>), pure)
import Data.Typeable (Typeable)
import Control.Monad.Logger (runStdoutLoggingT)
```

First, we'll set up our Persistent entities. We're going to create our data types (via mkPersist) and a migration function, which will automatically create and update our SQL schema (if we were using the MongoDB backend, migration would not be needed):

```
share [mkPersist sqlSettings, mkMigrate "migrateAll"] [persistLowerCase|
```

The following keeps track of users (in a more robust application, we would also keep the account creation date, display name, etc.):

```
User
    email Text
    UniqueUser email
```

In order to work with yesod-auth's caching, our User type must be an instance of Typeable:

```
deriving Typeable
```

An individual blog entry has this format (I've avoided using the word "post" due to the confusion with the request method POST):

```
Entry
    title Text
    posted UTCTime
    content Html
```

And a comment on the blog post looks like this:

```
Comment
    entry EntryId
    posted UTCTime
    user UserId
    name Text
    text Textarea
|]
```

Every site has a foundation data type. This value is initialized before launching your application, and is available throughout. We'll store a database connection pool and HTTP connection manager in ours. See the very end of the file for how those are initialized:

```
data Blog = Blog
    { connPool    :: ConnectionPool
    , httpManager :: Manager
    }
```

To make i18n easy and translator-friendly, we have a special file format for translated messages. There is a single file for each language, and each file is named based on the language code (e.g., en, es, de-DE) and placed in that folder. We also specify the main language file (here, "en") as a default language:

```
mkMessage "Blog" "blog-messages" "en"
```

Our *blog-messages/en.msg* file contains the following content:

```
-- @blog-messages/en.msg
NotAnAdmin: You must be an administrator to access this page.

WelcomeHomepage: Welcome to the homepage
SeeArchive: See the archive

NoEntries: There are no entries in the blog
LoginToPost: Admins can login to post
NewEntry: Post to blog
NewEntryTitle: Title
NewEntryContent: Content

PleaseCorrectEntry: Your submitted entry had some errors,
                    please correct and try again.
EntryCreated title@Text: Your new blog post, #{title}, has been created

EntryTitle title@Text: Blog post: #{title}
CommentsHeading: Comments
NoComments: There are no comments
AddCommentHeading: Add a Comment
LoginToComment: You must be logged in to comment
AddCommentButton: Add comment

CommentName: Your display name
CommentText: Comment
CommentAdded: Your comment has been added
PleaseCorrectComment: Your submitted comment had some errors,
                      please correct and try again.

HomepageTitle: Yesod Blog Demo
BlogArchiveTitle: Blog Archive
```

Now we're going to set up our routing table. We have four entries: a homepage, an entry list page (BlogR), an individual entry page (EntryR), and our authentication subsite. Note that BlogR and EntryR both accept GET and POST methods. The POST methods are for adding a new blog post and adding a new comment, respectively:

```
mkYesod "Blog" [parseRoutes|
/              HomeR  GET
/blog          BlogR  GET POST
/blog/#EntryId EntryR GET POST
/auth          AuthR  Auth getAuth
|]
```

Every foundation needs to be an instance of the Yesod typeclass. This is where we configure various settings:

```
instance Yesod Blog where
```

This is the base of our application (note that in order to make BrowserID work properly, a valid URL must be used):

```
approot = ApprootStatic "http://localhost:3000"
```

For our authorization scheme, we want to have the following rules:

- Only admins can add a new entry.
- Only logged-in users can add a new comment.
- All other pages can be accessed by anyone.

We set up our routes in a RESTful way, where the actions that could make changes are always using a POST method. As a result, we can simply check for whether a request is a write request, given by the True in the second field.

First, we'll authorize requests to add a new entry:

```
isAuthorized BlogR True = do
    mauth <- maybeAuth
    case mauth of
        Nothing -> return AuthenticationRequired
        Just (Entity _ user)
            | isAdmin user -> return Authorized
            | otherwise    -> unauthorizedI MsgNotAnAdmin
```

Now we'll authorize requests to add a new comment:

```
isAuthorized (EntryR _) True = do
    mauth <- maybeAuth
    case mauth of
        Nothing -> return AuthenticationRequired
        Just _  -> return Authorized
```

And for all other requests, the result is always authorized:

```
isAuthorized _ _ = return Authorized
```

We'll also specify where users should be redirected to if they get an AuthenticationRequired:

```
authRoute _ = Just (AuthR LoginR)
```

Next is where we define our site's look and feel. The function is given the content for the individual page, and wraps it up with a standard template:

```
defaultLayout inside = do
```

Yesod encourages the get-following-post pattern, where after a POST, the user is redirected to another page. In order to allow the POST page to give the user some kind of feedback, we have the getMessage and setMessage functions. It's a good idea to always check for pending messages in your defaultLayout function:

```
mmsg <- getMessage
```

We use widgets to compose HTML, CSS, and JavaScript resources. At the end of the day, we need to unwrap all of that into simple HTML. That's what the widgetToPageContent function is for. We're going to give it a widget consisting of the content we received from the individual page (inside), plus a standard CSS stylesheet for all pages. We'll use the Lucius template language to create the latter:

```
pc <- widgetToPageContent $ do
    toWidget [lucius|
body {
    width: 760px;
    margin: 1em auto;
    font-family: sans-serif;
}
textarea {
    width: 400px;
    height: 200px;
}
#message {
  color: #900;
}
|]
        inside
```

And finally, we'll use a new Hamlet template to wrap up the individual components (title, head data, and body data) into the final output:

```
withUrlRenderer [hamlet|
$doctype 5
<html>
    <head>
        <title>#{pageTitle pc}
        ^{pageHead pc}
    <body>
        $maybe msg <- mmsg
            <div #message>#{msg}
        ^{pageBody pc}
|]
```

This is a simple function to check if a user is the admin. In a real application, we would likely store the admin bit in the database itself, or check with some external system. For now, I've just hardcoded my own email address:

```
isAdmin :: User -> Bool
isAdmin user = userEmail user == "michael@snoyman.com"
```

In order to access the database we need to create a `YesodPersist` instance, which says which backend we're using and how to run an action:

```
instance YesodPersist Blog where
    type YesodPersistBackend Blog = SqlBackend
    runDB f = do
        master <- getYesod
        let pool = connPool master
        runSqlPool f pool
```

This is a convenience synonym. It is defined automatically for you in the scaffolding:

```
type Form x = Html -> MForm Handler (FormResult x, Widget)
```

In order to use `yesod-form` and `yesod-auth`, we need an instance of `RenderMessage` for `FormMessage`. This allows us to control the i18n of individual form messages:

```
instance RenderMessage Blog FormMessage where
    renderMessage _ _ = defaultFormMessage
```

In order to use the built-in Nic HTML editor, we need this instance. We just take the default values, which use a CDN-hosted version of Nic:

```
instance YesodNic Blog
```

In order to use `yesod-auth`, we need a `YesodAuth` instance:

```
instance YesodAuth Blog where
    type AuthId Blog = UserId
    loginDest _ = HomeR
    logoutDest _ = HomeR
    authHttpManager = httpManager
```

We'll use BrowserID (*https://browserid.org/*) (a.k.a., Mozilla Persona), which is a third-party system using email addresses as identifiers. This makes it easy to switch to other systems in the future, such as locally authenticated email addresses (also included with `yesod-auth`):

```
authPlugins _ = [authBrowserId def]
```

This function takes someone's login credentials (i.e., email address) and gives back a `UserId`:

```
getAuthId creds = do
    let email = credsIdent creds
        user = User email
    res <- runDB $ insertBy user
    return $ Just $ either entityKey id res
```

We also need to provide a `YesodAuthPersist` instance to work with Persistent:

```
instance YesodAuthPersist Blog
```

The one important detail in the homepage handler is our usage of setTitleI, which allows us to use i18n messages for the title. We also use this message with a _{Msg…} interpolation in Hamlet:

```
getHomeR :: Handler Html
getHomeR = defaultLayout $ do
    setTitleI MsgHomepageTitle
    [whamlet|
<p>_{MsgWelcomeHomepage}
<p>
  <a href=@{BlogR}>_{MsgSeeArchive}
|]
```

Next, we define a form for adding new entries. We want the user to provide the title and content, and then we fill in the post date automatically via getCurrentTime.

Note that slightly strange lift (liftIO getCurrentTime) manner of running an IO action. The reason is that applicative forms are not monads, and therefore cannot be instances of MonadIO. Instead, we use lift to run the action in the underlying Handler monad, and liftIO to convert the IO action into a Handler action:

```
entryForm :: Form Entry
entryForm = renderDivs $ Entry
    <$> areq textField (fieldSettingsLabel MsgNewEntryTitle) Nothing
    <*> lift (liftIO getCurrentTime)
    <*> areq nicHtmlField (fieldSettingsLabel MsgNewEntryContent) Nothing
```

Here we get the list of all blog entries, and present an admin with a form to create a new entry:

```
getBlogR :: Handler Html
getBlogR = do
    muser <- maybeAuth
    entries <- runDB $ selectList [] [Desc EntryPosted]
    (entryWidget, enctype) <- generateFormPost entryForm
    defaultLayout $ do
        setTitleI MsgBlogArchiveTitle
        [whamlet|
$if null entries
    <p>_{MsgNoEntries}
$else
    <ul>
        $forall Entity entryId entry <- entries
            <li>
                <a href=@{EntryR entryId}>#{entryTitle entry}
```

We have three possibilities: the user is logged in as an admin, the user is logged in and is not an admin, and the user is not logged in. In the first case, we should display the entry form. In the second, we'll do nothing. In the third, we'll provide a login link:

```
$maybe Entity _ user <- muser
    $if isAdmin user
```

```
                <form method=post enctype=#{enctype}>
                    ^{entryWidget}
                    <div>
                        <input type=submit value=_{MsgNewEntry}>
    $nothing
        <p>
            <a href=@{AuthR LoginR}>_{MsgLoginToPost}
    |]
```

Next, we need to process an incoming entry addition. We don't do any permissions checking, because isAuthorized handles it for us. If the form submission was valid, we add the entry to the database and redirect to the new entry. Otherwise, we ask the user to try again:

```
postBlogR :: Handler Html
postBlogR = do
    ((res, entryWidget), enctype) <- runFormPost entryForm
    case res of
        FormSuccess entry -> do
            entryId <- runDB $ insert entry
            setMessageI $ MsgEntryCreated $ entryTitle entry
            redirect $ EntryR entryId
        _ -> defaultLayout $ do
            setTitleI MsgPleaseCorrectEntry
            [whamlet|
<form method=post enctype=#{enctype}>
    ^{entryWidget}
    <div>
        <input type=submit value=_{MsgNewEntry}>
|]
```

Next up is a form for comments, very similar to our entryForm. It takes the EntryId of the entry the comment is attached to. By using pure, we embed this value in the resulting Comment output, without having it appear in the generated HTML:

```
commentForm :: EntryId -> Form Comment
commentForm entryId = renderDivs $ Comment
    <$> pure entryId
    <*> lift (liftIO getCurrentTime)
    <*> lift requireAuthId
    <*> areq textField (fieldSettingsLabel MsgCommentName) Nothing
    <*> areq textareaField (fieldSettingsLabel MsgCommentText) Nothing
```

We show an individual entry, comments, and an add comment form if the user is logged in:

```
getEntryR :: EntryId -> Handler Html
getEntryR entryId = do
    (entry, comments) <- runDB $ do
        entry <- get404 entryId
        comments <- selectList [CommentEntry ==. entryId] [Asc CommentPosted]
        return (entry, map entityVal comments)
```

```
        muser <- maybeAuth
        (commentWidget, enctype) <-
            generateFormPost (commentForm entryId)
        defaultLayout $ do
            setTitleI $ MsgEntryTitle $ entryTitle entry
            [whamlet|
    <h1>#{entryTitle entry}
    <article>#{entryContent entry}
        <section .comments>
            <h1>_{MsgCommentsHeading}
            $if null comments
                <p>_{MsgNoComments}
            $else
                $forall Comment _entry posted _user name text <- comments
                    <div .comment>
                        <span .by>#{name}
                        <span .at>#{show posted}
                        <div .content>#{text}
            <section>
                <h1>_{MsgAddCommentHeading}
                $maybe _ <- muser
                    <form method=post enctype=#{enctype}>
                        ^{commentWidget}
                        <div>
                            <input type=submit value=_{MsgAddCommentButton}>
                $nothing
                    <p>
                        <a href=@{AuthR LoginR}>_{MsgLoginToComment}
    |]
```

Here's how we receive an incoming comment submission:

```
postEntryR :: EntryId -> Handler Html
postEntryR entryId = do
    ((res, commentWidget), enctype) <-
        runFormPost (commentForm entryId)
    case res of
        FormSuccess comment -> do
            _ <- runDB $ insert comment
            setMessageI MsgCommentAdded
            redirect $ EntryR entryId
        _ -> defaultLayout $ do
            setTitleI MsgPleaseCorrectComment
            [whamlet|
    <form method=post enctype=#{enctype}>
        ^{commentWidget}
        <div>
            <input type=submit value=_{MsgAddCommentButton}>
    |]
```

Finally, our main function:

```
main :: IO ()
main = do
```

```
pool <- runStdoutLoggingT $ createSqlitePool "blog.db3" 10
-- create a new pool
-- perform any necessary migration
runSqlPersistMPool (runMigration migrateAll) pool
manager <- newManager tlsManagerSettings -- create a new HTTP manager
warp 3000 $ Blog pool manager -- start our server
```

CHAPTER 23

Wiki: Markdown, Chat Subsite, Event Source

This chapter ties together a few different ideas. We'll start with a chat subsite, which allows us to embed a chat widget on any page. We'll use the HTML5 event source API to handle sending events from the server to the client. You can view the entire project on FP Haskell Center (*http://www.bit.ly/fp-h-center*).

Subsite: Data

In order to define a subsite, we first need to create a foundation type for the subsite, the same as we would do for a normal Yesod application. In our case, we want to keep a channel of all the events to be sent to the individual participants of a chat. This ends up looking like:

```
-- @Chat/Data.hs
{-# LANGUAGE FlexibleContexts    #-}
{-# LANGUAGE FlexibleInstances   #-}
{-# LANGUAGE OverloadedStrings   #-}
{-# LANGUAGE QuasiQuotes         #-}
{-# LANGUAGE RankNTypes          #-}
{-# LANGUAGE TemplateHaskell     #-}
{-# LANGUAGE TypeFamilies        #-}
module Chat.Data where

import           Blaze.ByteString.Builder.Char.Utf8  (fromText)
import           Control.Concurrent.Chan
import           Data.Monoid                         ((<>))
import           Data.Text                           (Text)
import           Network.Wai.EventSource
import           Network.Wai.EventSource.EventStream
import           Yesod
```

```
-- | Our subsite foundation. We keep a channel of events that all connections
-- will share.
data Chat = Chat (Chan ServerEvent)
```

We also need to define our subsite routes in the same module. We need to have two commands—one to send a new message to all users, and another to receive the stream of messages:

```
-- @Chat/Data.hs
mkYesodSubData "Chat" [parseRoutes|
/send SendR POST
/recv ReceiveR GET
|]
```

Subsite: Handlers

Now that we've defined our foundation and routes, we need to create a separate module for providing the subsite dispatch functionality. We'll call this module Chat, and it's where we'll start to see how a subsite functions.

A subsite always sits as a layer on top of some master site, which will be provided by the user. In many cases, a subsite will require specific functionality to be present in the master site. In the case of our chat subsite, we want user authentication to be provided by the master site. The subsite needs to be able to query whether the current user is logged into the site, and to get the user's name.

The way we represent this concept is by defining a typeclass that encapsulates the necessary functionality. Let's have a look at our YesodChat typeclass:

```
-- @Chat/Data.hs
class (Yesod master, RenderMessage master FormMessage)
      => YesodChat master where
    getUserName :: HandlerT master IO Text
    isLoggedIn :: HandlerT master IO Bool
```

Any master site that wants to use the chat subsite will need to provide a YesodChat instance. (We'll see in a bit how this requirement is enforced.)

There are a few interesting things to note:

- We can put further constraints on the master site, such as providing a Yesod instance and allowing rendering of form messages. The former allows us to use defaultLayout, while the latter allows us to use standard form widgets.

- Previously in the book, we've used the Handler monad quite a bit. Remember that Handler is just an application-specific type synonym for HandlerT. This code is intended to work with many different applications, so we use the full `HandlerT` form of the transformer.

Speaking of the `Handler` type synonym, we're going to want to have something similar for our subsite. The question is: what does this monad look like? In a subsite situation, we end up with two layers of `HandlerT` transformers: one for the subsite, and one for the master site. We want to have a synonym that works for any master site that is an instance of `YesodChat`, so we end up with:

```
-- @Chat/Data.hs
type ChatHandler a =
    forall master. YesodChat master =>
    HandlerT Chat (HandlerT master IO) a
```

Now that we have our machinery out of the way, it's time to write our subsite handler functions. We had two routes: one for sending messages, and one for receiving messages. Let's start with sending. We need to:

1. Get the username for the person sending the message.

2. Parse the message from the incoming parameters. (Note that we're going to use `GET` parameters for simplicity of the client-side Ajax code.)

3. Write the message to the `Chan`.

The trickiest bit of all this code is knowing when to use `lift`. Let's look at the implementation, and then discuss those `lift` usages:

```
-- @Chat/Data.hs
postSendR :: ChatHandler ()
postSendR = do
    from <- lift getUserName
    body <- lift $ runInputGet $ ireq textField "message"
    Chat chan <- getYesod
    liftIO $ writeChan chan $ ServerEvent Nothing Nothing $ return $
        fromText from <> fromText ": " <> fromText body
```

`getUserName` is the function we defined in our `YesodChat` typeclass earlier. If we look at that type signature, we see that it lives in the master site's `Handler` monad. Therefore, we need to `lift` that call out of the subsite.

The call to `runInputGet` is a little more subtle. Theoretically, we could run this in either the subsite or the master site. However, we use `lift` here as well, for one specific reason: message translations. By using the master site, we can take advantage of whatever `RenderMessage` instance the master site defines. This also explains why we have a `RenderMessage` constraint on the `YesodChat` typeclass.

The next call to `getYesod` is *not* lifted. The reasoning here is simple: we want to get the subsite's foundation type in order to access the message channel. If we instead lifted that call, we'd get the master site's foundation type instead, which is not what we want in this case.

The final line puts the new message into the channel. Because this is an IO action, we use liftIO. ServerEvent is part of the wai-eventsource package and is the means by which we're providing server-sent events in this example.

The receiving side is similarly simple:

```
-- @Chat/Data.hs
getReceiveR :: ChatHandler ()
getReceiveR = do
    Chat chan0 <- getYesod
    chan <- liftIO $ dupChan chan0
    sendWaiApplication $ eventSourceAppChan chan
```

We use dupChan so that each new connection receives its own copy of newly generated messages. This is a standard method in concurrent Haskell of creating broadcast channels. The last line in our function exposes the underlying wai-eventsource application as a Yesod handler, using the sendWaiApplication function to promote a WAI application to a Yesod handler.

Now that we've defined our handler functions, we can set up our dispatch. In a normal application, dispatching is handled by calling mkYesod, which creates the appropriate YesodDispatch instance. In subsites, things are a little bit more complicated, because you'll often want to place constraints on the master site. The formula we use is the following:

```
-- @Chat.hs
{-# LANGUAGE FlexibleContexts      #-}
{-# LANGUAGE FlexibleInstances     #-}
{-# LANGUAGE MultiParamTypeClasses #-}
{-# LANGUAGE OverloadedStrings     #-}
{-# LANGUAGE QuasiQuotes           #-}
{-# LANGUAGE RankNTypes            #-}
{-# LANGUAGE TemplateHaskell       #-}
{-# LANGUAGE TypeFamilies          #-}
module Chat where

import           Chat.Data
import           Yesod

instance YesodChat master => YesodSubDispatch Chat (HandlerT master IO) where
    yesodSubDispatch = $(mkYesodSubDispatch resourcesChat)
```

We're stating that our chat subsite can live on top of any master site that is an instance of YesodChat. We then use the mkYesodSubDispatch Template Haskell function to generate all of our dispatching logic. This is a bit more difficult to write than mkYesod, but it provides the necessary flexibility and is mostly identical for any subsite you'll write.

Subsite: Widget

We now have a fully working subsite. The final component we want as part of our chat library is a widget to be embedded inside a page that will provide chat functionality. By creating this as a widget, we can include all of our HTML, CSS, and Javascript as a reusable component.

Our widget will need to take in one argument: a function to convert a chat subsite URL into a master site URL. The reasoning here is that an application developer could place the chat subsite anywhere in the URL structure, and this widget needs to be able to generate Javascript that will point at the correct URLs. Let's start off our widget:

```
-- @Chat.hs
chatWidget :: YesodChat master
           => (Route Chat -> Route master)
           -> WidgetT master IO ()
chatWidget toMaster = do
```

Next, we're going to generate some identifiers to be used by our widget. It's always good practice to let Yesod generate unique identifiers for you instead of creating them manually, to avoid name collisions:

```
-- @Chat.hs
    chat <- newIdent    -- the containing div
    output <- newIdent -- the box containing the messages
    input <- newIdent  -- input field from the user
```

And next, we need to check if the user is logged in, using the isLoggedIn function in our YesodChat typeclass. We're in a Widget and that function lives in the Handler monad, so we need to use handlerToWidget:

```
-- @Chat.hs
    ili <- handlerToWidget isLoggedIn  -- check if we're already logged in
```

If the user is logged in, we want to display the chat box, style it with some CSS, and then make it interactive using some Javascript. This is mostly client-side code wrapped in a Widget:

```
-- @Chat.hs
    if ili
        then do
            -- Logged in: show the widget
            [whamlet|
                <div ##{chat}>
                    <h2>Chat
                    <div ##{output}>
                    <input ##{input} type=text placeholder="Enter Message">
            |]
            -- Just some CSS
            toWidget [lucius|
```

```
                ##{chat} {
                    position: absolute;
                    top: 2em;
                    right: 2em;
                }
                ##{output} {
                    width: 200px;
                    height: 300px;
                    border: 1px solid #999;
                    overflow: auto;
                }
            |]
        -- And now that Javascript
        toWidgetBody [julius|
            // Set up the receiving end
            var output = document.getElementById(#{toJSON output});
            var src = new EventSource("@{toMaster ReceiveR}");
            src.onmessage = function(msg) {
                // This function will be called for each new message.
                var p = document.createElement("p");
                p.appendChild(document.createTextNode(msg.data));
                output.appendChild(p);

                // And now scroll down within the output div
                    so the most recent message
                // is displayed.
                output.scrollTop = output.scrollHeight;
            };

            // Set up the sending end: send a message via Ajax
                whenever the user hits Enter.
            var input = document.getElementById(#{toJSON input});
            input.onkeyup = function(event) {
                var keycode = (event.keyCode ? event.keyCode : event.which);
                if (keycode == '13') {
                    var xhr = new XMLHttpRequest();
                    var val = input.value;
                    input.value = "";
                    var params = "?message=" + encodeURI(val);
                    xhr.open("POST", "@{toMaster SendR}" + params);
                    xhr.send(null);
                }
            }
        |]
```

And finally, if the user isn't logged in, we'll ask her to log in to use the chat app:

```
    -- @Chat.hs
        else do
            -- User isn't logged in, give a not-logged-in message.
            master <- getYesod
            [whamlet|
                <p>
```

```
                You must be #
                $maybe ar <- authRoute master
                    <a href=@{ar}>logged in
                $nothing
                    logged in
                \ to chat.
    |]
```

Master Site: Data

Now we can proceed with writing our main application. This application will include the chat subsite and a wiki. The first thing we need to consider is how to store the wiki contents. Normally, we'd want to put this in some kind of a Persistent database. For simplicity, we'll just use an in-memory representation. Each wiki page is indicated by a list of names, and the content of each page is going to be a piece of Text. So, our full foundation data type is:

```haskell
-- @ChatMain.hs
{-# LANGUAGE MultiParamTypeClasses #-}
{-# LANGUAGE OverloadedStrings     #-}
{-# LANGUAGE QuasiQuotes           #-}
{-# LANGUAGE TemplateHaskell       #-}
{-# LANGUAGE TypeFamilies          #-}
{-# LANGUAGE ViewPatterns          #-}
module ChatMain where

import                Chat
import                Chat.Data
import                Control.Concurrent.Chan (newChan)
import                Data.IORef
import                Data.Map                (Map)
import qualified      Data.Map                as Map
import                Data.Text               (Text)
import qualified      Data.Text.Lazy          as TL
import                Text.Markdown
import                Yesod
import                Yesod.Auth
import                Yesod.Auth.Dummy

data App = App
    { getChat     :: Chat
    , wikiContent :: IORef (Map [Text] Text)
    }
```

Next, we want to set up our routes:

```haskell
-- @ChatMain.hs
mkYesod "App" [parseRoutes|
/           HomeR GET      -- the homepage
/wiki/*Texts WikiR GET POST -- note the multipiece for the wiki hierarchy
```

```
/chat        ChatR Chat getChat    -- the chat subsite
/auth        AuthR Auth getAuth    -- the auth subsite
|]
```

Master Site: Instances

We need to make two modifications to the default Yesod instance. First, we want to
provide an implementation of authRoute, so that our chat subsite widget can provide
a proper link to a login page. Second, we'll provide an override to the defaultLayout.
Besides providing login/logout links, this function will add in the chat widget on
every page:

```
-- @ChatMain.hs
instance Yesod App where
    authRoute _ = Just $ AuthR LoginR -- get a working login link

    -- Our custom defaultLayout will add the chat widget to every page.
    -- We'll also add login and logout links to the top.
    defaultLayout widget = do
        pc <- widgetToPageContent $ do
            widget
            chatWidget ChatR
        mmsg <- getMessage
        withUrlRenderer
            [hamlet|
                $doctype 5
                <html>
                    <head>
                        <title>#{pageTitle pc}
                        ^{pageHead pc}
                    <body>
                        $maybe msg <- mmsg
                            <div .message>#{msg}
                        <nav>
                            <a href=@{AuthR LoginR}>Login
                            \ | #
                            <a href=@{AuthR LogoutR}>Logout
                        ^{pageBody pc}
            |]
```

Because we're using the chat subsite, we have to provide an instance of YesodChat:

```
-- @ChatMain.hs
instance YesodChat App where
    getUserName = do
        muid <- maybeAuthId
        case muid of
            Nothing -> do
                setMessage "Not logged in"
                redirect $ AuthR LoginR
            Just uid -> return uid
```

```
    isLoggedIn = do
        ma <- maybeAuthId
        return $ maybe False (const True) ma
```

Our `YesodAuth` and `RenderMessage` instances, as well as the homepage handler, are rather bland:

```
-- @ChatMain.hs
-- Fairly standard YesodAuth instance. We'll use the dummy plug-in so that you
-- can create any name you want, and store the login name as the AuthId.
instance YesodAuth App where
    type AuthId App = Text
    authPlugins _ = [authDummy]
    loginDest _ = HomeR
    logoutDest _ = HomeR
    getAuthId = return . Just . credsIdent
    authHttpManager = error "authHttpManager" -- not used by authDummy
    maybeAuthId = lookupSession "_ID"

instance RenderMessage App FormMessage where
    renderMessage _ _ = defaultFormMessage

-- Nothing special here, just giving a link to the root of the wiki.
getHomeR :: Handler Html
getHomeR = defaultLayout
    [whamlet|
        <p>Welcome to the Wiki!
        <p>
            <a href=@{wikiRoot}>Wiki root
    |]
  where
    wikiRoot = WikiR []
```

Master Site: Wiki Handlers

Now it's time to write our wiki handlers: a GET for displaying a page, and a POST for updating a page. We'll also define a `wikiForm` function to be used on both handlers:

```
-- @ChatMain.hs
-- A form for getting wiki content
wikiForm :: Maybe Textarea -> Html -> MForm Handler (FormResult Textarea, Widget)
wikiForm mtext = renderDivs $ areq textareaField "Page body" mtext

-- Show a wiki page and an edit form
getWikiR :: [Text] -> Handler Html
getWikiR page = do
    -- Get the reference to the contents map
    icontent <- fmap wikiContent getYesod

    -- And read the map from inside the reference
    content <- liftIO $ readIORef icontent
```

```
        -- Look up the contents of the current page, if available
        let mtext = Map.lookup page content

        -- Generate a form with the current contents as the default value.
        -- Note that we use the Textarea wrapper to get a <textarea>.
        (form, _) <- generateFormPost $ wikiForm $ fmap Textarea mtext
        defaultLayout $ do
            case mtext of
                -- We're treating the input as markdown. The markdown package
                -- automatically handles XSS protection for us.
                Just text -> toWidget $ markdown def $ TL.fromStrict text
                Nothing -> [whamlet|<p>Page does not yet exist|]
            [whamlet|
                <h2>Edit page
                <form method=post>
                    ^{form}
                    <div>
                        <input type=submit>
            |]

-- Get a submitted wiki page and update the contents.
postWikiR :: [Text] -> Handler Html
postWikiR page = do
    icontent <- fmap wikiContent getYesod
    content <- liftIO $ readIORef icontent
    let mtext = Map.lookup page content
    ((res, form), _) <- runFormPost $ wikiForm $ fmap Textarea mtext
    case res of
        FormSuccess (Textarea t) -> do
            liftIO $ atomicModifyIORef icontent $
                \m -> (Map.insert page t m, ())
            setMessage "Page updated"
            redirect $ WikiR page
        _ -> defaultLayout
                [whamlet|
                    <form method=post>
                        ^{form}
                        <div>
                            <input type=submit>
                |]
```

Master Site: Running

Finally, we're ready to run our application. Unlike many of the previous examples in this book, we need to perform some real initialization in the main function. The chat subsite requires an empty Chan to be created, and we need to create a mutable variable to hold the wiki contents. Once we have those values, we can create an App value and pass it to the warp function:

```
-- @ChatMain.hs
main :: IO ()
```

```
main = do
    -- Create our server event channel
    chan <- newChan

    -- Initially have a blank database of wiki pages
    icontent <- newIORef Map.empty

    -- Run our app
    warpEnv App
        { getChat = Chat chan
        , wikiContent = icontent
        }
```

Summary

This chapter demonstrated the creation of a nontrivial subsite. Some important points to notice include the usage of typeclasses to express constraints on the master site, how data initialization was performed in the main function, and how lifting allowed us to operate in either the subsite or master site context.

If you're looking for a way to test out your subsite skills, I'd recommend modifying this example so that the wiki code also lives in its own subsite.

CHAPTER 24

JSON Web Service

Let's create a very simple web service: it takes a JSON request and returns a JSON response. We're going to write the server in WAI/Warp and the client in http-conduit. We'll be using aeson for JSON parsing and rendering. We could also write the server in Yesod itself, but for such a simple example, the extra features of Yesod don't add much.

Server

WAI uses the conduit package to handle streaming request bodies and efficiently generates responses using blaze-builder. aeson uses attoparsec for parsing; by using attoparsec-conduit we get easy interoperability with WAI. This plays out as:

```
{-# LANGUAGE OverloadedStrings #-}
import           Control.Exception        (SomeException)
import           Control.Exception.Lifted (handle)
import           Control.Monad.IO.Class   (liftIO)
import           Data.Aeson               (Value, encode, object, (.=))
import           Data.Aeson.Parser        (json)
import           Data.ByteString          (ByteString)
import           Data.Conduit             (($$))
import           Data.Conduit.Attoparsec  (sinkParser)
import           Network.HTTP.Types       (status200, status400)
import           Network.Wai              (Application, Response, responseLBS)
import           Network.Wai.Conduit      (sourceRequestBody)
import           Network.Wai.Handler.Warp (run)

main :: IO ()
main = run 3000 app

app :: Application
app req sendResponse = handle (sendResponse . invalidJson) $ do
```

```
    value <- sourceRequestBody req $$ sinkParser json
    newValue <- liftIO $ modValue value
    sendResponse $ responseLBS
        status200
        [("Content-Type", "application/json")]
        $ encode newValue

invalidJson :: SomeException -> Response
invalidJson ex = responseLBS
    status400
    [("Content-Type", "application/json")]
    $ encode $ object
        [ ("message" .= show ex)
        ]

-- Application-specific logic would go here.
modValue :: Value -> IO Value
modValue = return
```

Client

http-conduit was written as a companion to WAI. It too uses conduit and blaze-builder pervasively, meaning we once again get easy interop with aeson. A few extra comments for those not familiar with http-conduit:

- A Manager is present to keep track of open connections, so that multiple requests to the same server use the same connection. You usually want to use the withManager function to create and clean up this Manager, as it is exception-safe.

- We need to know the size of our request body, which can't be determined directly from a Builder. Instead, we convert the Builder into a lazy ByteString and take the size from there.

- There are a number of different functions for initiating a request. We use http, which allows us to directly access the data stream. There are other higher-level functions (such as httpLbs) that let you ignore the issue of sources and get the entire body directly.

```
{-# LANGUAGE OverloadedStrings #-}
import           Control.Monad.IO.Class  (liftIO)
import           Data.Aeson              (Value (Object, String))
import           Data.Aeson              (encode, object, (.=))
import           Data.Aeson.Parser       (json)
import           Data.Conduit            (($$+-))
import           Data.Conduit.Attoparsec (sinkParser)
import           Network.HTTP.Conduit    (RequestBody (RequestBodyLBS),
                                          Response (..), http, method, parseUrl,
                                          requestBody, withManager)
```

```
main :: IO ()
main = withManager $ \manager -> do
    value <- liftIO makeValue
    -- We need to know the size of the request body, so we convert to a
    -- ByteString
    let valueBS = encode value
    req' <- liftIO $ parseUrl "http://localhost:3000/"
    let req = req' { method = "POST", requestBody = RequestBodyLBS valueBS }
    res <- http req manager
    resValue <- responseBody res $$+- sinkParser json
    liftIO $ handleResponse resValue

-- Application-specific function to make the request value
makeValue :: IO Value
makeValue = return $ object
    [ ("foo" .= ("bar" :: String))
    ]

-- Application-specific function to handle the response from the server
handleResponse :: Value -> IO ()
handleResponse = print
```

CHAPTER 25

Case Study: Sphinx-Based Search

Sphinx (*http://sphinxsearch.com/*) is a search server, and it powers the search feature on many sites. The actual code necessary to integrate Yesod with Sphinx is relatively short, but it touches on a number of complicated topics and is therefore a great case study on how to play with some of the under-the-surface details of Yesod.

There are essentially three different pieces at play here:

Storing the content we wish to search
> This is fairly straightforward Persistent code, and we won't dwell on it much in this chapter.

Accessing Sphinx search results from inside Yesod
> Thanks to the Sphinx package, this is actually very easy.

Providing the document content to Sphinx
> This is where the interesting stuff happens. We'll show how to deal with streaming content from a database to XML, which then gets sent directly over the wire to the client.

The full code for this example can be found on FP Haskell Center (*http://www.bit.ly/ fp-h-center*).

Sphinx Setup

Unlike in many of our other examples, to start with here we'll need to actually configure and run our external Sphinx server. I'm not going to go into all the details of Sphinx, partly because it's not relevant to our point here, but mostly because I'm not an expert on Sphinx.

Sphinx provides three main command-line utilities: searchd is the actual search daemon that receives requests from the client (in this case, our web app) and returns the search results; indexer parses the set of documents and creates the search index; and search is a debugging utility that will run simple queries against Sphinx.

There are two important settings: the source and the index. The source tells Sphinx where to read document information from. It has direct support for MySQL and PostgreSQL, as well as a more general XML format known as *xmlpipe2*. We're going to use the last one. This not only will give us more flexibility with choosing Persistent backends, but will also demonstrate some more powerful Yesod concepts.

The second setting is the index. Sphinx can handle multiple indices simultaneously, which allows it to provide search functionality for multiple services at once. Each index will have a source it pulls from.

In our case, we're going to provide a URL from our application (*/search/xmlpipe*) that provides the XML file required by Sphinx, and then pipe that through to the indexer. So, we'll add the following to our Sphinx config file:

```
source searcher_src
{
        type = xmlpipe2
        xmlpipe_command = curl http://localhost:3000/search/xmlpipe
}

index searcher
{
        source = searcher_src
        path = /var/data/searcher
        docinfo = extern
        charset_type = utf-8
}

searchd
{
        listen              = 9312
        pid_file            = /var/run/sphinxsearch/searchd.pid
}
```

In order to build your search index, you would run indexer searcher. Obviously, this won't work until you have your web app running. For a production site, it would make sense to run this command via a cron job so the index is regularly updated.

Basic Yesod Setup

Let's get our basic Yesod setup going. We're going to have a single table in the database for holding documents, which each consist of a title and content. We'll store this in a SQLite database and provide routes for searching, adding documents, viewing documents, and providing the *xmlpipe* file to Sphinx:

```
share [mkPersist sqlSettings, mkMigrate "migrateAll"] [persistLowerCase|
Doc
    title Text
    content Textarea
|]

data Searcher = Searcher
    { connPool :: ConnectionPool
    }

mkYesod "Searcher" [parseRoutes|
/ HomeR GET
/doc/#DocId DocR GET
/add-doc AddDocR POST
/search SearchR GET
/search/xmlpipe XmlpipeR GET
|]

instance Yesod Searcher

instance YesodPersist Searcher where
    type YesodPersistBackend Searcher = SqlBackend

    runDB action = do
        Searcher pool <- getYesod
        runSqlPool action pool

instance YesodPersistRunner Searcher where -- see below
    getDBRunner = defaultGetDBRunner connPool

instance RenderMessage Searcher FormMessage where
    renderMessage _ _ = defaultFormMessage
```

Hopefully all of this looks pretty familiar by now. The one new thing we've defined here is an instance of YesodPersistRunner. This is a typeclass necessary for creating streaming database responses. The default implementation (defaultGetDBRunner) is almost always appropriate.

Next, we'll define some forms—one for creating documents, and one for searching:

```
addDocForm :: Html -> MForm Handler (FormResult Doc, Widget)
addDocForm = renderTable $ Doc
    <$> areq textField "Title" Nothing
    <*> areq textareaField "Contents" Nothing

searchForm :: Html -> MForm Handler (FormResult Text, Widget)
searchForm = renderDivs $ areq (searchField True) "Query" Nothing
```

The True parameter to searchField makes the field autofocus on page load. Finally, we have some standard handlers for the homepage (shows the add document form and the search form), the document display, and adding a document:

```
getHomeR :: Handler Html
getHomeR = do
    docCount <- runDB $ count ([] :: [Filter Doc])
    ((_, docWidget), _) <- runFormPost addDocForm
    ((_, searchWidget), _) <- runFormGet searchForm
    let docs = if docCount == 1
                then "There is currently 1 document."
                else "There are currently " ++ show docCount ++ " documents."
    defaultLayout
        [whamlet|
            <p>Welcome to the search application. #{docs}
            <form method=post action=@{AddDocR}>
                <table>
                    ^{docWidget}
                    <tr>
                        <td colspan=3>
                            <input type=submit value="Add document">
            <form method=get action=@{SearchR}>
                ^{searchWidget}
                <input type=submit value=Search>
        |]

postAddDocR :: Handler Html
postAddDocR = do
    ((res, docWidget), _) <- runFormPost addDocForm
    case res of
        FormSuccess doc -> do
            docid <- runDB $ insert doc
            setMessage "Document added"
            redirect $ DocR docid
        _ -> defaultLayout
            [whamlet|
                <form method=post action=@{AddDocR}>
                    <table>
                        ^{docWidget}
                        <tr>
                            <td colspan=3>
                                <input type=submit value="Add document">
            |]

getDocR :: DocId -> Handler Html
getDocR docid = do
    doc <- runDB $ get404 docid
    defaultLayout
        [whamlet|
            <h1>#{docTitle doc}
            <div .content>#{docContent doc}
        |]
```

Searching

Now that we've got the boring stuff out of the way, let's jump into the actual searching. We're going to need three pieces of information for displaying a result: the ID of the document it comes from, the title of that document, and the excerpts. Excerpts are the highlighted portions of the document that contain the search term (see Figure 25-1).

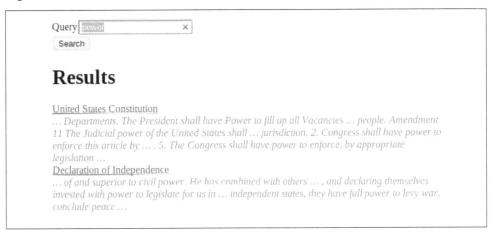

Figure 25-1. Search result

So, let's start off by defining a `Result` data type:

```
data Result = Result
    { resultId      :: DocId
    , resultTitle   :: Text
    , resultExcerpt :: Html
    }
```

Next, we'll look at the search handler:

```
getSearchR :: Handler Html
getSearchR = do
    ((formRes, searchWidget), _) <- runFormGet searchForm
    searchResults <-
        case formRes of
            FormSuccess qstring -> getResults qstring
            _ -> return []
    defaultLayout $ do
        toWidget
            [lucius|
                .excerpt {
                    color: green; font-style: italic
                }
                .match {
                    background-color: yellow;
```

```
            }
        |]
    [whamlet|
        <form method=get action=@{SearchR}>
            ^{searchWidget}
            <input type=submit value=Search>
        $if not $ null searchResults
            <h1>Results
            $forall result <- searchResults
                <div .result>
                    <a href=@{DocR $ resultId result}>#{resultTitle result}
                    <div .excerpt>#{resultExcerpt result}
    |]
```

Nothing magical here; we're just relying on the `searchForm` defined earlier and the `getResults` function, which hasn't been defined yet. This function just takes a search string and returns a list of results. This is where we first interact with the Sphinx API. We'll be using two functions: `query` will return a list of matches, and `buildExcerpts` will return the highlighted excerpts. Let's first look at `getResults`:

```
getResults :: Text -> Handler [Result]
getResults qstring = do
    sphinxRes' <- liftIO $ S.query config "searcher" qstring
    case sphinxRes' of
        ST.Ok sphinxRes -> do
            let docids = map (toSqlKey . ST.documentId) $ ST.matches sphinxRes
            fmap catMaybes $ runDB $ forM docids $ \docid -> do
                mdoc <- get docid
                case mdoc of
                    Nothing -> return Nothing
                    Just doc -> liftIO $ Just <$> getResult docid doc qstring
        _ -> error $ show sphinxRes'
  where
    config = S.defaultConfig
        { S.port = 9312
        , S.mode = ST.Any
        }
```

`query` takes three parameters: the configuration options, the index to search against (searcher in this case), and the search string. It returns a list of document IDs that contain the search string. The tricky bit here is that those documents are returned as `Int64` values, whereas we need `DocIds`. Fortunately, for the SQL Persistent backends, we can just use the `toSqlKey` function to perform the conversion.

 If you're dealing with a backend that has nonnumeric IDs, like MongoDB, you'll need to work out something a bit cleverer than this.

We then loop over the resulting IDs to get a [Maybe Result] value, and use cat Maybes to turn it into a [Result]. In the where clause, we define our local settings, which override the default port and set up the search to work when *any* term matches the document.

Let's finally look at the getResult function:

```
getResult :: DocId -> Doc -> Text -> IO Result
getResult docid doc qstring = do
    excerpt' <- S.buildExcerpts
        excerptConfig
        [escape $ docContent doc]
        "searcher"
        qstring
    let excerpt =
            case excerpt' of
                ST.Ok texts -> preEscapedToHtml $ mconcat texts
                _ -> ""
    return Result
        { resultId = docid
        , resultTitle = docTitle doc
        , resultExcerpt = excerpt
        }
  where
    excerptConfig = E.altConfig { E.port = 9312 }

escape :: Textarea -> Text
escape =
    T.concatMap escapeChar . unTextarea
  where
    escapeChar '<' = "&lt;"
    escapeChar '>' = "&gt;"
    escapeChar '&' = "&amp;"
    escapeChar c   = T.singleton c
```

buildExcerpts takes four parameters: the configuration options, the textual contents of the document, the search index, and the search term. The interesting bit is that we entity-escape the text content. Sphinx won't automatically escape these for us, so we must do it explicitly.

Similarly, the result from Sphinx is a list of Texts. But of course, we'd rather have HTML, so we concat that list into a single Text and use preEscapedToHtml to make sure that the tags inserted for matches are not escaped. Here's a sample of this HTML:

```
&#8230; Departments.  The President shall have <span class='match'>Power</span>
to fill up all Vacancies
&#8230;  people. Amendment 11 The Judicial <span class='match'>power</span>
of the United States shall
&#8230; jurisdiction. 2. Congress shall have <span class='match'>power</span>
to enforce this article by
&#8230; 5. The Congress shall have <span class='match'>power</span>
```

```
to enforce, by appropriate legislation
&#8230;
```

Streaming xmlpipe Output

I've saved the best for last. For the majority of Yesod handlers, the recommended approach is to load up the database results into memory and then produce the output document based on that. It's simpler to work with, but more importantly it's more resilient to exceptions. If there's a problem loading the data from the database, the user will get a proper 500 response code.

 What do I mean by "proper 500 response code?" If you start streaming a response to a client and encounter an exception halfway through, there's no way to change the status code; the user will see a 200 response that simply stops in the middle. Not only can this partial content be confusing, but it's an invalid usage of the HTTP spec.

However, generating the *xmlpipe* output is a perfect example of the alternative. There are potentially a huge number of documents, and documents could easily be several hundred kilobytes each. If we take a non-streaming approach, this can lead to huge memory usage and slow response times.

So how exactly do we create a streaming response? Yesod provides a helper function for this case: `responseSourceDB`. This function takes two arguments: a content type, and a `conduit Source` providing a stream of `blaze-builder Builders`. Yesod then handles all of the issues of grabbing a database connection from the connection pool, starting a transaction, and streaming the response to the user.

Now we know we want to create a stream of `Builders` from some XML content. Fortunately, the `xml-conduit` package provides this interface directly. `xml-conduit` provides some high-level interfaces for dealing with documents as a whole, but in our case, we're going to need to use the low-level `Event` interface to ensure minimal memory impact. So, the function we're interested in is:

```
renderBuilder :: Monad m => RenderSettings -> Conduit Event m Builder
```

In plain English, that means `renderBuilder` takes some settings (we'll just use the defaults), and will then convert a stream of `Events` to a stream of `Builders`. This is looking pretty good; all we need now is a stream of `Events`.

Speaking of which, what should our XML document actually look like? It's pretty simple: we have a `<sphinx:docset>` root element, a `<sphinx:schema>` element containing a single `<sphinx:field>` (which defines the content field), and then a

`<sphinx:document>` for each document in our database. That last element will have an `id` attribute and a child `content` element. Here is an example of such a document:

```
<sphinx:docset xmlns:sphinx="http://sphinxsearch.com/">
    <sphinx:schema>
        <sphinx:field name="content"/>
    </sphinx:schema>
    <sphinx:document id="1">
        <content>bar</content>
    </sphinx:document>
    <sphinx:document id="2">
        <content>foo bar baz</content>
    </sphinx:document>
</sphinx:docset>
```

 If you're not familiar with XML namespaces, the `xmlns:` syntax and `sphinx:` prefixes may look pretty weird. I don't want to get into an XML tutorial in this chapter, so I'll avoid an explanation. If you're curious, feel free to look up the XML namespace specification.

Every document is going to start off with the same events (start the `docset`, start the schema, etc.) and end with the same event (end the `docset`). We'll start off by defining those:

```
toName :: Text -> X.Name
toName x = X.Name x (Just "http://sphinxsearch.com/") (Just "sphinx")

docset, schema, field, document, content :: X.Name
docset = toName "docset"
schema = toName "schema"
field = toName "field"
document = toName "document"
content = "content" -- no prefix

startEvents, endEvents :: [X.Event]
startEvents =
    [ X.EventBeginDocument
    , X.EventBeginElement docset []
    , X.EventBeginElement schema []
    , X.EventBeginElement field [("name", [X.ContentText "content"])]
    , X.EventEndElement field
    , X.EventEndElement schema
    ]

endEvents =
    [ X.EventEndElement docset
    ]
```

Now that we have the shell of our document, we need to get the `Events` for each individual document. This is actually a fairly simple function:

```
entityToEvents :: Entity Doc -> [X.Event]
entityToEvents (Entity docid doc) =
    [ X.EventBeginElement document [("id", [X.ContentText $ toPathPiece docid])]
    , X.EventBeginElement content []
    , X.EventContent $ X.ContentText $ unTextarea $ docContent doc
    , X.EventEndElement content
    , X.EventEndElement document
    ]
```

We start the document element with an id attribute, start the content, insert the content, and then close both elements. We use toPathPiece to convert a DocId into a Text value. Next, we need to be able to convert a stream of these entities into a stream of events. For this, we can use the built-in concatMap function from Data.Conduit.List: CL.concatMap entityToEvents.

But what we *really* want is to stream those events directly from the database. For most of this book, we've used the selectList function, but Persistent also provides the (more powerful) selectSource function. So we end up with the function:

```
docSource :: Source (YesodDB Searcher) X.Event
docSource = selectSource [] [] $= CL.concatMap entityToEvents
```

The $= operator joins together a source and a conduit into a new source. Now that we have our Event source, all we need to do is surround it with the document start and end events. With Source's Monad instance, this is a piece of cake:

```
fullDocSource :: Source (YesodDB Searcher) X.Event
fullDocSource = do
    mapM_ yield startEvents
    docSource
    mapM_ yield endEvents
```

Now we need to tie it together in getXmlpipeR. We can do so by using the respond SourceDB function mentioned earlier. The last trick we need to do is convert our stream of Events into a stream of Chunk Builders. Converting to a stream of Builders is achieved with renderBuilder, and finally we'll just wrap each Builder in its own Chunk:

```
getXmlpipeR :: Handler TypedContent
getXmlpipeR =
    respondSourceDB "text/xml"
    $  fullDocSource
    $= renderBuilder def
    $= CL.map Chunk
```

Full Code

```
{-# LANGUAGE FlexibleContexts           #-}
{-# LANGUAGE GADTs                      #-}
{-# LANGUAGE GeneralizedNewtypeDeriving #-}
```

```
{-# LANGUAGE MultiParamTypeClasses    #-}
{-# LANGUAGE OverloadedStrings        #-}
{-# LANGUAGE QuasiQuotes              #-}
{-# LANGUAGE TemplateHaskell          #-}
{-# LANGUAGE TypeFamilies             #-}
{-# LANGUAGE ViewPatterns             #-}
import            Control.Applicative              ((<$>), (<*>))
import            Control.Monad                    (forM)
import            Control.Monad.Logger             (runStdoutLoggingT)
import            Data.Conduit
import qualified  Data.Conduit.List                as CL
import            Data.Maybe                       (catMaybes)
import            Data.Monoid                      (mconcat)
import            Data.Text                        (Text)
import qualified  Data.Text                        as T
import            Data.Text.Lazy.Encoding          (decodeUtf8)
import qualified  Data.XML.Types                   as X
import            Database.Persist.Sqlite
import            Text.Blaze.Html                  (preEscapedToHtml)
import qualified  Text.Search.Sphinx               as S
import qualified  Text.Search.Sphinx.ExcerptConfiguration as E
import qualified  Text.Search.Sphinx.Types         as ST
import            Text.XML.Stream.Render           (def, renderBuilder)
import            Yesod

share [mkPersist sqlSettings, mkMigrate "migrateAll"] [persistLowerCase|
Doc
    title Text
    content Textarea
|]

data Searcher = Searcher
    { connPool :: ConnectionPool
    }

mkYesod "Searcher" [parseRoutes|
/ HomeR GET
/doc/#DocId DocR GET
/add-doc AddDocR POST
/search SearchR GET
/search/xmlpipe XmlpipeR GET
|]

instance Yesod Searcher

instance YesodPersist Searcher where
    type YesodPersistBackend Searcher = SqlBackend

    runDB action = do
        Searcher pool <- getYesod
        runSqlPool action pool
```

```
instance YesodPersistRunner Searcher where
    getDBRunner = defaultGetDBRunner connPool

instance RenderMessage Searcher FormMessage where
    renderMessage _ _ = defaultFormMessage

addDocForm :: Html -> MForm Handler (FormResult Doc, Widget)
addDocForm = renderTable $ Doc
    <$> areq textField "Title" Nothing
    <*> areq textareaField "Contents" Nothing

searchForm :: Html -> MForm Handler (FormResult Text, Widget)
searchForm = renderDivs $ areq (searchField True) "Query" Nothing

getHomeR :: Handler Html
getHomeR = do
    docCount <- runDB $ count ([] :: [Filter Doc])
    ((_, docWidget), _) <- runFormPost addDocForm
    ((_, searchWidget), _) <- runFormGet searchForm
    let docs = if docCount == 1
                then "There is currently 1 document."
                else "There are currently " ++ show docCount ++ " documents."
    defaultLayout
        [whamlet|
            <p>Welcome to the search application. #{docs}
            <form method=post action=@{AddDocR}>
                <table>
                    ^{docWidget}
                    <tr>
                        <td colspan=3>
                            <input type=submit value="Add document">
            <form method=get action=@{SearchR}>
                ^{searchWidget}
                <input type=submit value=Search>
        |]

postAddDocR :: Handler Html
postAddDocR = do
    ((res, docWidget), _) <- runFormPost addDocForm
    case res of
        FormSuccess doc -> do
            docid <- runDB $ insert doc
            setMessage "Document added"
            redirect $ DocR docid
        _ -> defaultLayout
            [whamlet|
                <form method=post action=@{AddDocR}>
                    <table>
                        ^{docWidget}
                        <tr>
                            <td colspan=3>
                                <input type=submit value="Add document">
```

```
            |]

getDocR :: DocId -> Handler Html
getDocR docid = do
    doc <- runDB $ get404 docid
    defaultLayout
        [whamlet|
            <h1>#{docTitle doc}
            <div .content>#{docContent doc}
        |]

data Result = Result
    { resultId      :: DocId
    , resultTitle   :: Text
    , resultExcerpt :: Html
    }

getResult :: DocId -> Doc -> Text -> IO Result
getResult docid doc qstring = do
    excerpt' <- S.buildExcerpts
        excerptConfig
        [escape $ docContent doc]
        "searcher"
        qstring
    let excerpt =
            case excerpt' of
                ST.Ok texts -> preEscapedToHtml $ mconcat texts
                _ -> ""
    return Result
        { resultId = docid
        , resultTitle = docTitle doc
        , resultExcerpt = excerpt
        }
  where
    excerptConfig = E.altConfig { E.port = 9312 }

escape :: Textarea -> Text
escape =
    T.concatMap escapeChar . unTextarea
  where
    escapeChar '<' = "&lt;"
    escapeChar '>' = "&gt;"
    escapeChar '&' = "&amp;"
    escapeChar c   = T.singleton c

getResults :: Text -> Handler [Result]
getResults qstring = do
    sphinxRes' <- liftIO $ S.query config "searcher" qstring
    case sphinxRes' of
        ST.Ok sphinxRes -> do
            let docids = map (toSqlKey . ST.documentId) $ ST.matches sphinxRes
            fmap catMaybes $ runDB $ forM docids $ \docid -> do
```

```
                    mdoc <- get docid
                    case mdoc of
                         Nothing -> return Nothing
                         Just doc -> liftIO $ Just <$> getResult docid doc qstring
              _ -> error $ show sphinxRes'
    where
      config = S.defaultConfig
          { S.port = 9312
          , S.mode = ST.Any
          }

getSearchR :: Handler Html
getSearchR = do
    ((formRes, searchWidget), _) <- runFormGet searchForm
    searchResults <-
        case formRes of
            FormSuccess qstring -> getResults qstring
            _ -> return []
    defaultLayout $ do
        toWidget
            [lucius|
                .excerpt {
                    color: green; font-style: italic
                }
                .match {
                    background-color: yellow;
                }
            |]
        [whamlet|
            <form method=get action=@{SearchR}>
                ^{searchWidget}
                <input type=submit value=Search>
            $if not $ null searchResults
                <h1>Results
                $forall result <- searchResults
                    <div .result>
                        <a href=@{DocR $ resultId result}>#{resultTitle result}
                        <div .excerpt>#{resultExcerpt result}
        |]

getXmlpipeR :: Handler TypedContent
getXmlpipeR =
    respondSourceDB "text/xml"
  $  fullDocSource
  $= renderBuilder def
  $= CL.map Chunk

entityToEvents :: (Entity Doc) -> [X.Event]
entityToEvents (Entity docid doc) =
    [ X.EventBeginElement document [("id", [X.ContentText $ toPathPiece docid])]
    , X.EventBeginElement content []
    , X.EventContent $ X.ContentText $ unTextarea $ docContent doc
```

```
    , X.EventEndElement content
    , X.EventEndElement document
    ]

fullDocSource :: Source (YesodDB Searcher) X.Event
fullDocSource = do
    mapM_ yield startEvents
    docSource
    mapM_ yield endEvents

docSource :: Source (YesodDB Searcher) X.Event
docSource = selectSource [] [] $= CL.concatMap entityToEvents

toName :: Text -> X.Name
toName x = X.Name x (Just "http://sphinxsearch.com/") (Just "sphinx")

docset, schema, field, document, content :: X.Name
docset = toName "docset"
schema = toName "schema"
field = toName "field"
document = toName "document"
content = "content" -- no prefix

startEvents, endEvents :: [X.Event]
startEvents =
    [ X.EventBeginDocument
    , X.EventBeginElement docset []
    , X.EventBeginElement schema []
    , X.EventBeginElement field [("name", [X.ContentText "content"])]
    , X.EventEndElement field
    , X.EventEndElement schema
    ]

endEvents =
    [ X.EventEndElement docset
    ]

main :: IO ()
main = runStdoutLoggingT $ withSqlitePool "searcher.db3" 10 $
 \pool -> liftIO $ do
    runSqlPool (runMigration migrateAll) pool
    warp 3000 $ Searcher pool
```

Visitor Counter

Remember back in the good ol' days of the Internet, when no website was complete without a little "you are visitor number 32" thingy? Ahh, those were the good times! Let's re-create that wonderful experience in Yesod!

Now, if we wanted to do this properly, we'd store this information in some kind of persistent storage layer, like a database, so that the information could be shared across multiple horizontally scaled web servers and would survive an app restart.

But our goal here isn't to demonstrate good practice (after all, if it was about good practice, I wouldn't be demonstrating a visitor counter, right?). Instead, this is meant to provide a simple example of sharing some state among multiple handlers. A real-world use case would be caching information across requests. Just remember that when you use the technique shown here, you need to be careful about multiple app servers and app restarts.

The technique is simple: we create a new field in the foundation data type for a mutable reference to some data, and then access it in each handler. The technique is so simple, it's worth just diving into the code:

```
{-# LANGUAGE OverloadedStrings #-}
{-# LANGUAGE QuasiQuotes       #-}
{-# LANGUAGE TemplateHaskell   #-}
{-# LANGUAGE TypeFamilies      #-}
import           Data.IORef
import           Yesod

data App = App
    { visitors :: IORef Int
    }

mkYesod "App" [parseRoutes|
/ HomeR GET
```

```
|]

instance Yesod App

getHomeR :: Handler Html
getHomeR = do
    visitorsRef <- fmap visitors getYesod
    visitors <-
        liftIO $ atomicModifyIORef visitorsRef $ \i ->
        (i + 1, i + 1)
    defaultLayout
        [whamlet|
            <p>Welcome, you are visitor number #{visitors}.
        |]

main :: IO ()
main = do
    visitorsRef <- newIORef 0
    warp 3000 App
        { visitors = visitorsRef
        }
```

I used IORef here, because we didn't need anything more than it provided, but you're free to use MVars or TVars as well. In fact, a good exercise for the reader is to modify this program to store the visitor count in a TVar instead.

Single-Process Pub/Sub

The example in the previous chapter was admittedly quite simple. Let's build on that foundation (pun intended) to do something a bit more interesting. Suppose we have a workflow on our site like the following:

1. Enter some information on page X, and submit.
2. Submission starts a background job, and the user is redirected to a page to view the status of that job.
3. That second page will subscribe to updates from the background job and display them to the user.

The core principle here is the ability to let one thread publish updates, and have another thread subscribe to receive those updates. This is known generally as *pub/sub*, and fortunately is very easy to achieve in Haskell via STM (the Software Transactional Memory library).

Like in the previous chapter, let me start off with the following caveat: this technique only works properly if you have a single web application process. If you have two different servers and a load balancer, you'll either need sticky sessions or some other solution to make sure that the requests from a single user are going to the same machine. In those situations, you may want to consider using an external pub/sub solution, such as Redis.

With that caveat out of the way, let's get started.

Foundation Data Type

We'll need two different mutable references in our foundation. The first will keep track of the next "job ID" we'll hand out. Each of these background jobs will be represented by a unique identifier that will be used in our URLs. The second piece of data will be a map from the job ID to the broadcast channel used for publishing updates. In code:

```
data App = App
    { jobs    :: TVar (IntMap (TChan (Maybe Text)))
    , nextJob :: TVar Int
    }
```

Notice that our `TChan` contains `Maybe Text` values. The reason for the `Maybe` wrapper is so that we can indicate that the channel is complete, by providing a `Nothing` value.

Allocate a Job

In order to allocate a job, we need to:

1. Get a job ID.

2. Create a new broadcast channel.

3. Add the channel to the channel map.

Due to the beauty of STM, this is pretty easy:

```
(jobId, chan) <- liftIO $ atomically $ do
    jobId <- readTVar nextJob
    writeTVar nextJob $! jobId + 1
    chan <- newBroadcastTChan
    m <- readTVar jobs
    writeTVar jobs $ IntMap.insert jobId chan m
    return (jobId, chan)
```

Fork Our Background Job

There are many different ways we could go about this, and they depend entirely on what the background job is going to be. Here's a minimal example of a background job that prints out a few messages, with a one-second delay between each message. Note how after our final message, we broadcast a `Nothing` value and remove our channel from the map of channels:

```
liftIO $ forkIO $ do
    threadDelay 1000000
    atomically $ writeTChan chan $ Just "Did something\n"
    threadDelay 1000000
    atomically $ writeTChan chan $ Just "Did something else\n"
    threadDelay 1000000
    atomically $ do
        writeTChan chan $ Just "All done\n"
        writeTChan chan Nothing
```

```
    m <- readTVar jobs
    writeTVar jobs $ IntMap.delete jobId m
```

View Progress

For this demonstration, I've elected for a very simple progress viewing: a plain text page with a streaming response. There are a few other possibilities here: an HTML page that autorefreshes every X seconds, or using EventSource or WebSockets. I encourage you to give those a shot also, but here's the simplest implementation I can think of:

```
getViewProgressR jobId = do
    App {..} <- getYesod
    mchan <- liftIO $ atomically $ do
        m <- readTVar jobs
        case IntMap.lookup jobId m of
            Nothing -> return Nothing
            Just chan -> fmap Just $ dupTChan chan
    case mchan of
        Nothing -> notFound
        Just chan -> respondSource typePlain $ do
            let loop = do
                    mtext <- liftIO $ atomically $ readTChan chan
                    case mtext of
                        Nothing -> return ()
                        Just text -> do
                            sendChunkText text
                            sendFlush
                            loop
            loop
```

We start off by looking up the channel in the map. If we can't find it, it means the job either never existed, or has already been completed. In either event, we return a 404. (Another possible enhancement would be to store some information on all previously completed jobs and let the user know if the job is done.)

Assuming the channel exists, we use `respondSource` to start a streaming response. We then repeatedly call `readTChan` until we get a `Nothing` value, at which point we exit (via `return ()`). Notice that on each iteration, we call both `sendChunkText` and `sendFlush`. Without that second call, the user won't receive any updates until the output buffer completely fills up, which is not acceptable for a real-time update system.

Complete Application

For completeness, here's the full source code for this application:

```
{-# LANGUAGE OverloadedStrings #-}
{-# LANGUAGE QuasiQuotes       #-}
{-# LANGUAGE RecordWildCards   #-}
```

```
{-# LANGUAGE TemplateHaskell    #-}
{-# LANGUAGE TypeFamilies       #-}
{-# LANGUAGE ViewPatterns       #-}
import              Control.Concurrent    (forkIO, threadDelay)
import              Control.Concurrent.STM
import              Data.IntMap           (IntMap)
import qualified    Data.IntMap           as IntMap
import              Data.Text             (Text)
import              Yesod

data App = App
    { jobs    :: TVar (IntMap (TChan (Maybe Text)))
    , nextJob :: TVar Int
    }

mkYesod "App" [parseRoutes|
/ HomeR GET POST
/view-progress/#Int ViewProgressR GET
|]

instance Yesod App

getHomeR :: Handler Html
getHomeR = defaultLayout $ do
    setTitle "PubSub example"
    [whamlet|
        <form method=post>
            <button>Start new background job
    |]

postHomeR :: Handler ()
postHomeR = do
    App {..} <- getYesod
    (jobId, chan) <- liftIO $ atomically $ do
        jobId <- readTVar nextJob
        writeTVar nextJob $! jobId + 1
        chan <- newBroadcastTChan
        m <- readTVar jobs
        writeTVar jobs $ IntMap.insert jobId chan m
        return (jobId, chan)
    liftIO $ forkIO $ do
        threadDelay 1000000
        atomically $ writeTChan chan $ Just "Did something\n"
        threadDelay 1000000
        atomically $ writeTChan chan $ Just "Did something else\n"
        threadDelay 1000000
        atomically $ do
            writeTChan chan $ Just "All done\n"
            writeTChan chan Nothing
            m <- readTVar jobs
            writeTVar jobs $ IntMap.delete jobId m
    redirect $ ViewProgressR jobId
```

```
getViewProgressR :: Int -> Handler TypedContent
getViewProgressR jobId = do
    App {..} <- getYesod
    mchan <- liftIO $ atomically $ do
        m <- readTVar jobs
        case IntMap.lookup jobId m of
            Nothing -> return Nothing
            Just chan -> fmap Just $ dupTChan chan
    case mchan of
        Nothing -> notFound
        Just chan -> respondSource typePlain $ do
            let loop = do
                    mtext <- liftIO $ atomically $ readTChan chan
                    case mtext of
                        Nothing -> return ()
                        Just text -> do
                            sendChunkText text
                            sendFlush
                            loop
            loop

main :: IO ()
main = do
    jobs <- newTVarIO IntMap.empty
    nextJob <- newTVarIO 1
    warp 3000 App {..}
```

Environment Variables for Configuration

There's a recent move, perhaps most prominently advocated by the twelve-factor app (*http://12factor.net/config*), to store all app configuration in environment variables instead of using config files or hardcoding them into the application source code (you don't do that, right?).

Yesod's scaffolding comes built in with some support for this—most specifically, for respecting the APPROOT environment variable to indicate how URLs should be generated, the PORT environment variable for which port to listen for requests on, and database connection settings. (Incidentally, this ties in nicely with the Keter deployment manager (*https://github.com/snoyberg/keter*).)

The technique for doing this is quite easy: just do the environment variable lookup in your main function. The following example demonstrates this technique, along with the slightly special handling necessary for setting the application root:

```
{-# LANGUAGE OverloadedStrings #-}
{-# LANGUAGE QuasiQuotes       #-}
{-# LANGUAGE RecordWildCards   #-}
{-# LANGUAGE TemplateHaskell   #-}
{-# LANGUAGE TypeFamilies      #-}
import          Data.Text         (Text, pack)
import          System.Environment
import          Yesod

data App = App
    { myApproot      :: Text
    , welcomeMessage :: Text
    }

mkYesod "App" [parseRoutes|
/ HomeR GET
|]
```

```
instance Yesod App where
    approot = ApprootMaster myApproot

getHomeR :: Handler Html
getHomeR = defaultLayout $ do
    App {..} <- getYesod
    setTitle "Environment variables"
    [whamlet|
        <p>Here's the welcome message: #{welcomeMessage}
        <p>
            <a href=@{HomeR}>And a link to: @{HomeR}
    |]

main :: IO ()
main = do
    myApproot <- fmap pack $ getEnv "APPROOT"
    welcomeMessage <- fmap pack $ getEnv "WELCOME_MESSAGE"
    warp 3000 App {..}
```

The only tricky things here are:

- You need to convert the String value returned by getEnv into a Text by using pack.

- We use the ApprootMaster constructor for approot, which says "Apply this function to the foundation data type to get the actual application root."

Route Attributes

Route attributes allow you to set some metadata on each of your routes, in the route description itself. The syntax is trivial: just an exclamation point followed by a value. Using it is also trivial: just use the routeAttrs function.

It's easiest to understand how all this fits together, and when you might want to use it, with a motivating example. The case I personally most use this for is annotating administrative routes. Imagine having a website with about 12 different admin actions. You could manually add a call to requireAdmin or some such at the beginning of each action, but:

- It's tedious.
- It's error prone: you could easily forget one.
- Worse yet, it's not easy to notice that you've missed one.

Modifying your isAuthorized method with an explicit list of administrative routes is a bit better, but it's still difficult to see at a glance when you've missed one.

This is why I like to use route attributes for this: you add a single word to each relevant part of the route definition, and then you just check for that attribute in isAuthorized. Let's see the code!

```
{-# LANGUAGE MultiParamTypeClasses #-}
{-# LANGUAGE OverloadedStrings     #-}
{-# LANGUAGE QuasiQuotes           #-}
{-# LANGUAGE TemplateHaskell       #-}
{-# LANGUAGE TypeFamilies          #-}
import           Data.Set           (member)
import           Data.Text          (Text)
import           Yesod
import           Yesod.Auth
```

```
import             Yesod.Auth.Dummy

data App = App

mkYesod "App" [parseRoutes|
/ HomeR GET
/unprotected UnprotectedR GET
/admin1 Admin1R GET !admin
/admin2 Admin2R GET !admin
/admin3 Admin3R GET
/auth AuthR Auth getAuth
|]

instance Yesod App where
    authRoute _ = Just $ AuthR LoginR
    isAuthorized route _writable
        | "admin" `member` routeAttrs route = do
            muser <- maybeAuthId
            case muser of
                Nothing -> return AuthenticationRequired
                Just ident
                    -- Just a hack because we're using the dummy module
                    | ident == "admin" -> return Authorized
                    | otherwise -> return $ Unauthorized "Admin access only"
        | otherwise = return Authorized

instance RenderMessage App FormMessage where
    renderMessage _ _ = defaultFormMessage

-- Hacky YesodAuth instance for just the dummy auth plug-in
instance YesodAuth App where
    type AuthId App = Text

    loginDest _ = HomeR
    logoutDest _ = HomeR
    getAuthId = return . Just . credsIdent
    authPlugins _ = [authDummy]
    maybeAuthId = lookupSession credsKey
    authHttpManager = error "no http manager provided"

getHomeR :: Handler Html
getHomeR = defaultLayout $ do
    setTitle "Route attr homepage"
    [whamlet|
        <p>
            <a href=@{UnprotectedR}>Unprotected
        <p>
            <a href=@{Admin1R}>Admin 1
        <p>
            <a href=@{Admin2R}>Admin 2
        <p>
            <a href=@{Admin3R}>Admin 3
```

```
|]

getUnprotectedR, getAdmin1R, getAdmin2R, getAdmin3R :: Handler Html
getUnprotectedR = defaultLayout [whamlet|Unprotected|]
getAdmin1R = defaultLayout [whamlet|Admin1|]
getAdmin2R = defaultLayout [whamlet|Admin2|]
getAdmin3R = defaultLayout [whamlet|Admin3|]

main :: IO ()
main = warp 3000 App
```

And it was so glaring, I bet you even caught the security hole about Admin3R.

Alternative Approach: Hierarchical Routes

Another approach that can be used in some cases is *hierarchical routes*. This allows
you to group a number of related routes under a single parent. If you want to keep all
of your admin routes under a single URL structure (e.g., */admin*), this can be a good
solution. Using hierarchical routes is fairly simple. You need to add a line to your
routes declaration with a path, a name, and a colon:

```
/admin AdminR:
```

Then, you place all child routes beneath that line, indented at least one space:

```
/1 Admin1R GET
/2 Admin2R GET
/3 Admin3R GET
```

To refer to these routes using type-safe URLs, you simply wrap them with the AdminR
constructor (e.g., AdminR Admin1R). Here is the previous route attribute example
rewritten to use hierarchical routes:

```
{-# LANGUAGE MultiParamTypeClasses #-}
{-# LANGUAGE OverloadedStrings     #-}
{-# LANGUAGE QuasiQuotes           #-}
{-# LANGUAGE TemplateHaskell       #-}
{-# LANGUAGE TypeFamilies          #-}
import        Data.Set        (member)
import        Data.Text       (Text)
import        Yesod
import        Yesod.Auth
import        Yesod.Auth.Dummy

data App = App

mkYesod "App" [parseRoutes|
/ HomeR GET
/unprotected UnprotectedR GET
/admin AdminR:
    /1 Admin1R GET
    /2 Admin2R GET
```

```
    /3 Admin3R GET
/auth AuthR Auth getAuth
|]

instance Yesod App where
    authRoute _ = Just $ AuthR LoginR
    isAuthorized (AdminR _) _writable = do
        muser <- maybeAuthId
        case muser of
            Nothing -> return AuthenticationRequired
            Just ident
                -- Just a hack because we're using the dummy module
                | ident == "admin" -> return Authorized
                | otherwise -> return $ Unauthorized "Admin access only"
    isAuthorized _route _writable = return Authorized

instance RenderMessage App FormMessage where
    renderMessage _ _ = defaultFormMessage

-- Hacky YesodAuth instance for just the dummy auth plug-in
instance YesodAuth App where
    type AuthId App = Text

    loginDest _ = HomeR
    logoutDest _ = HomeR
    getAuthId = return . Just . credsIdent
    authPlugins _ = [authDummy]
    maybeAuthId = lookupSession credsKey
    authHttpManager = error "no http manager provided"

getHomeR :: Handler Html
getHomeR = defaultLayout $ do
    setTitle "Route attr homepage"
    [whamlet|
        <p>
            <a href=@{UnprotectedR}>Unprotected
        <p>
            <a href=@{AdminR Admin1R}>Admin 1
        <p>
            <a href=@{AdminR Admin2R}>Admin 2
        <p>
            <a href=@{AdminR Admin3R}>Admin 3
    |]

getUnprotectedR, getAdmin1R, getAdmin2R, getAdmin3R :: Handler Html
getUnprotectedR = defaultLayout [whamlet|Unprotected|]
getAdmin1R = defaultLayout [whamlet|Admin1|]
getAdmin2R = defaultLayout [whamlet|Admin2|]
getAdmin3R = defaultLayout [whamlet|Admin3|]

main :: IO ()
main = warp 3000 App
```

Appendices

monad-control

monad-control is used in a few places within Yesod, most notably to ensure proper exception handling within Persistent. It is a general-purpose package to extend standard functionality in monad transformers.

Overview

One of the powerful, and sometimes confusing, features in Haskell is monad transformers. They allow you to take different pieces of functionality—such as mutable state, error handling, or logging—and compose them easily. Though I swore I'd never write a monad tutorial, I'm going to employ a painful analogy here: monads are like onions. (Monads are *not* like cakes.) By that, I mean *layers*.

We have the core monad, also known as the innermost or bottom monad. On top of this core, we add layers, each adding a new feature and spreading outward/upward. As a motivating example, let's consider an ErrorT transformer stacked on top of the IO monad:

```
newtype ErrorT e m a = ErrorT { runErrorT :: m (Either e a) }
type MyStack = ErrorT MyError IO
```

Now pay close attention here: ErrorT is just a simple newtype around an Either wrapped in a monad. Getting rid of the newtype, we have:

```
type ErrorTUnwrapped e m a = m (Either e a)
```

At some point, we'll need to actually perform some I/O inside our MyStack. If we went with the unwrapped approach, it would be trivial, as there would be no ErrorT constructor in the way. However, we need that newtype wrapper for a whole bunch of type reasons I won't go into here (this isn't a monad transformer tutorial, after all). So the solution is the MonadTrans typeclass:

```
class MonadTrans t where
    lift :: Monad m => m a -> t m a
```

I'll admit, the first time I saw that type signature my response was stunned confusion, and incredulity that it actually meant anything. But looking at an instance helps a bit:

```
instance (Error e) => MonadTrans (ErrorT e) where
    lift m = ErrorT $ do
        a <- m
        return (Right a)
```

All we're doing is wrapping the inside of the IO with a Right value, and then applying our newtype wrapper. This allows us to take an action that lives in IO and "lift" it to the outer/upper monad.

But now to the point at hand. This works very well for simple functions. For example:

```
sayHi :: IO ()
sayHi = putStrLn "Hello"

sayHiError :: ErrorT MyError IO ()
sayHiError = lift $ putStrLn "Hello"
```

But let's take something slightly more complicated, like a callback:

```
withMyFile :: (Handle -> IO a) -> IO a
withMyFile = withFile "test.txt" WriteMode

sayHi :: Handle -> IO ()
sayHi handle = hPutStrLn handle "Hi there"

useMyFile :: IO ()
useMyFile = withMyFile sayHi
```

So far so good, right? Now let's say that we need a version of sayHi that has access to the Error monad:

```
sayHiError :: Handle -> ErrorT MyError IO ()
sayHiError handle = do
    lift $ hPutStrLn handle "Hi there, error!"
    throwError MyError
```

We would like to write a function that combines withMyFile and sayHiError. Unfortunately, GHC doesn't like this very much:

```
useMyFileErrorBad :: ErrorT MyError IO ()
useMyFileErrorBad = withMyFile sayHiError

    Couldn't match expected type `ErrorT MyError IO ()'
                with actual type `IO ()'
```

Why does this happen, and how can we work around it?

Intuition

Let's try and develop an external intuition of what's happening here. The `ErrorT` monad transformer adds extra functionality to the `IO` monad. We've defined a way to "tack on" that extra functionality to normal `IO` actions: we add that `Right` constructor and wrap it all in `ErrorT`. Wrapping in `Right` is our way of saying "it went OK"; i.e., there wasn't anything wrong with this action.

Now this intuitively makes sense: because the `IO` monad doesn't have the concept of returning a `MyError` when something goes wrong, it will always succeed in the lifting phase. (Note: This has *nothing* to do with runtime exceptions, so don't even think about them.) What we have is a guaranteed one-directional translation up the monad stack.

Let's take another example: the `Reader` monad. A `Reader` has access to some extra piece of data that's floating around. Whatever is running in the inner monad doesn't know about that extra piece of information. So how would you do a lift? You just ignore that extra information. The `Writer` monad? Don't write anything. `State`? Don't change anything. I'm seeing a pattern here.

But now let's try and go in the opposite direction: I have something in a `Reader`, and I'd like to run it in the base monad (e.g., `IO`). Well… that's not going to work, is it? I need that extra piece of information; I'm relying on it, and it's not there. There's simply no way to go in the opposite direction without providing that extra value.

Or is there? If you remember, we pointed out earlier that `ErrorT` is just a simple wrapper around the inner monad. In other words, if I have `errorValue :: ErrorT MyError IO MyValue`, I can apply `runErrorT` and get a value of type `IO (Either MyError MyValue)`. The looks quite a bit like bidirectional translation, doesn't it?

Well, not exactly. We originally had an `ErrorT MyError IO` monad, with a value of type `MyValue`. Now we have a monad of type `IO` with a value of type `Either MyError MyValue`. So, this process has in fact changed the value, while the lifting process leaves it the same.

But still, with a little fancy footwork we can unwrap the `ErrorT`, do some processing, and then wrap it back up again:

```
useMyFileError1 :: ErrorT MyError IO ()
useMyFileError1 =
    let unwrapped :: Handle -> IO (Either MyError ())
        unwrapped handle = runErrorT $ sayHiError handle
        applied :: IO (Either MyError ())
        applied = withMyFile unwrapped
        rewrapped :: ErrorT MyError IO ()
        rewrapped = ErrorT applied
     in rewrapped
```

This is the crucial point of this whole discussion, so look closely. We first unwrap our monad. This means that, to the outside world, it's now just a plain old IO value. Internally, we've stored all the information from our `ErrorT` transformer. Now that we have a plain old IO, we can easily pass it off to `withMyFile`. `withMyFile` takes in the internal state and passes it back out unchanged. Finally, we wrap everything back up into our original `ErrorT`.

This is the entire pattern of `monad-control`. We embed the extra features of our monad transformer inside the value. Once in the value, the type system ignores it and focuses on the inner monad. When we're done playing around with that inner monad, we can pull our state back out and reconstruct our original monad stack.

Types

I purposely started with the `ErrorT` transformer, as it is one of the simplest for this inversion mechanism. Unfortunately, others are a bit more complicated. Take, for instance, `ReaderT`. It is defined as `newtype ReaderT r m a = ReaderT { runRea derT :: r -> m a }`. If we apply `runReaderT` to it, we get a function that returns a monadic value. We're going to need some extra machinery to deal with all that stuff. And this is when we leave Kansas behind.

There are a few approaches to solving these problems. In the past, I implemented a solution using type families in the `neither` package. Anders Kaseorg implemented a much more straightforward solution in `monad-peel`. And for efficiency, in `monad-control`, Bas van Dijk uses CPS (continuation passing style) and existential types.

 The code taken from `monad-control` actually applies to version 0.2. 0.3 changed things just a bit, by making the state explicit with an associated type and generalizing `MonadControlIO` to `MonadBaseCon trol`, but the concepts are still the same.

The first type we're going to look at is the following:

```
type Run t = forall n o b. (Monad n, Monad o, Monad (t o)) => t n b -> n (t o b)
```

That's incredibly dense, so let's talk it out. The only "input" data type to this thing is `t`, a monad transformer. A `Run` is a function that will then work with *any* combination of types `n`, `o`, and `b` (that's what the `forall` means). `n` and `o` are both monads, while `b` is a simple value contained by them.

The lefthand side of the `Run` function, `t n b`, is our monad transformer wrapped around the `n` monad and holding a `b` value. So, for example, that could be a `MyTrans FirstMonad MyValue`. It then returns a value with the transformer "popped" inside, with a brand new monad at its core. In other words, FirstMonad (MyTrans NewMonad MyValue).

That might sound pretty scary at first, but it actually isn't as foreign as you'd think: this is essentially what we did with ErrorT. We started with ErrorT on the outside, wrapping around IO, and ended up with an IO by itself containing an Either. Well guess what: another way to represent an Either is ErrorT MyError Identity. So essentially, we pulled the IO to the outside and plunked an Identity in its place. We're doing the same thing in a Run—pulling the FirstMonad outside and replacing it with a NewMonad:

```
errorRun :: Run (ErrorT MyError)
errorRun = undefined

useMyFileError2 :: IO (ErrorT MyError Identity ())
useMyFileError2 =
    let afterRun :: Handle -> IO (ErrorT MyError Identity ())
        afterRun handle = errorRun $ sayHiError handle
        applied :: IO (ErrorT MyError Identity ())
        applied = withMyFile afterRun
    in applied
```

This looks eerily similar to our previous example. In fact, errorRun is acting almost identically to runErrorT. However, we're still left with two problems: we don't know where to get that errorRun value from, and we still need to restructure the original ErrorT after we're done.

MonadTransControl

Obviously, in the specific case we have before us we could use our knowledge of the ErrorT transformer to beat the types into submission and create our Run function manually. But what we *really* want is a general solution for many transformers. At this point, you know we need a typeclass.

So let's review what we need: access to a Run function, and some way to restructure our original transformer after the fact. And thus was born MonadTransControl, with its single method liftControl:

```
class MonadTrans t => MonadTransControl t where
    liftControl :: Monad m => (Run t -> m a) -> t m a
```

Let's look at this closely. liftControl takes a function (the one we'll be writing). That function is provided with a Run function, and must return a value in some monad (m). liftControl will then take the result of that function and reinstate the original transformer on top of everything:

```
useMyFileError3 :: Monad m => ErrorT MyError IO (ErrorT MyError m ())
useMyFileError3 =
```

```
        liftControl inside
      where
        inside :: Monad m => Run (ErrorT MyError) -> IO (ErrorT MyError m ())
        inside run = withMyFile $ helper run
        helper :: Monad m
              => Run (ErrorT MyError) -> Handle -> IO (ErrorT MyError m ())
        helper run handle = run (sayHiError handle :: ErrorT MyError IO ())
```

Close, but not exactly what I had in mind. What's up with the double monads? Well, let's start at the end. The sayHiError handle returns a value of type ErrorT MyError IO (). This we knew already; no surprises. What might be a little surprising (it got me, at least) is the next two steps.

First, we apply run to that value. Like we discussed before, the result is that the IO inner monad is popped to the outside, to be replaced by some arbitrary monad (represented by m here). So we end up with an IO (ErrorT MyError m ()). OK... we then get the same result after applying withMyFile. Not surprising.

The last step took me a long time to understand correctly. Remember how we said that we reconstruct the original transformer? Well, so we do: by plopping it right on top of everything else we have. So our end result is the previous type—IO (ErrorT MyError m ())—with an ErrorT MyError stuck on the front.

That seems just about utterly worthless, right? Well, almost. But don't forget, that m can be any monad, including IO. If we treat it that way, we get ErrorT MyError IO (ErrorT MyError IO ()). That looks a lot like m (m a), and we want just plain old m a. Fortunately, now we're in luck:

```
useMyFileError4 :: ErrorT MyError IO ()
useMyFileError4 = join useMyFileError3
```

And it turns out that this usage is so common, that Bas had mercy on us and defined a helper function:

```
control :: (Monad m, Monad (t m), MonadTransControl t)
        => (Run t -> m (t m a)) -> t m a
control = join . liftControl
```

So all we need to write is the following:

```
useMyFileError5 :: ErrorT MyError IO ()
useMyFileError5 =
    control inside
  where
    inside :: Monad m => Run (ErrorT MyError) -> IO (ErrorT MyError m ())
    inside run = withMyFile $ helper run
    helper :: Monad m
          => Run (ErrorT MyError) -> Handle -> IO (ErrorT MyError m ())
    helper run handle = run (sayHiError handle :: ErrorT MyError IO ())
```

And just to make it a little shorter:

```
useMyFileError6 :: ErrorT MyError IO ()
useMyFileError6 = control $ \run -> withMyFile $ run . sayHiError
```

MonadControlIO

The MonadTrans class provides the lift method, which allows us to lift an action one level in the stack. There is also the MonadIO class: this provides liftIO, which lifts an IO action as far in the stack as desired. We have the same breakdown in monad-control. But first, we need a corollary to Run:

```
type RunInBase m base = forall b. m b -> base (m b)
```

Instead of dealing with a transformer, we're dealing with two monads. base is the underlying monad, and m is a stack built on top of it. RunInBase is a function that takes the entire stack as a value, pops out that base, and puts in on the outside. Unlike in the Run type, we don't replace it with an arbitrary monad, but with the original one. To use some more concrete types:

```
RunInBase (ErrorT MyError IO) IO = forall b. ErrorT MyError IO b
                                   -> IO (ErrorT MyError IO b)
```

This should look fairly similar to what we've been looking at so far; the only difference is that we want to deal with a specific inner monad. Our MonadControlIO class is really just an extension of MonadControlTrans using this RunInBase:

```
class MonadIO m => MonadControlIO m where
    liftControlIO :: (RunInBase m IO -> IO a) -> m a
```

Simply put, liftControlIO takes a function that receives a RunInBase. That RunIn Base can be used to strip down our monad to just an IO, and then liftControlIO builds everything back up again. And like MonadControlTrans, it comes with a helper function:

```
controlIO :: MonadControlIO m => (RunInBase m IO -> IO (m a)) -> m a
controlIO = join . liftControlIO
```

We can easily rewrite our previous example with it:

```
useMyFileError7 :: ErrorT MyError IO ()
useMyFileError7 = controlIO $ \run -> withMyFile $ run . sayHiError
```

And as an advantage, it easily scales to multiple transformers:

```
sayHiCrazy :: Handle -> ReaderT Int (StateT Double (ErrorT MyError IO)) ()
sayHiCrazy handle = liftIO $ hPutStrLn handle "Madness!"

useMyFileCrazy :: ReaderT Int (StateT Double (ErrorT MyError IO)) ()
useMyFileCrazy = controlIO $ \run -> withMyFile $ run . sayHiCrazy
```

Real-Life Examples

Let's solve some real-life problems with this code. Probably the biggest motivating use case is exception handling in a transformer stack. For example, let's say that we want to automatically run some cleanup code when an exception is thrown. If this were normal IO code, we'd use:

```
onException :: IO a -> IO b -> IO a
```

But if we're in the ErrorT monad, we can't pass in either the action or the cleanup. In comes controlIO to the rescue:

```
onExceptionError :: ErrorT MyError IO a
                 -> ErrorT MyError IO b
                 -> ErrorT MyError IO a
onExceptionError action after = controlIO $ \run ->
    run action `onException` run after
```

Let's say we need to allocate some memory to store a Double in. In the IO monad, we could just use the alloca function. Once again, our solution is simple:

```
allocaError :: (Ptr Double -> ErrorT MyError IO b)
            -> ErrorT MyError IO b
allocaError f = controlIO $ \run -> alloca $ run . f
```

Lost State

Let's rewind a bit to our onExceptionError. It uses onException under the surface, which has a type signature of IO a -> IO b -> IO a. Let me ask you something: what happened to the b in the output? Well, it was thoroughly ignored. But that seems to cause us a bit of a problem. After all, we store our transformer state information in the value of the inner monad. If we ignore it, we're essentially ignoring the monadic side effects as well!

And yes, this does happen with monad-control. Certain functions will drop some of the monadic side effects. This is put best by Bas, in the comments on the relevant functions:

> Note, any monadic side effects in m of the "release" computation will be discarded; it is run only for its side effects in IO.

In practice, monad-control will usually be doing the right thing for you, but you need to be aware that some side effects may disappear.

More Complicated Cases

In order to make our tricks work so far, we've needed to have functions that give us full access to play around with their values. Sometimes, this isn't the case. Take, for instance:

```
addMVarFinalizer :: MVar a -> IO () -> IO ()
```

In this case, we are required to have no value inside our finalizer function. Intuitively, the first thing we should notice is that there will be no way to capture our monadic side effects. So how do we get something like this to compile? Well, we need to explicitly tell it to drop all of its state-holding information:

```
addMVarFinalizerError :: MVar a -> ErrorT MyError IO () -> ErrorT MyError IO ()
addMVarFinalizerError mvar f = controlIO $ \run ->
    return $ liftIO $ addMVarFinalizer mvar (run f >> return ())
```

Another case from the same module is:

```
modifyMVar :: MVar a -> (a -> IO (a, b)) -> IO b
```

Here, we have a restriction on the return type in the second argument: it must be a tuple of the value passed to that function and the final return value. Unfortunately, I can't see a way of writing a little wrapper around modifyMVar to make it work for ErrorT. Instead, in this case, I copied the definition of modifyMVar and modified it:

```
modifyMVar :: MVar a
           -> (a -> ErrorT MyError IO (a, b))
           -> ErrorT MyError IO b
modifyMVar m io =
  Control.Exception.Control.mask $ \restore -> do
    a      <- liftIO $ takeMVar m
    (a',b) <- restore (io a) `onExceptionError` liftIO (putMVar m a)
    liftIO $ putMVar m a'
    return b
```

Web Application Interface

It is a problem almost every language used for web development has dealt with: the low level interface between the web server and the application. The earliest example of a solution is the venerable and battle-worn Common Gateway Interface (CGI), providing a language-agnostic interface using only standard input, standard output, and environment variables.

 This chapter covers WAI version 3.0, which has a number of changes from previous versions.

Back when Perl was becoming the de facto web programming language, a major shortcoming of CGI became apparent: the process needed to be started anew for each request. When dealing with an interpreted language and an application requiring a database connection, this overhead became unbearable. FastCGI (and later SCGI) arose as a successor to CGI, but it seems that much of the programming world went in a different direction.

Each language began creating its own standard for interfacing with servers: mod_perl, mod_python, mod_php, mod_ruby. Within the same language, multiple interfaces arose. In some cases, we even had interfaces on top of interfaces. And all of this led to much duplicated effort: a Python application designed to work with FastCGI wouldn't work with mod_python; mod_python only exists for certain web servers; and these programming language-specific web server extensions need to be written for each programming language.

Haskell has its own history. We originally had the `cgi` package, which provided a monadic interface. The `fastcgi` package then provided the same interface. Meanwhile, it seemed that the majority of Haskell web development focused on the stand-alone server. The problem here is that each server comes with its own interface, meaning that you need to target a specific backend. This means that it is impossible to share common features, like gzip encoding, development servers, and testing frameworks.

WAI attempts to solve this, by providing a generic and efficient interface between web servers and applications. Any handler supporting the interface can serve any WAI application, while any application using the interface can run on any handler.

At the time of writing, there are various backends, including Warp, FastCGI, and the development server. There are even more esoteric backends, like `wai-handler-webkit` for creating desktop apps. `wai-extra` provides many common middleware components like gzip, JSON-P, and virtual hosting. `wai-test` makes it easy to write unit tests, and `wai-handler-devel` lets you develop your applications without worrying about stopping to compile. Yesod targets WAI, as well as other Haskell web frameworks such as Scotty and MFlow. It's also used by some applications that skip the framework entirely, including Hoogle.

 Yesod provides an alternative approach for a devel server, known as `yesod devel`. The difference from `wai-handler-devel` is that `yesod devel` actually compiles your code each time, respecting all settings in your cabal file. This is the recommended approach for general Yesod development.

The Interface

The interface itself is very straightforward: an application takes a request and returns a response. A response consists of an HTTP status, a list of headers, and a response body. A request contains various information: the requested path, query string, request body, HTTP version, and so on.

In order to handle resource management in an exception-safe manner, we use continuation passing style for returning the response, similar to how the `bracket` function works. This makes our definition of an application look like:

```
type Application =
    Request ->
    (Response -> IO ResponseReceived) ->
    IO ResponseReceived
```

The first argument is a `Request`, which shouldn't be too surprising. The second argument is the continuation, or what we should *do* with a `Response`. Generally speaking, this will just be sending it to the client. We use the special `ResponseReceived` type to ensure that the application does in fact call the continuation.

This may seem a little strange, but usage is pretty straightforward, as we'll demonstrate next.

Response Body

Haskell has a data type known as a "lazy" ByteString. By utilizing laziness, you can create large values without exhausting memory. Using lazy I/O, you can do such tricks as having a value that represents the entire contents of a file, yet only occupies a small memory footprint. In theory, a lazy ByteString is the only representation necessary for a response body.

In practice, while lazy ByteStrings are wonderful for generating "pure" values, the lazy I/O necessary to read a file introduces some nondeterminism into our programs. When serving thousands of small files a second, the limiting factor is not memory, but file handles. Using lazy I/O, file handles may not be freed immediately, leading to resource exhaustion. To deal with this, WAI provides its own streaming data interface.

The core of this streaming interface is the Builder. A Builder represents an action to fill up a buffer with bytes of data. This is more efficient than simply passing Byte Strings around, as it can avoid multiple copies of data. In many cases, an application needs to provide only a single Builder value. For that simple case, we have the ResponseBuilder constructor.

However, there are times when an application will need to interleave IO actions with yielding of data to the client. For that case, we have ResponseStream. With Response Stream, you provide a *function*. This function in turn takes two actions: a "yield more data" action, and a "flush the buffer" action. This allows you to yield data, perform IO actions, and flush, as many times as you need, and with any interleaving desired.

There is one further optimization: many operating systems provide a sendfile system call, which sends a file directly to a socket, bypassing a lot of the memory copying inherent in more general I/O system calls. For that case, we have ResponseFile.

Finally, there are some cases where we need to break out of the HTTP mode entirely. Two examples are WebSockets, where we need to upgrade a half-duplex HTTP connection to a full-duplex connection and HTTPS proxying, which requires our proxy server to establish a connection, and then become a dumb data transport agent. For these cases, we have the ResponseRaw constructor. Note that not all WAI handlers can in fact support ResponseRaw, though the most commonly used handler, Warp, does provide this support.

Request Body

Like with response bodies, we could theoretically use a lazy `ByteString` for request bodies, but in practice we want to avoid lazy I/O. Instead, the request body is represented with an `IO ByteString` action (`ByteString` here being a *strict* `ByteString`). Note that this does *not* return the entire request body, but rather just the next chunk of data. Once you've consumed the entire request body, further calls to this action will return an empty `ByteString`.

Note that, unlike with response bodies, we have no need for using `Builders` on the request side, as our purpose is purely for reading.

The request body could in theory contain any type of data, but the most common are URL-encoded and multipart form data. The `wai-extra` package contains built-in support for parsing these in a memory-efficient manner.

Hello, World

To demonstrate the simplicity of WAI, let's look at a Hello, World example. In this example, we're going to use the `OverloadedStrings` language extension to avoid explicitly packing string values into `ByteStrings`:

```
{-# LANGUAGE OverloadedStrings #-}
import Network.Wai
import Network.HTTP.Types (status200)
import Network.Wai.Handler.Warp (run)

application _ respond = respond $
  responseLBS status200 [("Content-Type", "text/plain")] "Hello, World"

main = run 3000 application
```

Lines 2 through 4 perform our imports. Warp is provided by the `warp` package, and is the premier WAI backend. WAI is also built on top of the `http-types` package, which provides a number of data types and convenience values, including `status200`.

First, we define our application. Because we don't care about the specific request parameters, we ignore the first argument to the function, which contains the request value. The second argument is our "send a response" function, which we immediately use. The response value we send is built from a lazy `ByteString` (thus `responseLBS`), with status code of 200 OK, a `text/plain` content type, and a body containing the words "Hello, World". Pretty straightforward.

Resource Allocation

Let's make this a little more interesting, and try to allocate a resource for our response. We'll create an MVar in our main function to track the number of requests, and then hold that MVar while sending each response:

```
{-# LANGUAGE OverloadedStrings #-}
import           Blaze.ByteString.Builder          (fromByteString)
import           Blaze.ByteString.Builder.Char.Utf8 (fromShow)
import           Control.Concurrent.MVar
import           Data.Monoid                        ((<>))
import           Network.HTTP.Types                 (status200)
import           Network.Wai
import           Network.Wai.Handler.Warp           (run)

application countRef _ respond = do
    modifyMVar countRef $ \count -> do
        let count' = count + 1
            msg = fromByteString "You are visitor number: " <>
                    fromShow count'
        responseReceived <- respond $ responseBuilder
            status200
            [("Content-Type", "text/plain")]
            msg
        return (count', responseReceived)

main = do
    visitorCount <- newMVar 0
    run 3000 $ application visitorCount
```

This is where WAI's continuation interface shines. We can use the standard modifyM Var function to acquire the MVar lock and send our response. Note how we thread the responseReceived value through, though we never actually use the value for anything. It is merely witness to the fact that we have, in fact, sent a response.

Notice also how we take advantage of Builders in constructing our msg value. Instead of concatenating two ByteStrings together directly, we monoidally append two different Builder values. The advantage to this is that the results will end up being copied directly into the final output buffer, instead of first being copied into a temporary ByteString buffer to only later be copied into the final buffer.

Streaming Response

Let's give our streaming interface a test as well:

```
{-# LANGUAGE OverloadedStrings #-}
import           Blaze.ByteString.Builder (fromByteString)
import           Control.Concurrent       (threadDelay)
import           Network.HTTP.Types       (status200)
```

```
import          Network.Wai
import          Network.Wai.Handler.Warp (run)

application _ respond = respond $ responseStream status200
    [("Content-Type", "text/plain")]
    $ \send flush -> do
        send $ fromByteString "Starting the response...\n"
        flush
        threadDelay 1000000
        send $ fromByteString "All done!\n"

main = run 3000 application
```

We use `responseStream`, and our third argument is a function that takes our "send a builder" and "flush the buffer" functions. Notice how we flush after our first chunk of data, to make sure the client sees the data immediately. However, there's no need to flush at the end of a response. WAI requires that the handler automatically flush at the end of a stream.

Middleware

In addition to allowing our applications to run on multiple backends without code changes, WAI allows us another benefit: middleware. Middleware is essentially an application transformer, taking one application and returning another one.

Middleware components can be used to provide lots of services: cleaning up URLs, authentication, caching, JSON-P requests. But perhaps the most useful and most intuitive middleware is the one for gzip compression. This middleware works very simply: it parses the request headers to determine if a client supports compression, and if so, it compresses the response body and adds the appropriate response header.

The great thing about middleware is that it is unobtrusive. Let's see how we would apply the `gzip` middleware to our Hello, World application:

```
{-# LANGUAGE OverloadedStrings #-}
import Network.Wai
import Network.Wai.Handler.Warp (run)
import Network.Wai.Middleware.Gzip (gzip, def)
import Network.HTTP.Types (status200)

application _ respond = respond $ responseLBS status200
                        [("Content-Type", "text/plain")]
                        "Hello, World"

main = run 3000 $ gzip def application
```

We added an import line to actually have access to the middleware, and then simply applied `gzip` to our application. You can also *chain together* multiple middleware components: a line such as `gzip False $ jsonp $ othermiddleware $ myapplica`

---

tion is perfectly valid. One word of warning: the order the middleware is applied in can be important. For example, `jsonp` needs to work on uncompressed data, so if you apply it after you apply `gzip`, you'll have trouble.

Settings Types

Let's say you're writing a web server. You want the server to take a port to listen on, and an application to run. So you create the following function:

```
run :: Int -> Application -> IO ()
```

But suddenly you realize that some people will want to customize their timeout durations. So you modify your API:

```
run :: Int -> Int -> Application -> IO ()
```

So, which Int is the timeout, and which is the port? Well, you could create some type aliases, or comment your code. But there's another problem creeping into the code: this run function is getting unmanageable. Soon you'll need to take an extra parameter to indicate how exceptions should be handled, and then another one to control which host to bind to, and so on.

A more extensible solution is to introduce a settings data type:

```
data Settings = Settings
    { settingsPort :: Int
    , settingsHost :: String
    , settingsTimeout :: Int
    }
```

And this makes the calling code almost self-documenting:

```
run Settings
    { settingsPort = 8080
    , settingsHost = "127.0.0.1"
    , settingsTimeout = 30
    } myApp
```

Great—couldn't be clearer, right? True, but what happens when you have 50 settings to your web server? Do you really want to have to specify all of those each time? Of course not. So instead, the web server should provide a set of defaults:

```
defaultSettings = Settings 3000 "127.0.0.1" 30
```

And now, instead of needing to write that long bit of code, you can get away with:

```
run defaultSettings { settingsPort = 8080 } myApp -- (1)
```

This is great, except for one minor hitch. Let's say you now decide to add an extra record to `Settings`. Any code out in the wild looking like this:

```
run (Settings 8080 "127.0.0.1" 30) myApp -- (2)
```

will be broken, because the `Settings` constructor now takes four arguments. The proper thing to do would be to bump the major version number so that dependent packages don't get broken. But having to change major versions for every minor setting you add is a nuisance. The solution? Don't export the `Settings` constructor:

```
module MyServer
    ( Settings
    , settingsPort
    , settingsHost
    , settingsTimeout
    , run
    , defaultSettings
    ) where
```

With this approach, no one can write code like (2), so you can freely add new records without any fear of code breaking.

The one downside of this approach is that it's not immediately obvious from the Haddocks that you can actually change the settings via record syntax. That's the point of this chapter: to clarify what's going on in the libraries that use this technique.

I personally use this technique in a few places—feel free to have a look at the Haddocks to see what I mean:

- Warp: `Settings`
- `http-conduit`: `Request` and `ManagerSettings`
- `xml-conduit`
- Parsing: `ParseSettings`
- Rendering: `RenderSettings`

As a tangential issue, `http-conduit` and `xml-conduit` actually create instances of the `Default` typeclass instead of declaring brand new identifiers. This means you can just type `def` instead of `defaultParserSettings`.

http-conduit

Most of Yesod is about serving content over HTTP. But that's only half the story: someone has to receive it. And even when you're writing a web app, sometimes that someone will be you. If you want to consume content from other services or interact with RESTful APIs, you'll need to write client code. And the recommended approach for that is http-conduit.

This chapter is not directly connected to Yesod, and will be generally useful for anyone wanting to make HTTP requests.

Synopsis

```
{-# LANGUAGE OverloadedStrings #-}
import Network.HTTP.Conduit -- the main module

-- The streaming interface uses conduits
import Data.Conduit
import Data.Conduit.Binary (sinkFile)

import qualified Data.ByteString.Lazy as L
import Control.Monad.IO.Class (liftIO)
import Control.Monad.Trans.Resource (runResourceT)

main :: IO ()
main = do
    -- Simplest query: just download the information from the given URL as a
    -- lazy ByteString.
    simpleHttp "http://www.example.com/foo.txt" >>= L.writeFile "foo.txt"
```

```
-- Use the streaming interface instead. We need to run all of this inside a
-- ResourceT, to ensure that all our connections get properly cleaned up in
-- the case of an exception.
runResourceT $ do
    -- We need a Manager, which keeps track of open connections. simpleHttp
    -- creates a new manager on each run (i.e., it never reuses
    -- connections).
    manager <- liftIO $ newManager conduitManagerSettings

    -- A more efficient version of the simpleHttp query above. First we
    -- parse the URL to a request.
    req <- liftIO $ parseUrl "http://www.example.com/foo.txt"

    -- Now get the response
    res <- http req manager

    -- And finally stream the value to a file
    responseBody res $$+- sinkFile "foo.txt"

    -- Make it a POST request, don't follow redirects, and accept any
    -- status code
    let req2 = req
            { method = "POST"
            , redirectCount = 0
            , checkStatus = \_ _ _ -> Nothing
            }
    res2 <- http req2 manager
    responseBody res2 $$+- sinkFile "post-foo.txt"
```

Concepts

The simplest way to make a request in http-conduit is with the simpleHttp function. This function takes a String giving a URL and returns a ByteString with the contents of that URL. But under the surface, there are a few more steps:

- A new connection Manager is allocated.
- The URL is parsed to a Request. If the URL is invalid, then an exception is thrown.
- The HTTP request is made, following any redirects from the server.
- If the response has a status code outside the 200 range, an exception is thrown.
- The response body is read into memory and returned.
- runResourceT is called, which will free up any resources (e.g., the open socket to the server).

If you want more control over what's going on, you can configure any of these steps (plus a few more) by explicitly creating a Request value, allocating your Manager manually, and using the http and httpLbs functions.

Request

The easiest way to create a Request is with the parseUrl function. This function will return a value in any Failure monad, such as Maybe or IO. The last of those is the most commonly used, and results in a runtime exception whenever an invalid URL is provided. However, you can use a different monad if, for example, you want to validate user input:

```
import Network.HTTP.Conduit
import System.Environment (getArgs)
import qualified Data.ByteString.Lazy as L
import Control.Monad.IO.Class (liftIO)

main :: IO ()
main = do
    args <- getArgs
    case args of
        [urlString] ->
            case parseUrl urlString of
                Nothing -> putStrLn "Sorry, invalid URL"
                Just req -> withManager $ \manager -> do
                    res <- httpLbs req manager
                    liftIO $ L.putStr $ responseBody res
        _ -> putStrLn "Sorry, please provide exactly one URL"
```

The Request type is abstract, so that http-conduit can add new settings in the future without breaking the API (see Appendix C for more information). In order to make changes to individual records, you use record notation. For example, a modification to our program that issues HEAD requests and prints the response headers would be:

```
{-# LANGUAGE OverloadedStrings #-}
import Network.HTTP.Conduit
import System.Environment (getArgs)
import qualified Data.ByteString.Lazy as L
import Control.Monad.IO.Class (liftIO)

main :: IO ()
main = do
    args <- getArgs
    case args of
        [urlString] ->
            case parseUrl urlString of
                Nothing -> putStrLn "Sorry, invalid URL"
                Just req -> withManager $ \manager -> do
                    let reqHead = req { method = "HEAD" }
                    res <- http reqHead manager
```

```
                liftIO $ do
                    print $ responseStatus res
                    mapM_ print $ responseHeaders res
        _ -> putStrLn "Sorry, please provide example one URL"
```

There are a number of different configuration settings in the API; some noteworthy ones are:

proxy
> Allows you to pass the request through the given proxy server.

redirectCount
> Indicates how many redirects to follow. The default is 10.

checkStatus
> Checks the status code of the return value. By default, gives an exception for any non-2XX response.

requestBody
> Specifies the request body to be sent. Be sure to also update the method. For the common case of URL-encoded data, you can use the urlEncodedBody function.

Manager

The connection manager allows you to reuse connections. When making multiple queries to a single server (e.g., accessing Amazon S3), this can be critical for creating efficient code. A manager will keep track of multiple connections to a given server (taking into account ports and SSL as well), automatically reaping unused connections as needed. When you make a request, http-conduit first tries to check out an existing connection. When you're finished with the connection (if the server allows keep-alive), the connection is returned to the manager. If anything goes wrong, the connection is closed.

To keep our code exception-safe, we use the ResourceT monad transformer. All this means for you is that your code needs to be wrapped inside a call to runResourceT, either implicitly or explicitly, and that code inside that block will need to use liftIO to perform normal IO actions.

There are two ways you can get ahold of a manager. newManager will return a manager that will not be automatically closed (you can use closeManager to do so manually), while withManager will start a new ResourceT block, allow you to use the manager, and then automatically close the ResourceT when you're done. If you want to use a ResourceT for an entire application, and have no need to close it, you should probably use newManager.

One other thing to point out: you obviously don't want to create a new manager for each and every request; that would defeat the whole purpose. You should create your Manager early and then share it.

Response

The Response data type contains three pieces of information: the status code, the response headers, and the response body. The first two are straightforward; let's discuss the body.

The Response type has a type variable to allow the response body to be of multiple types. If you want to use http-conduit's streaming interface, you want this to be a Source. For the simple interface, it will be a lazy ByteString. One thing to note is that, even though we use a lazy ByteString, *the entire response is held in memory*. In other words, we perform no lazy I/O in this package.

The conduit package does provide a lazy module that will allow you to read this value in lazily, but like any lazy I/O, it's a bit unsafe, and definitely nondeterministic. If you need it, though, you can use it.

http and httpLbs

So let's tie it together. The http function gives you access to the streaming interface (i.e., it returns a Response using a ResumableSource), while httpLbs returns a lazy ByteString. Both of these return values in the ResourceT transformer so that they can access the Manager and have connections handled properly in the case of exceptions.

If you want to ignore the remainder of a large response body, you can connect to the sinkNull sink. The underlying connection will automatically be closed, preventing you from having to read a large response body over the network.

xml-conduit

Many developers cringe at the thought of dealing with XML files. XML has the reputation of having a complicated data model, with obfuscated libraries and huge layers of complexity sitting between you and your goal. I'd like to posit that a lot of that pain is actually a language and library issue, not inherent to XML.

Once again, Haskell's type system allows us to easily break down the problem to its most basic form. The xml-types package neatly deconstructs the XML data model (both a streaming and a DOM-based approach) into some simple algebraic data types. Haskell's standard immutable data structures make it easier to apply transforms to documents, and a simple set of functions makes parsing and rendering a breeze.

We're going to be covering the xml-conduit package. Under the surface, this package uses a lot of the approaches Yesod in general does for high performance: blaze-builder, text, conduit, and attoparsec. But from a user perspective, it provides everything from the simplest APIs (readFile/writeFile) through full control of XML event streams.

In addition to xml-conduit, there are a few related packages that come into play, like xml-hamlet and xml2html. We'll cover both how to use all these packages, and when they should be used.

Synopsis

```
<!-- Input XML file -->
<document title="My Title">
    <para>This is a paragraph. It has <em>emphasized</em>
          and <strong>strong</strong> words.</para>
    <image href="myimage.png"/>
</document>
```

```
{-# LANGUAGE OverloadedStrings #-}
{-# LANGUAGE QuasiQuotes       #-}
import qualified Data.Map       as M
import           Prelude        hiding (readFile, writeFile)
import           Text.Hamlet.XML
import           Text.XML

main :: IO ()
main = do
    -- readFile will throw any parse errors as runtime exceptions.
    -- def uses the default settings.
    Document prologue root epilogue <- readFile def "input.xml"

    -- root is the root element of the document; let's modify it
    let root' = transform root

    -- And now we write out. Let's indent our output.
    writeFile def
        { rsPretty = True
        } "output.html" $ Document prologue root' epilogue

-- We'll turn our <document> into an XHTML document
transform :: Element -> Element
transform (Element _name attrs children) = Element "html" M.empty
    [xml|
        <head>
            <title>
                $maybe title <- M.lookup "title" attrs
                    \#{title}
                $nothing
                    Untitled Document
        <body>
            $forall child <- children
                ^{goNode child}
    |]

goNode :: Node -> [Node]
goNode (NodeElement e) = [NodeElement $ goElem e]
goNode (NodeContent t) = [NodeContent t]
goNode (NodeComment _) = [] -- hide comments
goNode (NodeInstruction _) = [] -- and hide processing instructions too

-- convert each source element to its XHTML equivalent
goElem :: Element -> Element
goElem (Element "para" attrs children) =
    Element "p" attrs $ concatMap goNode children
goElem (Element "em" attrs children) =
    Element "i" attrs $ concatMap goNode children
goElem (Element "strong" attrs children) =
    Element "b" attrs $ concatMap goNode children
goElem (Element "image" attrs _children) =
    Element "img" (fixAttr attrs) [] -- images can't have children
```

```
      where
        fixAttr mattrs
            | "href" `M.member` mattrs  =
              M.delete "href" $ M.insert "src" (mattrs M.! "href") mattrs
            | otherwise                 = mattrs
    goElem (Element name attrs children) =
        -- don't know what to do, just pass it through...
        Element name attrs $ concatMap goNode children

<?xml version="1.0" encoding="UTF-8"?>
<!-- Output XHTML -->
<html>
    <head>
        <title>
            My Title
        </title>
    </head>
    <body>
        <p>
            This is a paragraph. It has
            <i>
                emphasized
            </i>
            and
            <b>
                strong
            </b>
            words.
        </p>
        <img src="myimage.png"/>
    </body>
</html>
```

Types

Let's take a bottom-up approach to analyzing types. This section will also serve as a primer on the XML data model itself, so don't worry if you're not completely familiar with it.

I think the first place where Haskell really shows its strength is with the `Name` data type. Many languages (like Java) struggle with properly expressing names. The issue is that there are, in fact, three components to a name: its local name, its namespace (optional), and its prefix (also optional). Let's look at some XML to explain:

```
<no-namespace/>
<no-prefix xmlns="first-namespace" first-attr="value1"/>
<foo:with-prefix xmlns:foo="second-namespace" foo:second-attr="value2"/>
```

The first tag has a local name of `no-namespace`, and no namespace or prefix. The second tag (local name: `no-prefix`) *also* has no prefix, but it does have a namespace (first-namespace). first-attr, however, does *not* inherit that namespace: attribute namespaces must always be explicitly set with a prefix.

 Namespaces are almost always URIs of some sort, though there is nothing in any specification requiring that it be so.

The third tag has a local name of with-prefix, a prefix of foo, and a namespace of second-namespace. Its attribute has a second-attr local name and the same prefix and namespace. The xmlns and xmlns:foo attributes are part of the namespace specification, and are not considered attributes of their respective elements.

So let's review what we need from a name: every name has a local name, and it can optionally have a prefix and namespace. Seems like a simple fit for a record type:

```
data Name = Name
    { nameLocalName :: Text
    , nameNamespace :: Maybe Text
    , namePrefix    :: Maybe Text
    }
```

According to the XML namespace standard, two names are considered equivalent if they have the same local name and namespace. In other words, the prefix is not important. Therefore, xml-types defines Eq and Ord instances that ignore the prefix.

The last class instance worth mentioning is IsString. It would be very tedious to have to manually type out Name "p" Nothing Nothing every time we want a paragraph. If you turn on OverloadedStrings, "p" will resolve to that all by itself! In addition, the IsString instance recognizes something called Clark notation, which allows you to prefix the namespace surrounded in curly brackets. In other words:

```
"{namespace}element" == Name "element" (Just "namespace") Nothing
"element" == Name "element" Nothing Nothing
```

The Four Types of Nodes

An XML document is a tree of nested nodes. There are in fact four different types of nodes allowed: elements, content (i.e., text), comments, and processing instructions.

You may not be familiar with that last one, as it's less commonly used. It is marked up as:

```
<?target data?>
```

There are two surprising facts about processing instructions (PIs):

- PIs don't have attributes. Although you'll often see processing instructions that appear to have attributes, there are in fact no rules about that data of an instruction.

- The `<?xml …?>` stuff at the beginning of a document is not a processing instruction. It is simply the beginning of the document (known as the XML declaration), and happens to look an awful lot like a PI. The difference is that the `<?xml …?>` line will not appear in your parsed content.

Processing instructions have two pieces of text associated with them (the target and the data), so we have a simple data type:

```
data Instruction = Instruction
    { instructionTarget :: Text
    , instructionData :: Text
    }
```

Comments have no special data type, because they are just text. But content is an interesting one: it can contain either plain text or unresolved entities (e.g., `&copyright-statement;`). xml-types keeps those unresolved entities in all the data types in order to completely match the spec. However, in practice, it can be very tedious to program against those data types. And in most use cases, an unresolved entity is going to end up as an error anyway.

Therefore, the `Text.XML` module defines its own set of data types for nodes, elements, and documents that remove all unresolved entities. If you need to deal with unresolved entities instead, you should use the `Text.XML.Unresolved` module. From now on, we'll be focusing only on the `Text.XML` data types, though they are almost identical to the xml-types versions.

Anyway, after that detour: content is just a piece of text, and therefore it too does not have a special data type. The last node type is an element, which contains three pieces of information: a name, a map of attribute name/value pairs, and a list of child nodes. (In xml-types, this value could contain unresolved entities as well.) So our `Element` is defined as:

```
data Element = Element
    { elementName :: Name
    , elementAttributes :: Map Name Text
    , elementNodes :: [Node]
    }
```

Which of course begs the question: what does a Node look like? This is where Haskell really shines—its sum types model the XML data model perfectly:

```
data Node
    = NodeElement Element
    | NodeInstruction Instruction
    | NodeContent Text
    | NodeComment Text
```

Documents

So now we have elements and nodes, but what about an entire document? Let's just lay out the data types:

```
data Document = Document
    { documentPrologue :: Prologue
    , documentRoot :: Element
    , documentEpilogue :: [Miscellaneous]
    }

data Prologue = Prologue
    { prologueBefore :: [Miscellaneous]
    , prologueDoctype :: Maybe Doctype
    , prologueAfter :: [Miscellaneous]
    }

data Miscellaneous
    = MiscInstruction Instruction
    | MiscComment Text

data Doctype = Doctype
    { doctypeName :: Text
    , doctypeID :: Maybe ExternalID
    }

data ExternalID
    = SystemID Text
    | PublicID Text Text
```

The XML spec says that a document has a single root element (documentRoot). It also has an optional DOCTYPE statement. Before and after both the DOCTYPE and the root element, you are allowed to have comments and processing instructions. (You can also have whitespace, but that is ignored in the parsing.)

So what's up with the DOCTYPE? Well, it specifies the root element of the document, and then optional public and system identifiers. These are used to refer to document type definition (DTD) files, which give more information about the file (e.g., validation rules, default attributes, entity resolution). Let's take a look at some examples:

```
<!-- no external identifier -->
<!DOCTYPE root>
```

```
<!-- a system identifier -->
<!DOCTYPE root SYSTEM "root.dtd">
<!-- public identifiers have a system ID as well -->
<!DOCTYPE root PUBLIC "My Root Public Identifier" "root.dtd">
```

And that, my friends, is the entire XML data model. For many parsing purposes, you'll be able to simply ignore the entire Document data type and go immediately to the documentRoot.

Events

In addition to the document API, xml-types defines an Event data type. This can be used for constructing streaming tools, which can be much more memory-efficient for certain kinds of processing (e.g., adding an extra attribute to all elements). We will not be covering the streaming API here, though it should look very familiar after analyzing the document API.

You can see an example of the streaming API in the Sphinx case study (Chapter 25).

Text.XML

The recommended entry point to xml-conduit is the Text.XML module. This module exports all of the data types you'll need to manipulate XML in a DOM fashion, as well as a number of different approaches for parsing and rendering XML content. Let's start with the simple ones:

```
readFile  :: ParseSettings  -> FilePath -> IO Document
writeFile :: RenderSettings -> FilePath -> Document -> IO ()
```

This introduces the ParseSettings and RenderSettings data types. You can use these to modify the behavior of the parser and renderer, such as adding character entities and turning on pretty (i.e., indented) output. Both these types are instances of the Default typeclass, so you can simply use def when these need to be supplied. That is how we will supply these values throughout the rest of this appendix; see the API docs for more information.

It's worth pointing out that in addition to the file-based API, there is also a Text- and ByteString-based API. The BytesString-powered functions all perform intelligent encoding detections and support UTF-8, UTF-16, and UTF-32, in either big- or little-endian format, with and without a byte-order marker (BOM). All output is generated in UTF-8.

For complex data lookups, we recommend using the higher-level cursor API. The standard Text.XML API not only forms the basis for that higher level, but is also a great API for simple XML transformations and for XML generation. See the synopsis for an example.

A Note About File Paths

In the type signature, we have a type called FilePath. However, this isn't Prelude.FilePath. The standard Prelude defines a type synonym type FilePath = [Char]. Unfortunately, there are many limitations to using such an approach, including confusion of filename character encodings and differences in path separators.

Instead, xml-conduit uses the system-filepath package, which defines an abstract FilePath type. I've personally found this to be a much nicer approach to work with. The package is fairly easy to follow, so I won't go into details here, but I do want to give a few quick explanations of how to use it:

- Because a FilePath is an instance of IsString, you can type in regular strings and they will be treated properly, as long as the OverloadedStrings extension is enabled. (I highly recommend enabling it anyway, as it makes dealing with Text values much more pleasant.)

- If you need to explicitly convert to or from Prelude's FilePath, you should use encodeString and decodeString, respectively. This takes into account file path encodings.

- Instead of manually splicing together directory names and filenames with extensions, use the operators in the Filesystem.Path.CurrentOS module—for example, myfolder </> filename <.> extension.

Cursor

Suppose you want to pull the title out of an XHTML document. You could do so with the Text.XML interface we just described, using standard pattern matching on the children of elements. But that would get very tedious, very quickly. Probably the gold standard for these kinds of lookups is XPath, where you would be able to write /html/head/title. And that's exactly what inspired the design of the Text.XML.Cursor combinators.

A cursor is an XML node that knows its location in the tree; it's able to traverse up, down, and side-to-side (under the surface, this is achieved by tying the knot (*http://www.haskell.org/haskellwiki/Tying_the_Knot*)). There are two functions available for creating cursors from Text.XML types: fromDocument and fromNode.

We also have the concept of an axis, defined as type `Axis = Cursor -> [Cursor]`. It's easiest to get started by looking at example axes: `child` returns zero or more cursors that are the child of the current one, `parent` returns the single parent cursor of the input (or an empty list if the input is the root element), and so on.

In addition, there are some axes that take predicates. `element` is a commonly used function that filters down to only elements that match the given name. For example, `element "title"` will return the input element if its name is "title", or an empty list otherwise.

Another common function that isn't quite an axis is `content :: Cursor -> [Text]`. For all content nodes, it returns the contained text; otherwise, it returns an empty list.

And thanks to the monad instance for lists, it's easy to string all of these together. For example, to do our title lookup, we would write the following program:

```
{-# LANGUAGE OverloadedStrings #-}
import Prelude hiding (readFile)
import Text.XML
import Text.XML.Cursor
import qualified Data.Text as T

main :: IO ()
main = do
    doc <- readFile def "test.xml"
    let cursor = fromDocument doc
    print $ T.concat $
            child cursor >>= element "head" >>= child
                    >>= element "title" >>= descendant >>= content
```

What this says is:

1. Get me all the child nodes of the root element.
2. Filter down to only the elements named "head".
3. Get all the children of all those head elements.
4. Filter down to only the elements named "title".
5. Get all the descendants of all those title elements. (A descendant is a child, or a descendant of a child. Yes, that was a recursive definition.)
6. Get only the text nodes.

So for the input document:

```
<html>
    <head>
        <title>My <b>Title</b></title>
    </head>
    <body>
        <p>Foo bar baz</p>
```

```
        </body>
    </html>
```

we end up with the output My Title. This is all well and good, but it's much more verbose than the XPath solution. To combat this verbosity, Aristid Breitkreuz added a set of operators to the Cursor module to handle many common cases. So, we can rewrite our example as:

```
{-# LANGUAGE OverloadedStrings #-}
import Prelude hiding (readFile)
import Text.XML
import Text.XML.Cursor
import qualified Data.Text as T

main :: IO ()
main = do
    doc <- readFile def "test.xml"
    let cursor = fromDocument doc
    print $ T.concat $
        cursor $/ element "head" &/ element "title" &// content
```

$/ says to apply the axis on the right to the children of the cursor on the left. &/ is almost identical, but is instead used to combine two axes together. This is a general rule in Text.XML.Cursor: operators beginning with $ directly apply an axis, while & will combine two together. &// is used for applying an axis to all descendants.

Let's go for a more complex, if more contrived, example. We have a document that looks like:

```
<html>
    <head>
        <title>Headings</title>
    </head>
    <body>
        <hgroup>
            <h1>Heading 1 foo</h1>
            <h2 class="foo">Heading 2 foo</h2>
        </hgroup>
        <hgroup>
            <h1>Heading 1 bar</h1>
            <h2 class="bar">Heading 2 bar</h2>
        </hgroup>
    </body>
</html>
```

We want to get the content of all the <h1> tags that precede an <h2> tag with a class attribute of "bar". To perform this convoluted lookup, we can write:

```
{-# LANGUAGE OverloadedStrings #-}
import Prelude hiding (readFile)
import Text.XML
import Text.XML.Cursor
```

```
import qualified Data.Text as T

main :: IO ()
main = do
    doc <- readFile def "test2.xml"
    let cursor = fromDocument doc
    print $ T.concat $
        cursor $// element "h2"
                >=> attributeIs "class" "bar"
                >=> precedingSibling
                >=> element "h1"
                &// content
```

Let's step through that. First we get all <h2> elements in the document. ($// gets all descendants of the root element.) Then we filter out only those with class=bar. That >=> operator is actually the standard operator from Control.Monad; yet another advantage of the monad instance of lists. precedingSibling finds all nodes that come before our node *and* share the same parent. (There is also a preceding axis, which takes all elements earlier in the tree.) We then take just the <h1> elements, and grab their content.

The equivalent XPath, for comparison, would be //h2[@class = 'bar']/preceding-sibling::h1//text().

While the cursor API isn't quite as succinct as XPath, it has the advantages of being standard Haskell code and of type safety.

xml-hamlet

Thanks to the simplicity of Haskell's data type system, creating XML content with the Text.XML API is easy, if a bit verbose. The following code:

```
{-# LANGUAGE OverloadedStrings #-}
import           Data.Map (empty)
import           Prelude  hiding (writeFile)
import           Text.XML

main :: IO ()
main =
    writeFile def "test3.xml" $ Document (Prologue [] Nothing []) root []
  where
    root = Element "html" empty
        [ NodeElement $ Element "head" empty
            [ NodeElement $ Element "title" empty
                [ NodeContent "My "
                , NodeElement $ Element "b" empty
```

```
                    [ NodeContent "Title"
                    ]
                ]
            ]
        , NodeElement $ Element "body" empty
            [ NodeElement $ Element "p" empty
                [ NodeContent "foo bar baz"
                ]
            ]
        ]
```

produces:

```
<?xml version="1.0" encoding="UTF-8"?>
<html><head><title>My <b>Title</b></title></head>
<body><p>foo bar baz</p></body></html>
```

This is leaps and bounds easier than having to deal with an imperative, mutable-value-based API (cough, Java, cough), but it's far from pleasant and obscures what we're really trying to achieve. To simplify things, we have the xml-hamlet package, which uses quasiquotation to allow you to type in your XML in a natural syntax. For example, the preceding code could be rewritten as:

```
{-# LANGUAGE OverloadedStrings #-}
{-# LANGUAGE QuasiQuotes       #-}
import           Data.Map       (empty)
import           Prelude        hiding (writeFile)
import           Text.Hamlet.XML
import           Text.XML

main :: IO ()
main =
    writeFile def "test3.xml" $ Document (Prologue [] Nothing []) root []
  where
    root = Element "html" empty [xml|
<head>
    <title>
        My #
        <b>Title
<body>
    <p>foo bar baz
|]
```

There are a few points to keep in mind:

- The syntax is almost identical to normal Hamlet, except URL interpolation (@{…}) has been removed. As such:

    — There are no close tags.

    — It's whitespace-sensitive.

— If you want to have whitespace at the end of a line, use a # at the end. At the beginning, use a backslash.

- An xml interpolation will return a list of Nodes, so you still need to wrap up the output in all the normal Document and root Element constructs.

- There is no support for the special .class and #id attribute forms.

Like in normal Hamlet, you can use variable interpolation and control structures. So, a slightly more complex example would be:

```
{-# LANGUAGE OverloadedStrings #-}
{-# LANGUAGE QuasiQuotes #-}
import Text.XML
import Text.Hamlet.XML
import Prelude hiding (writeFile)
import Data.Text (Text, pack)
import Data.Map (empty)

data Person = Person
    { personName :: Text
    , personAge :: Int
    }

people :: [Person]
people =
    [ Person "Michael" 26
    , Person "Miriam" 25
    , Person "Eliezer" 3
    , Person "Gavriella" 1
    ]

main :: IO ()
main =
    writeFile def "people.xml" $ Document (Prologue [] Nothing []) root []
  where
    root = Element "html" empty [xml|
<head>
    <title>Some People
<body>
    <h1>Some People
    $if null people
        <p>There are no people.
    $else
        <dl>
            $forall person <- people
                ^{personNodes person}
|]

personNodes :: Person -> [Node]
personNodes person = [xml|
<dt>#{personName person}
```

```
<dd>#{pack $ show $ personAge person}
|]
```

A few more notes:

- The caret interpolation (^{...}) takes a list of nodes, so it can easily embed other xml quotations.

- Unlike in Hamlet, hash interpolations (#{...}) are not polymorphic and can *only* accept Text values.

xml2html

The preceding examples have revolved around XHTML. I've done that so far simply because it is likely to be the most familiar form of XML for most readers. But there's an ugly side to all this that we must acknowledge: not all XHTML will be correct HTML. The following discrepancies exist:

- There are some void tags (e.g., <img>, <br>) in HTML that do not need to have close tags, and in fact are not allowed to.

- HTML does not understand self-closing tags, so <script></script> and <script/> mean very different things.

- Combining the previous two points: you are free to self-close void tags, though to a browser it won't mean anything.

- In order to avoid quirks mode, you should start your HTML documents with a DOCTYPE statement.

- We do not want the XML declaration <?xml ...?> at the top of an HTML page.

- We do not want any namespaces used in HTML, while XHTML is fully name-spaced.

- The contents of <style> and <script> tags should not be escaped.

Fortunately, xml-conduit provides ToHtml instances for Nodes, Documents, and Elements that respect these discrepancies. So by just using toHtml, we can get the correct output:

```
{-# LANGUAGE OverloadedStrings #-}
{-# LANGUAGE QuasiQuotes       #-}
import         Data.Map                         (empty)
import         Text.Blaze.Html                  (toHtml)
import         Text.Blaze.Html.Renderer.String (renderHtml)
import         Text.Hamlet.XML
import         Text.XML

main :: IO ()
```

```
main = putStr $ renderHtml $ toHtml $ Document (Prologue [] Nothing []) root []

root :: Element
root = Element "html" empty [xml|
<head>
    <title>Test
    <script>if (5 < 6 || 8 > 9) alert("Hello, World!");
    <style>body > h1 { color: red }
<body>
    <h1>Hello World!
|]
```

Here is the output (with whitespace added):

```
<!DOCTYPE HTML>
<html>
    <head>
        <title>Test</title>
        <script>if (5 < 6 || 8 > 9) alert("Hello, World!");</script>
        <style>body > h1 { color: red }</style>
    </head>
    <body>
        <h1>Hello, World!</h1>
    </body>
</html>
```

Index

Symbols

! (exclamation point)
    !!! for doctype statement, 33
    != (not equal) operator, 121
    turning off overlap checking for routes, 68
(hash)
    beginning dynamic single pieces of paths, 66
    using for id attributes in Hamlet, 31
$ (dollar sign)
    $(), 11
    $= operator, 294
&&& (fan-out) operator, 88
() (parentheses), representing an empty
    response, 71
* (asterisk), beginning dynamic multi pieces, 66
+ (plus sign), indicating dynamic multi pieces,
    67
. (period), using for class attributes in Hamlet,
    31
/<-. (is not member) operator, 121
/=. (divide and set) operator, 121
: (colon), using to add attributes in Hamlet, 32
<$> operator, 85
<*> operator, 85
<-. (is member) operator, 121
= (equals sign), in attributes in Hamlet, 31
@ (at sign)
    @?{…}, using to embed query string param-
        eters, 30
    interpolation (@{…}), 20, 30
^. (projection) operator, 224
_ (underscore)
    interpolation with, 38
    _{Msg…} interpolation in Hamlet, 265
    _{…} i18n interpolation, 200
{…}, variable interpolation in Shakespeare, 25
|| (OR) operator, 121
∧ (caret)
    embedding templates in Hamlet, 30
    using for embedding in simplified Hamlet,
        38
    using for interpolation in Lucius, 34

A

absolute URLs, 54
Accept header, 153, 240
Accept-Encoding header, 160
Accept-Language header, 160
addStaticContent function, 60
    on scaffold site, capabilities of, 61
aeson package, 21, 154, 281
    documentation, 155
∧Forms, 83
    creating, 84
        optional fields, 85
    features, 83
alreadyExpired function, 75
ALTER TABLE command, 117
Amazon SES, 179
AND operator, 121
AnyMethodR, 214
aopt function, 85
Apache web server, CGI on, 146
API documentation, Haskell, 12
App type, 235
App {..}, 256
Application class, 208, 230

converting HandlerT stacks to Applications, 238

converting instance of YesodDispatch to, 211

return type for yesodDispatch, 236

Application module, 190

application/json mime type, 153

applicative forms, 82, 83, 265

    (see also AForms)

    monadic forms and, 91

APPROOT environment variable, 54

approot, value of, 54

ApprootMaster typeclass, 54

ApprootRelative typeclass, 54

ApprootRequest typeclass, 54

AprootStatic typeclass, 54

areq function, 85

associated types, 234

at-sign interpolation (@{...}), 20, 30

attoparsec, 281

attributes

    HTML attributes, in Hamlet, 31

    in Persistent, 125-128

authentication and authorization, 173-185

    auhorization, 182

    authentication example, 174

    blog application (example), 262

    defined, 173

    email authentication, 178-182

    overview, 173

    with Yesod typeclass, 62

authHttpManager, 177

AuthId type, 174, 176

authPlugins, 176

authRoute function, 62, 182

axes, 353

B

badMethod function, 214

blaze-builder package, 230, 281

blaze-html packages, 26, 231, 249

    combinators, 250

blog application, 259-268

    authentication, 262

    authorization, 262

    comment on blog post, 260

    database, 264

    imports, 259

    individual blog entry, 260

    internationalization (i18n), 261

    language extensions in cabal file, 259

    routing table, setting up, 261

    setting up Persistent entities, 260

    users, tracking, 260

    widget, 263

blog post, form for, 95

blogs, multiauthor, 219

boundary issue, 1

    between application and storage layer, 107

        solving with Persistent, 109

Bounded type, 87

bracket function, 230

broadcast channels

    creating, 272

    for publishing updates, 304

    readTChannel function, 305

BrowserID, 173, 264

build tools

    Cabal, 7

    for JavaScript tools, 7

Builder type, 230, 282, 331

    creating stream of Builders from XML content, 292

buildExcerpts function, 290, 291

C

C preprocessors, 7

Cabal, 7

    cabal file, 188

    command to install necessary libraries, 7

    installation, common pitfalls, 7

    language pragmas in cabal file, 8

cabal clean command, 140

cabal install --only-dependencies command, 21

cacheSeconds function, 75

callbacks, 320

canonical URLs, 66

case statement, 33

Cassius, 18, 23

    example of use, 24

    syntax, 35

    using to construct widgets, 41

CGI, 142, 329

    on Apache, 146

    on lighttpd, 147

chat subsite (example), 269-275

    defining routes, 270

    foundation data type, 269

handler functions, 270
  widget, 273
check function, 86
checkBool function, 86
checkM function, 86
cleanPath function, 55, 57, 211
clearUltDest function, 104
client-session-key.aes, 100
client-side session cookies, server-side encryption for, 141
clientsession, 99
code generation
  in Yesod, 2
  with Template Haskell (TH), 10
combinators (blaze-html), 250
comment nodes (XML), 349
Common Gateway Interface (see CGI)
compiled languages versus interpreted languages, 22
compiling web applications, 140
concatMap function, 294
conditionals in Hamlet, 32
conduit library, 232, 281, 343
configuration, environment variables for, 309-310
content nodes (XML), 349
content system (Yesod), types, 239
Content type, 209, 239
content types, 71
ContentBuilder typeclass, 239
ContentDontEvaluate, 239
ContentFile typeclass, 239
ContentSource typeclass, 239
continuation passing style, 230, 232, 322
cookies, 243
  handler functions for, 74
  session information in, 99
counters (see visitor counter)
CRandT monad transformer, 168
cross-site request forgery (CSRF) attacks, 88
CSS
  Cassius and Lucius templating languages for, 23
  Cassius templating language, 35
  coordination with HTML and JavaScript, 41
  Css type and ToCSS typeclass, 26
  for widgets in static files, 193
  helper data types for colors and units, 26
  in external files, 60

Lucius templating language, 33
  producing using Cassius and Lucius (example), 24
curl commands, 154
CURRENT_TIME function, 126
Cursor module, 354
cursors (XML), 352

D

data constructors, 6
data declarations, 6
data types (see types)
database migrations, 115
database-driven navbar (example), 163
databases
  backend, selecting, 188
  blog application (example), 264
  data sent to and from, types representing, 110
  database queries in widgets, 221
  manipulating data in, 122
  SQLite, for Sphinx-based search, 286
  storing information in SQL database, 109
  supported by Persistent, 107
-ddump-splices GHC option, 11
debugging, using MonadIO and MonadLogger for, 75
declarations, generated by Template Haskell code, 11
default attribute, 126
defaultClientSessionBackend function, 100
defaultErrorHandler function, 60
defaultGetDBRunner, 287
defaultLayout function, 18
  for scaffolded site, 192
  getMessage in, 102
  overriding, 57
    wiki master site (example), 276
  use by subsite, 205
  using for widgets, 48, 252
delete function, 125
DELETE method, 152
deleteBy function, 125
deleteCookie function, 74
deleteWhere function, 125
dependencies, scaffolded site, 188
deploying web applications, 139-147
  CGI on Apache, 146
  CGI on lighttpd, 147

compiling, 140
desktop, 145
FastCGI on lighttpd, 146
files to deploy, 140
Keter, 139
Nginx and FastCGI, 144
SSL and static files, 141
Warp, 141
   Nginx configuration, 142
   server process, 144
derivePersistentField function, 132
development servers, 22, 142, 330
dispatch, 70
   arguments for handler function, 71
   complete code for non–Template Haskell
     approach, 216
   dispatch function, 189
   handling for requests, 210
   module for subsite dispatch code, 203
   return type for handler functions, 70
     Handler monad, 70
     Html, 71
   setting up for chat subsite (example), 272
   Template Haskell generated code, 212
   toWaiApp, toWaiAppPlain, and warp, 211
   using continuation passing style, 230
do notation, using to construct widget pieces,
   45
doctype statement, 33
drop-down lists, 87
dynamic multi pieces, 66
dynamic parameters, 245
dynamic single piece, 66

E

Either, 319
element nodes (XML), 349
else statement, 32
elseif statement, 32
email, authentication with, 178-182
encryption
   server-side, for client-side session cookies,
     141
   session information, 100
Enctype, 82, 88
   for form fields, 94
English, language codes for, 198
entities
   defining in Persistent, 127

defining routes for scaffolded site, 189
entity encodings, 25
Entity typeclass, 120
Enum tye, 87
environment information, 209
environment variables for configuration,
   309-310
error messages, monad transformers and, 167
Error monad, 161, 320
error pages, custom, 59
errorHandler function, 59
errorMessage function, 86
ErrorT monad transformer, 171, 319, 321
escapes (in Hamlet), 28
Esqueleto, 108, 136
   switching to streaming response, 225
   type-safe DSL for writing SQL queries, 223
Event interface, 292
events
   server-sent, for chat subsite (example), 272
   stream of, 292
   XML, 351
exceptions, 210
   running clean-up code when exception is
     thrown, 326
   streamed responses and, 232, 292
existingLinks function, 165
Expires header, 75
expiresAt function, 75
extensions (Haskell), 8
external files, calling Shakespeare from in Haskell code, 35

F

fan-out operator (&&&), 88
FastCGI, 142, 329
   Nginx and, 144
     specifying FastCGI variables, 145
   on lighttpd, 146
Field type, 83, 85, 93
fieldEnctype function, 94
FieldSettings type, 83, 85, 91
fieldView function, 94
FieldView type, 91
file descriptors, 144
FilePath type, 352
files, serving, 233
Filesystem.Path.CurrentOS module, 352
fileUpload function, 63

Filter typeclass, 120
filtering
    Persistent operators for, 121
    using in deleteWhere function, 125
    using with selectList function, 121
Flush Builder values, 226
forall statement, 32
FormInput, 83
    features, 84
FormMessage type, 83, 89, 264
FormResult type, 83, 88
forms, 79-97, 243
    categories of, 81
    converting between kinds of, 84
    creating AForms, 84
    custom fields, 93
    for blog application (example), 265
    input, 92
    internationalization (i18n), 89
    monadic, 89
    more sophisticated fields, 87
    naming conventions for form types, 82
    running, 88
    Sphinx-based search (example), 288
    types, 82
    validation, 86
    values not coming from the user, 95
foundation data type, 18, 190
    blog application (example), 260
    creating for chat subsite (example), 269
    creating for single process pub-sub (exam-
        ple), 303
    creating for visitor counter (example), 301
    for wiki master site (example), 275
    HelloSub (example), 205
    initializing data in, 255-258
        creating foundation value, 256
        defining foundation type, 256
        example, complete soure code, 257
        using foundation type, 256
    uses of, 234
Foundation module, 190
fragments, adding hash fragments to URLs, 76
FromJSON typeclass, 154
fromPathPiece function, 67, 215
functions
    for creating widgets, 44
    naming scheme for Shakespeare functions
        in Haskell code, 37

Template Haskell (TH), 11

G

GADT (generalized algebraic data type), 113
GCC preprocessor, 7
generateFormGet function, 88
generateFormPost function, 88
generic types, 130
get function, 114
GET requests, 151
    for forms, 88, 91
        handler code for, 96
    handler function for, 214
    information about, 73
    information on, getting inside a Widget, 165
    responses to, 18
get404 function, 136
getApplicationDev function, 190
getAuthId function, 176
getBy function, 120
getContentType function, 160
getHomeR function, 157
getMessage function, 58, 102, 263
getOnlyGetR function, 214
getRequest function, 73
getResults function, 290
getSession function, 101
getUrlRender function, 73
getUrlRenderParams function, 73
getXmlpipeR function, 294
getYesod function, 73
GHState typeclass, 209
Glasgow Haskell Compiler (GHC), 2, 7
    -ddump-splices option, 11
    installation, common pitfalls, 7
    language pragmas on the command line, 8
    viewing generated code with -ddump-
        splices, 207
gzip, 334

H

Hackage, 12
Haddock, 12
    documentation, 26
Hamlet, 18, 23
    blaze-html packages, 26
    converting a template to an Html value, 57
    database actions and, 221
    i18n interpolation (_{...}), 200

internationalization in, 38
syntax, 28-33
    attributes, 31
    case statement, 33
    conditionals, 32
    doctype statement, 33
    forall statement, 32
    interpolation, 29
    maybe, 32
    tags, 28
    with statement, 33
types, alternatives to HtmlUrl, 37
using to construct widgets, 41
    whamlet, 46
variable interpolation in, 25
hamlet (quasi-quoter), 12
handler functions, 17, 208
    arguments, 72
    dealing with content, 209
    defining for subsite route type, 205
    dispatch function and route type, 189
    for chat subsite (example), 270
    Handler modules for, 191
    in Handler monad, 72-75
        application information from, 73
        generating response headers, 74
        getting request information, 73
        short circuiting, 73
    information needed for, 208
    naming conventions, 18
    return type, 70
        HandlerT monad, 70
        Html, 71
    search handler, Sphinx-based search, 289
    short circuiting, 243
    short-circuit responses, 210
    specifying for resources, 69
    streaming responses, 243
    using in widgets, 50
    writing, 242-245
        getting request parameters, 242
        return type, ToTypedContext, 242
        wiki master site (example), 277
Handler monad, 161
    checkM function in, 87
    converting IO action to Handler action, 265
    isAuthorized method and, 184
HandlerContents typeclass, 210
HandlerData typeclass, 168

HandlerT monad transformer, 70, 162, 168,
        236-242
    (To)Content and (To)TypedContent, 239
    HandlerT App IO monad stack, 238
    HasContentType and representations, 240
    layering CRandT on top of, 169
    power of, 171
    warp function, 242
handlerToWidget . runDB, 165
handlerToWidget function, 51, 163, 222
    using in Chat widget (example), 273
    wrapping call to runInputGet, 167
HasContentType typeclass, 159, 240
hash fragments, 76
HashDB, 173
Haskell, xi
    API documentation, 12
    calling Shakespeare from, 35
    language pragmas, 8
    learning, resources for, 5
    overloaded strings, 8
    packages and libraries available in, 3
    QuasiQuotes (QQ), 12
    Template Haskell (TH), 10
    terminology, 5
    tools, Glasgow Haskell Compiler (GHC)
        and Cabal, 7
    type families, 9
Haskell Platform, 7
Haskell.org Hoogle instance, 12
head tags, external CSS and JavaScript in, 60
headers
    Content-Type, 249
    request, 160
    request and response, 243
Hello, World application, 15, 332
    subsite, 203
hierarchical routes, 313
Hoogle, 12
Host header, 160
HTML
    coordination with CSS and JavaScript, 41
    generation of, superficial approach to, 43
    Hamlet templating engine for, 18, 24
        how Hamlet produces HTML, 27
    handlers dealing with, 209
    Html response, 239
    in widgets, 43
    Nic editor, 264

representations of data, 152
result from Sphinx-based search, 291
xmltohtml, 358
Html type, 25, 249
as return type for handler functions, 71
HtmlUrl type, 37
HTTP
Accept request header, 240
connection manager, 177
methods, 151
Request and Response classes representing, 208
statelessness of, 99
http function, 282, 343
http-conduit package, 282, 339-343
http and httpLbs functions, 343
Manager, 342
Request, 341
Response, 343
httpLbs function, 282, 343
HTTPS, 141

I

i18n (see internationalization)
identifiers
email addresses as, 176, 264
generating for Chat widget (example), 273
IDs
AuthId, 174
database queries fetching by, 119
document IDs containing search string, 290
generating for widgets, 46
insert function and, 123
UserId for blog application, 264
if statement, 32
Import module, 190
Import.hs file, 189
index setting (Sphinx), 286
indexer, 286
indexer searcher command, 286
input forms, 82, 92
differences from applicative and monadic forms, 92
FormInput, 83
insert function, 114, 122
internationalization (i18n), 195-201
blog application (example)
setting title messages, 265
error messages, 86

form messages in blog application (example), 264
in blog application (example), 261
in forms, 89
in Hamlet, 38
interpolation, 200
message files, 198
specifying types, 199
overview, 197
RenderMessage typeclass, 199
translating phrases, not words, 201
interpolation, 29
(see also variable interpolation)
i18n (_{...}), 200
in Julius, 35
in Lucius, 33
in whamlet, 47
URL, 30
using a ʌ (caret), 30
variable, 29
_ (underscore), using, 38
interpreted languages versus compiled languages, 22
invalidArgs function, 74
IO base monad, 47, 86, 162
ErrorT transformer stacked on, 319
IO Response, 230
iopt function, 92
IORef typeclass, 168, 256, 302
ireq function, 92
is member operator (<-.), 121
is not member operator (/<-.), 121
isAuthorized function, 62, 182, 311
isLoggedIn function, 273
IsString type, 9, 85, 348
drawback to, 9
isWriteRequest function, 62

J

JavaScript
coordination with HTML and CSS, 41
for form controls, 97
for widgets in static files, 193
in external files, 60
Javascript type and ToJavascript typeclass, 26
Julius templating language for, 23
syntax, 35
minification, with hjsmin package, 35

joinPath function, 55, 57
JSON
    helper functions for, 154
    representations of data, 152
    responses, 21
JSON web service, creating, 281-283
    client, 282
    server, 281
Julius, 18, 23
    example of use, 25
    syntax, 35
    using to construct widgets, 41

K

Keter, 139
    deploying web applications, 139

L

language pragmas, 8
languages
    Accept-Language header, 160
    language codes, 198
languages function, 75
lazy bytestrings, 331
lift
    functions autolifted with MonadHandler,
        167
    in chat subsite handlers (example), 271
    lifting a call to next monad up, 162
    lifting IO action to upper monad, 320
    liftIO, 75
    liftIO getCurrentTime, 265
    running Handler actions in applicative
        form, 95
    using in subsite to get master site default-
        Layout, 205
liftControl function, 323
liftIO function, 325
lighttpd
    CGI on, 147
    FastCGI on, 146
LIKE operator (SQL), 133
limits and offsets, SelectOpt, 121
Linux, GHC and Haskell Platform packages on,
    7
LiteApp, 248
logging
    MonadLogger typeclass, 75
    shouldLog function, 63

loginDest, 176
logoutDest, 176
lookupCookie function, 74
lookupGetParam function, 50
lookupSession function, 101
Lucius, 18, 23
    example of use, 24
    syntax, 33-35
    using to construct widgets, 41

M

Mac OS X, installing GHC and Cabal, 7
main function, 236
    environment variable lookup in, 309
    for wiki master site (example), 278
    replacing with warp function, 242
makeApplication function, 190
makeSessionBackend function, 100
Manager type, 282, 342
many-to-many relationships, 128
maximumContentLength function, 63
maybe
    database query results, 119
    in Hamlet, 32
    in SQL, 126
    optional default value in AForm, 85
    optional fields in AForm, 85
maybeRoute, 238
message files, 190, 198
    blog application (example), 261
    specifying types, 199
messages
    in blog application (example), 263
    session, 102
    using i18n messages for title in blog applica-
        tion, 265
meta tags, 44
MForms, 83, 89
migrate function, 116
migrations (see database migrations)
mime types, 153
    discovering for a possible representation,
        159
mime-mail-ses package, 179
mixins (in Lucius), 34
mkMessage function, 199
mkMessages function, 190
mkMigrate function, 116
mkPersist function, 111

mkYesod TH function, 16, 189
mkYesodData function, 190
mkYesodDispatch function, 190
mkYesodSubData function, 205
mkYesodSubDispatch function, 272
MMVars, 302
Model.hs file, 189
modularity (Yesod), 3
modules for a subsite, 203
Monad instance (of Widget), 45
monad transformers, 47, 319
monad-control, 319-327
    lost state, 326
    more complicated cases, 327
    overview, 319
    real-life examples, 326
    types, 322
        MonadControlIO, 325
        MonadTransControl, 323
MonadBaseControl typeclass, 242
MonadControlIO typeclass, 325
MonadCRandom typeclass, 168
monadcryptorandom package, 168
MonadHandler typeclass, 51, 71, 167
monadic forms, 82, 83, 89
    (see also MForms)
MonadIO typeclass, 75, 163, 242, 325
MonadLogger typeclass, 75, 242
MonadResource typeclass, 167, 242
monads, 161-172
    adding a new monad transformer, 168-171
    database-driven navbar (example), 163
    HandlerT App IO monad stack, 238
    monad transformers, 161
    performance and error messages, 167
    request information (example), 165
MonadTrans typeclass, 242, 319, 325
MonadTransControl typeclass, 323
MongoDB, 114
    ByteStrings, use for IDs, 130
    mongoSettings, 131
    uniqueness constraints and, 119
mopt function, 91
mpsGeneric, 131
mreq function, 91

N

Name type, 347
namespaces (XML), 293, 348

neverExpires function, 75
newIdent function, 46
newtype declarations, 6
Nginx, 142
    and FastCGI, 144
        specifying FastCGI variables, 145
    server process, 144
Nic HTML editor, 264
NoImplicitPrelude extension, 191
notFound function, 74
Nothing, NULL versus, 119
NULL values, uniqueness and, 118

O

OAuth, 173
one-to-many relationships, 128
OpenID, 173
optionsEnum function, 88
OR operator, 121
overlapping in routes, 68
OverloadedStrings type, 9, 86, 332

P

pagination, 225
ParseRoute class and parseRoute function, 17
parsing routes, 238
paseUrl function, 341
path pieces, 66
    beginning with exclamation point (!), 68
    types of, 66
pathInfo, 214
    in a subsite, 216
PathMultiPiece typeclass, 66
    defining an instance, 67
PathPiece typeclass, 67, 245
paths
    converting requested path into route value,
        238
    in WAI, 230
performance
    advantage of using Esqueleto, 224
    advantages of Yesod and Haskell, 2
    monad transformer levels and, 167
permissionDenied function, 74
persistence, 255
Persistent, 107-137
    attributes, 125-128
    custom fields, 131
    database migrations, 115

cases not handled by Persistent, 117
 rules about, 117
features, 107
filtering operators, 121
integration with Yesod, 134
joins in, 222
manipulating database data, 122
 deleting data, 125
 insert function, 122
 update function, 124
monad transformers, 162
PostgreSQL, working with, 136
queries, 119
 fetching by ID, 119
 fetching by unique constraint, 120
 using select functions, 120
raw SQL, 132
relationships in data, 128
setting up entities for blog application, 260
solving the boundary issue, 109
 code generation, 111
 PersistStore, 114
 types, 110
types, closer examination of, 129
uniqueness constraints, 118
writing SQL queries in, using Esqueleto, 224
PersistEntity typeclass, 110, 130
 generating instance for each data type
  defined, 111
PersistField typeclass, 110
persistFileWith function, 111
persistLowerCase quasi-quoter, 111
PersistStore typeclass, 114, 162
PersistValue typeclass, 110, 130
pluralization, 197
PORT environment variable, 211
POST requests, 151
 for forms, 88, 91
  handler code for, 96
 information about, 73
Post/Redirect/Get, 58, 102, 263
PostgreSQL, 109, 114
 working with, 136
preEscapedToHtml, 291
Prelude, 190, 352
printMigration function, 117
processing instructions (PIs), 349
progress, viewing (publish/subscribe example),
 305

projections, 224
provideJson function, 155
provideRep function, 153, 240
provideRepType function, 160
publish/subscribe, single process, 303-307
 allocating a job, 304
 complete source code, 305-307
 forking the background job, 304
 foundation data type, 303
 viewing progress, 305
PUT method, 152

Q

QtWebkit, 145
QuasiQuotes (QQ), 12, 18
 persistLowerCase, 111
 using to embed Shakespeare in Haskell
  code, 35
  correct language extensions and syntax,
   36
queries, database, 119
 fetching by ID, 119
 fetching by unique constraint, 120
 in widgets, 221
 using select functions, 120
 writing SQL queries with Esqueleto, 223
query function, 290
query strings, 76
 embedding query string parameters in
  Hamlet, 30
 generating parameters for, 213
 handling by URL rendering functions, 27
 parameters produced by renderRoute function, 55
quotation marks, Hamlet attributes, 31

R

R suffix on resource names, 16
race conditions, 124
radio buttons, 88
rapid prototyping, 22
rawSql function, 223
Reader monad, 161, 321
ReaderT monad transformer, 162, 168, 171,
 209, 322
readTChannel function, 305
record wildcard syntax, 256
redirect function, 73, 246

calling during handler function execution, 210

redirects, indicated by cleanPath function, 56

RedirectUrl typeclass, 76

redirectUrlDest function, 104

redirectWith function, 73

relationships in database data, 128, 130

reload mode, calling Shakespeare from Haskell code, 36

renderBuilder function, 292, 294

rendering functions (URL), 27

renderMessage function, 200

RenderMessage typeclass, 89, 199
  creating instance for blog application (example), 264
  creating instance for wiki master site (example), 277

RenderRoute class, 17

renderRoute function, 17, 55, 236

RenderRoute typeclass, 55, 235

replace function, 124

representations, 240

Request class, 208, 230, 330, 341

request headers, 160

request methods, 69, 151

requests, 207-218
  auhorization in blog application (example), 262
  code changes in Yesod 1.2, 207
  dispatch, 210
    complete code for non-Template Haskell approach, 216
    generated code, 212
    toWaiApp, toWaiAppPlain, and warp, 211
  getting request parameters, 242
  handlers, 207
    content, 209
    layers, 208
    short-circuit responsed, 210
  handling, 236
  representations of data, 240
  request body (WAI), 332

resources, 19
  handler functions, specifying, 69
  HomeR route (example), 16
  names of, 68
  resource allocation in WAI, 333
  single URL for each resource, 153

writing, patterns for, 67

ResourceT monad transformer, 168, 208, 342

respondSource API, 244

respondSource function, 305

respondSourceDB function, 225

Response class, 208, 330, 343

response headers, handler functions generating, 74

responseFile function, 233

responseLBS function, 230

responses, 230
  generating streaming response bodies, 231
  non-HTML, 21
  response body (WAI), 331
  streaming response in WAI, 333

responseSource function, converting from WAI to Yesod, 244

responseSourceDB function, 292

RESTful features in Yesod, 151-160
  representations of data, 152
    JSON, conveniences for, 154
    new data types, 156
  request headers, 160
  request methods, 151

Result type, 289

returnJson function, 155

reverse proxy, running Warp via, 142

route attributes, 311-315
  alternative to, hierarchical routes, 313

routeAttrs function, 311

routing, 16, 20, 65-70
  blog application (example), 261
  converting requested path into route value, 238
  defining routes for chat subsite (example), 270
  defining routes for scaffolded site, 189
  generating routes for subsites, 213
  generating subsite route data type and parse and render functions, 205
  handler functions for routes, 191
  handler specification for requests, 69
  links and, 26
  mkYesod TH function, 16
  modeling route data type, 245
  overlap checking for routes, 68
  resource names, 68
  route data type, 234
  route syntax, 65

splitting requested path into pieces, 66

route type and route render function, 189

setting up routes for wiki master site (example), 275

subsite embedded in master site route definition, 205

using LiteApp, 248

using Template Haskell, 246

runDB function, 134, 163

runErrorT function, 321

runFormGet function, 88

runFormPost function, 88

runFormPostNoToken function, 88

runHandler function, 210

RunHandlerEnv typeclass, 209

RunInBase function, 325

runInputGet function, 92, 271

runInputPost function, 92

runMigration function, 116

printing of migrations on stderr, 117

runMigrationSilent function, 117

running applications, 19

runSqlite function, 114

S

scaffold sites, 21

scaffolded site

defaultLayout function, 192

file structure, 188

cabal file, 188

Foundation and Application modules, 189

Handler modules, 191

Import module, 190

routes and entities, 189

static files, 192

widgetFile function, 191

scaffolding, 187

SCGI, 142, 329

script tags

external JavaScript in, 60

fine-grained control over insertion of, 44

search (debugging utility), 286

search, Sphinx-based (see Sphinx-based search)

searchd, 286

select functions, 120

select, replacing with selectSource, 225

selectList, 120

selectSource, 294

SELECT statement, 223

SelectOpt typeclass, 120

constructors setting options, 122

selectRep function, 153, 240

sendChunkText function, 305

sendFile function, 74

sendfile system call, 233

sendFlush function, 305

sendmail executable, 179

sendResponse function, 74

sendWaiApplication function, 272

sendwaiResponse function, 74

sessions, 99-106

AuthId and, 174

clientsession, 99

controlling, 100

messages, 102

operations, 101

server-side, 174

session state, GHState typeclass, 209

ultimate destination, 104

Yesod user session framework, 243

setCookie function, 74

setHeader function, 74

setLanguage function, 75

setMessage function, 58, 102, 263

setSession function, 101

Settings types, 337-338

Settings.staticRoot function, 143

setTitleI function, 265

setUltDest function, 104

setUltDestCurrent function, 104

setUltDestReferer function, 104

Shakespearean family of template languages, 23, 249

calling Shakespeare from Haskell code, 35

getting the most from, guidelines for, 40

in widgets, 41

other Shakespeare languages, 39

synopsis of, 23

syntax, 27

Hamlet, 28-33

Lucius,

type-safe URLs, 26

types, 25

URL rendering function, 251

shamlet (quasiquoter), 38

Html value produced by, 153

shamletFile function, 38

share function, 117
short circuiting handler functions, 73, 243
short-circuit responses, 210
shouldLog function, 63
simpleHttp function, 340
single process pub-sub (see publish/subscribe, single process)
sinkNull sink, 343
site template, 188
source setting (Sphinx), 286
Source type, 244
Source typeclass, 120
spawn-fcgi program, 144
Sphinx package, 285
Sphinx-based search (case study), 285-299
    basic Yesod setup, 286
    complete code, 294-299
    searching, 289
    setting up Sphinx, 285
    streaming xmlpipe output, 292
SQL
    more complex, in Esqueleto library, 136
    raw SQL in Persistent, 132
    uniqueness, NULL values and, 118
SQL joins, 219-228
    database queries in widgets, 221
    multiauthor blogs, 219
    streaming, 224
    using Esqueleto, 223
    writing joins, 222
SqlBackend typeclass, 114, 130, 162
    Persistent and, 131
SQLite, 114
    Sphinx-based search database, 286
sqlSettings function, 130
SSL, 178
SSL certificates, 141
Stackage, 7
stage restriction, 11
statelessness of HTTP, 99
StateT monad transformer, 171
static files
    in scaffolded site, 192
    serving from a separate domain name, 143
    serving from a subsite, 70
    serving over HTTPS, 141
    smarter, 61
static pieces, 66
static root in Settings.hs file, 193

streaming, 224
    complete code for streaming HTML response, 226
    database responses, 287
    generating streaming response bodies, 231
    streaming response in WAI, 333
    xmlpipe output from Sphinx-based search, 292
strings
    interpolated, creating with shakespeare-text, 39
    overloaded Strings, 8
    String type, converting to raw content, 158
style tags, external CSS in, 60
subsites, 203-205
    creating, Hello, World (example), 203
    for authentication, 176
    generated code for dispatch of responses, 215
    generating query string parameters for, 213
    static, 70
    support for, in dispatch, 210
system libraries for GHC and Haskell Platform, 7
system-filepath package, 352

T
tags (HTML), 28
    closing tags furnished by Hamlet, 29
Template Haskell (TH), 10
    functions inserting source code location into log messages, 75
    generated code for dispatch of responses, 212
    parsing and rendering of routes, 17
    routing with, 246
templates, 2
text
    creating interpolated strings in shakespeare-text, 39
    RenderMessage instance for Text, 89
Text.XML module, 349, 351
Text.XML.Cursor module, 354
text/html mime type, 153
TH (see Template Haskell)
timeouts (session), 100
toContent function, 157
ToContent typeclass, 158, 209, 240
ToCss typeclass, 26

toHtml function, 25
ToJavascript typeclass, 26
ToJSON typeclass, 154
ToMarkup typeclass, 25
toPathPiece function, 67, 214, 294
toSqlKey function, 290
ToTypedContent typeclass, 158, 209, 240
    return type for handler functions, 242
toWaiApp function, 211, 234
toWaiAppPlain function, 211, 234
toWidget method, 44
ToWidget typeclass, 44
ToWidgetBody typeclass, 44
ToWidgetHead typeclass, 44
transactions, 115
translations
    message files, 198
    messages for chat subsite (example), 271
    translating phrases, not words, 201
TVars, 302
type constructors, 6
type safety, 1
type variables, 6
type-safe URLs, 20, 26, 234
    syntax, 30
Typeable type, 260
typeclasses, 234
    advantages over record type, 53
TypedContent typeclass, 71, 153, 156, 239
types
    associated, 234
    data sent to and from a database, 110
    foundation data type in Yesod, 234
    in Haskell, 6
        and data constructors, names of, 6
    in Persistent, 129
        more complicated, more generic, 130
    in Shakespearean templates, 25
    in whamlet, 47
    module for subsite data types, 203
    monad-control, 322
    new data types representing data, 156
    Settings, 337-338
    specifying for messages, 199
    textual data types in shakespeare-text exam-
        ple, 40
    type declarations in Haskell, 6
    type families, 9

U

ultimate destination, 104
unique identifiers, 273
Unique typeclass, 119
uniqueness constraints, 118
    database queries on, 120
update function, 124
Update typeclass, 124
updateWhere function, 124
urlEncodeBody function, 342
urlRenderOverride function, 62, 143
URLs
    adding information to, with RedirectUrl and
        Fragment, 76
    interpolation
        simplified Hamlet and, 38
    pieces, splitting requested path into, 66
        types of pieces, 66
    rendering and parsing with Yesod typeclass,
        53
        using cleanPath, 55
        using joinPath, 55
    rendering functions, 27, 251
    type-safe, 20, 26
    used in linking, types of, 26

V

validation (forms), 86
variable interpolation, 25
    in Hamlet, 25, 29
variables (in Lucius), 34
visitor counter (example), 301-302

W

WAI (Web Application Interface), 19, 229-233,
    229, 329-335
    handlers, 208
    Hello, World application (example), 332
    interface, 330
        request body, 332
        response body, 331
    interoperability with, JSON web service
        server (example), 281
    middleware, 334
    pathInfo, 214
    promoting WAI applicaion to a Yesod han-
        dler, 272
    resource allocation, 333

sending raw WAI response, 74
streaming response, 333
support for using WAI applications as sub-
    sites, 210
version 3.0, 329
Yesod interaction with, 234-236
WAI backends, 141
wai-conduit helper package, 232
wai-eventsource package, 272
wai-handler-launch, 146
wai-handler-webkit, 145
waiRequest function, 73
warp function, 211, 242, 278
Warp web server, 2, 19, 141
    advantages of using, 142
    Nginx configuration, 142
    server process, 144
    warp function, 22
warpEnv function, 211, 242
Web Application Interface (see WAI)
web development
    challenge of coordinating HTML, CSS, and
        JavaScript, 41
    type safety and, 1
    Yesod and Haskell, 1
WebKit, 142
    wai-handler-webkit, 145
whamlet, 46
    types, 47
whitespace
    escape rules in Hamlet, 28
    in Hamlet and Cassius, 23
Widget monad, 161
    getting request information in (example),
        165
Widget type synonyms, 47
widgetFile function, 191
widgets, 18, 41-51, 251
    capabilities of Widget and Handler, 163
    combining, 45
    components of, 43
    constructing, 44
        functions for, 44
    database queries in, 221
    for chat subsite (example), 273
    generating ids for, 46
    using, 48
    using handler fuctions in, 50
    using whamlet, 46

types, 47
Widget type, returned from running forms,
    88
WidgetT monad transformer, 71, 162, 168
widgetToPageContent function, 57, 263
wihUrlRenderer function, 251
wiki (example), 269-279
    chat subsite, 269-275
    handlers for master site, writing, 277
    master site data, 275
    master site instances, 276
    running the master site, 278
Windows systems, installing GHC and Cabal, 7
with statement, 33
withManager function, 282
withUrlRenderer function, 57, 263
write requests, 184, 262
Writer monad, 321
WriterT monad transformer, 171

X

XML
    representations of data, 152
    Sphinx search results document, 292
    streaming database content to, 285
xml-conduit package, 292, 345-359
    cursor, 352
    documents, 350
    file paths, 352
    Text.XML module, 351
    types, 347
        events, 351
        nodes, types of, 348
xml-hamlet package, 355-358
xml-types package, 345
xml2html, 358
xmlpipe2, 286
    streaming output, 292
XPath, 352

Y

Yesod, xi, 229-252
    1.2 release, 207
    code generation, 2
    concise code for web applications, 2
    dynamic parameters, 245
    handler functions, writing, 242-245
    HandlerT monad transformer, 236-242
    Hello, Warp application (example), 229

interaction with WAI, 234-236
    Yesod application (example), 234
language pragmas, handling of, 8
modularity, 3
MonadHandler typeclass, 51
monads (see monads)
performance advantages of, 2
powerful ecosystem available with, 3
quick start guide for GHC and Cabal, 7
scaffold site, 21
Shakespeare, 249
widgets, 251
yesod add-handler command, 191
yesod devel command, 21, 188, 330
    library-only and dev flags, 188
yesod executable, 187
yesod init command, 21, 188
Yesod typeclass, 53-63, 234
    advantages of typeclass over record type, 53
    authentication/authorization, 62
    cleanPath member function, 211
    creating instance for wiki master site (example), 276
    custom error pages, 59
    defaultLayout function, 57
    documentation, 63
    external CSS and JavaScript, 60
    methods handling authorization, 174
    rendering and parsing URLs, 53
        using cleanPath, 55
        using joinPath, 55
    simple settings, methods for, 63

smarter static files, 61
yesod-auth package, 62, 173
yesod-form package, 79
yesod-static command, 193
Yesod.Core, documentation, 100
Yesod.Core.Types, 168
YesodApp typeclass, 208
YesodAuth typeclass, 176
    creating instance for blog application (example), 264
    creating instance for wiki master site (example), 277
    required declarations in an instance, 176
YesodAuthPersist typeclass, 264
YesodDB monad, 161, 163
yesodDispatch function, 236
YesodDispatch typeclass, 17, 211, 234, 236
    instance of, 214
    writing an instance, 246
YesodMessage typeclass, 198
YesodPersist typeclass, 134
    creating instance for blog application (example), 264
YesodPersistentBackend typeclass, 163
YesodPersistRunner typeclass, 287
YesodRequest data type, 73, 208
YesodResponse data type, 208
yesodRunner function, 214, 238
YesodRunnerEnv typeclass, 210, 236, 238
yesodSubDispatch function, 215
YesodSubDispatch typeclass, 211
YesodSubRunnerEnv typeclass, 210

About the Author

Michael Snoyman, creator of Yesod, has been programming for about 15 years, using Haskell for the past five. He has ten years of web development experience in a wide variety of environments as well as time spent creating documentation.

Colophon

The animals on the cover of *Developing Web Apps with Haskell and Yesod, Second Edition* are a common rhinoceros beetle (*Xylotrupes ulysses*) and an Apollo butterfly (*Parnassius apollo*).

Common rhinoceros beetles are famous for their size and unique head shape—the males possess a set of large horns, one pointing from the top of the head and another from the center of the thorax. These horns are used to fight other males for mating rights, and also to dig in search of food. The size of the horn relative to the body is a good indication of physical health and nutrition.

Male rhinoceros beetles can reach up to six inches in length, and this large size provides protection from most predators. However, these beetles cannot bite or sting, which makes them popular pets in some Asian countries. Their violent bids for female attention also make them widely used for gambling fights.

The Apollo butterfly is a beautiful white butterfly with black spots on the forewings and red eyespots on the hindwings. The size, placement, and shade of these spots can vary depending on the region the butterfly is from. This makes them a very attractive species to collectors, who endeavor to capture one of each variant.

These butterflies are native to Europe, and can be found as far east as central Asia. They prefer a habitat of mountain meadows that contain many nectar-providing flowers and rocky outcroppings for cocoon formation.

Due in part to over-collecting, but mostly to habitat loss, these butterflies are listed as "vulnerable" on the IUCN Red List. There are laws in place to restrict trade of individual Apollo butterflies, but more conservation needs to be done to prevent further loss of habitat. Climate change, acid rain, and urbanization are all contributing factors to the displacement of this species, but thankfully countries like Poland and Germany have small groups of conservationists working to protect their local populations.

Many of the animals on O'Reilly covers are endangered; all of them are important to the world. To learn more about how you can help, go to *animals.oreilly.com*.

The cover fonts are URW Typewriter and Guardian Sans. The text font is Adobe Minion Pro; the heading font is Adobe Myriad Condensed; and the code font is Dalton Maag's Ubuntu Mono.

Get even more for your money.

Join the O'Reilly Community, and register the O'Reilly books you own. It's free, and you'll get:

- $4.99 ebook upgrade offer
- 40% upgrade offer on O'Reilly print books
- Membership discounts on books and events
- Free lifetime updates to ebooks and videos
- Multiple ebook formats, DRM FREE
- Participation in the O'Reilly community
- Newsletters
- Account management
- 100% Satisfaction Guarantee

Signing up is easy:

1. Go to: oreilly.com/go/register
2. Create an O'Reilly login.
3. Provide your address.
4. Register your books.

Note: English-language books only

To order books online:
oreilly.com/store

For questions about products or an order:
orders@oreilly.com

To sign up to get topic-specific email announcements and/or news about upcoming books, conferences, special offers, and new technologies:
elists@oreilly.com

For technical questions about book content:
booktech@oreilly.com

To submit new book proposals to our editors:
proposals@oreilly.com

O'Reilly books are available in multiple DRM-free ebook formats. For more information:
oreilly.com/ebooks